To Anita,
'Force-Fully Yours'!
Michael Sheard

YES, ADMIRAL

THE SECOND EDITION

CW01561285

MICHAEL SHEARD

SUMMERSDALE

Summersdale Publishers Ltd
46 West Street
Chichester
West Sussex
PO19 1RP
United Kingdom

www.summersdale.com

Printed and bound in Great Britain by Cox & Wyman, Reading.

ISBN 1 84024 122 5

Photographs by: George Bosnyak, Pamela Clarke, Mark Ford,
June Svenson, David Glyn Perkins.

YES, ADMIRAL

SCI-FI, CONVENTIONS, FRIENDS AND FURTHER MEMORIES

MICHAEL SHEARD

Forewords by:

Kenny Baker
Jeremy Bulloch
Nicholas Courtney
Peter Mayhew

This one is for you, the Appreciators,
every flippin' one of you

In memory of my dear friend

Declan Mulholland

Massive thanks also to my chums

Kenny 'R2 D2' Baker
Jeremy 'Boba Fett' Bulloch
Nicholas 'Brigadier Lethbridge Stewart' Courtney
Peter 'Chewbacca' Mayhew

For their great and kind forewords

Pamela Clarke
Proofreader Fantastique

And to my lovely new editor
Elizabeth Kershaw
and her assistant
Amy Charter
Bless you for putting up with me!

Dear Mike,

May I take this opportunity of wishing you All The Best for the release of your latest book. I'm sure it will be very interesting, with all your showbiz gossip and anecdotes. I can't wait to read it.

There's somebody on my shoulder, and he's saying, 'Bleep! Bleep! Bloop!' which presumably means 'Good Luck' in R2 D2 language!

See you soon mate,

Cheers for now.

Kenny Baker

Kenny Baker
25th February 1999

MICHAEL IS A MAN ONCE MET
IS NOT EASY TO FORGET.
A GENT FROM OVER THE BORDER
IN FIRST CLASS ORDER WHEN WE MEET.

Good luck with the book, 'Grandfather',
it may be the best yet.

BEST WISHES
Peter Mayhew

Peter Mayhew
2nd March 1999

It is only when someone you have known over a long period of time starts to send you up as soon as you enter the room that you know that person is probably someone who actually likes you. On one occasion – during one of his numerous appearances in *Dr Who* – Michael and I had a long argument about which of the two of us had featured in more episodes of the programme (I think I just won, but only just).

In recent years we have renewed our acquaintanceship, due to the fact that we tend to meet with regularity at *Dr Who* conventions. These are events where a great deal of socialising goes on, and on one occasion the two of us were interviewed together. At the conclusion of said interview – and for no apparent reason at all – Michael and I broke into a song and dance number, 'Me and My Shadow'.

It occurs to me that since this is Michael's second book and I have only written one – I had better be *his* 'shadow' and follow his example!

Nicholas Courtney
March 1999

NB: Nick's great book is titled *Five Rounds Rapid*, published by Virgin Publishing.

I have known Michael for twenty-five years, and he looks the same now as he did then (at least a hundred).

We first met whilst working together on an RAF documentary. Needless to say, he was my senior officer . . . He is one of the most enthusiastic people I know, always the first person to arrive, and the last to leave. His energy is boundless, and he is always ready to help anyone, whether it is organising a raffle, or helping out in the karaoke contest.

No one falls asleep when he is on stage, if you dare, his booming voice jerks you to attention. There is more than a touch of 'Bronson' in him, and I don't mean Charles!

In the last few years we have met up at various Sci-Fi conventions due to the popularity of the re-release of *Star Wars*. I thought I attended a lot of conventions, but Michael sometimes manages to attend two in a weekend, or is it three? I am sure his name is always top of the promoters' list, he is good value in every aspect. His varied career continues unabated, and not many actors can boast of appearing in eight *Dr Who* stories, and portraying Hitler on four separate occasions. I hope that we will work together again soon. I, for one, am very glad that he has followed his highly successful first book with this long-awaited second.

Good luck Michael.

Regards,

Jeremy Bulloch

Jeremy Bulloch
28th February 1999

Prologue

Let me make it abundantly clear from the start, this is not a sneaky way for me to begin the next volume of my memoirs before the second thirty years is up. (Please see, read and enjoy volume one, *Yes, Mr Bronson – Memoirs of a Bum Actor*, also published by Summersdale, the first edition of which sold out before it reached the shops!) No, give us a chance, I expect to enjoy those years first!

It has been pointed out, however, that although the excellent *Yes, Mr B.* covers more facets of my business than any other tome, before or since, and is affectionate, informative, detailed, and amusing (other reviewers' words, not mine); there are inevitably some bits and pieces which are either not mentioned, because they are a consequence of my profession rather than an integral part, or not given enough weight because there were, frankly, not enough pages in book one. *Dr Who, Star Wars, Space 1999, Blake's 7*, indeed all things Science-Fiction, certainly come into this category – shame on me!

So, do you remember Dearly Beloved? Those who have read the aforementioned masterpiece will certainly have heard of her, those who have not done so had better hurry; the third edition has also all but sold out. (But, shush, don't worry, the fourth will in fact be along soon.) Dearly Beloved, then, my missis, along with a great many others, including my publishers (and isn't that a recommendation), persuaded me to fill in those bits, gather the pieces, expand the weightiness, and give you The Untold Stories, tarra!

Before I continue, though, I must give mention to a couple or so sources of invaluable help, without whom it would not have been possible to give you these wee writings. The *Dr Who* Anorax from the Isle of Man; my old mate Chris Gardner (newspaper man extraordinaire); and Mr Iain Lowson, who hails from Edinburgh, hence the Scottish spelling of his name.

Many, many years ago I was doing, not a book signing, that was ages in the future, but an ordinary autograph session, way down somewhere on the south coast. This chap came up, and said, 'Can I have your autograph please, and will you personalise it?'

'Of course I will,' I replied. 'What's your name?'

'Iain,' (note the spelling).

'OK Ian,' quoth I, and I started to write.

'No' like that!' the guy shouted, 'I'm a Scotsman and proud of it. It's the Scottish Iain, with the extra 'I'.' From that day forward, if there is even the slightest doubt in my mind, I always ask people to spell their name.

Hey, I'm off at a tangent already! But that means I've got lots to tell. But before we go, I must first set the scene.

I did promise Anorax Anonymous, to give them their full title, that I would start thus: 'I was invited to the Isle of Man the other week to be the surprise guest at Andy's twenty-first birthday party', but it's such a super story that I'm sure they won't mind if I hold on to it for a while, so that I can give it its full weight.

Conventions will happily be one of the largest contributors this time, and I couldn't decide if I should put them at the beginning or at the end. At the beginning, and you readers might not bother with the other Sci-Fi gems to follow; at the end, and you might skip the first half and again fail to find the other delightful nuggets. At one stage I even considered bringing out a whole bag of separate booklets, but quickly discarded that as impracticable. The content of each of these smaller manuscripts would still be scintillating of course but it would be a Herculean task for the publishers. So I thought, what the convention, I'll stick with the one book.

Michael Sheard.
Ryde, Isle of Wight.

Chapter 1

I was just on the point of putting conventions first and Sci-Fi last, when I had an even better idea. I finally plumped for interspersion. A couple of conventions, followed by a thumbnail sketch of a Sci-Fi chum, then some interviews, another convention, more thumbnails, more conventions, etc. A large number of the conventions were also attended by my mates anyway and that, I thought, will give variety, and keep me laughing as I write. I'd better come clean from the start, although I very much enjoy doing interviews and personal appearances and all the rest, it's conventions I love most.

OK? Right, but just before we start – here I go on a tangent again! As many of you will already know, I don't like the label 'fan'. It stands for fanatic and I don't think you are fanatical. Can we please agree on another handle? How about 'Appreciator'? You, the apps, have always played a huge part in my life and this time you are very much the most important ingredient. An actor can, if he's lucky, have a goodish career without ever receiving even one app letter – it's not likely, but it is possible. But to be invited to conventions; to be a special guest; open penguin pools; give lectures, to be a guest on TV and radio chat shows and invited to open supermarkets; one must have appeared in something – or things – and have given a performance, or performances, which have been special, and deserving of praise and recognition by you, the audience, the appreciators.

Before I do finally get going therefore: Thanks, your appreciation is very much appreciated. This one is for you.

OK then. Let's start . . .

Chapter 2

I'm going to start with a wee convention I did in Essex a couple of months ago with 'The Men Behind the Mask'. How I could possibly think of leaving Sci-Fi to the end I don't know. I'm delighted to say that the Sci-Fi aroma will permeate this book like a mug of fragrant coffee. Of course it will, it's bound to. Sci-Fi has played a huge part in my life, still does. Wait until I tell you of *First Frontier* and *Manic Moonsters*!

Dr Who conventions may have come first, but as there are, alas, no more *Dr Who* planned (at this time), and it has to be said that the *Who* appreciators diminish in number, year by year. I was talking to a chap in America the other day who very reluctantly admitted that he doubted whether the States could give full justice to a (solely) *Dr Who* convention for much longer, and that they were already beginning to combine them with other Sci-Fis. It's a heck of a pity and we who are *Who* apps must hope that one of these days *Who* will be resurrected.

But in the meantime, there are lots of others keeping the flag flying. There are the wonderful 'Star Treks' of course. The first *Trek* convention was held in 1971 – they expected 300 and 3,000 arrived! And apart from the new digitalised trilogy of *Star Wars* (what a wonderful première that was – read *Yes, Mr B.* for more) there are the new *Star Wars* films, episodes one, two and three. There's *Babylon 5* too, *Highlander*, *Blake's 7* . . . you name it!

Well, blow me. Would you believe it? The phone has just rung and it was a chap from Exeter – Mark O'Grady – asking if I could help him with his new *Dr Who* convention. Honestly, I promise. Maybe I underestimated the power of *Who*. But I'm not going to scrub my previous observation. I still think it's true. But please don't misunderstand me, Andrew (Beech

– organiser of the super *Dr Who* convention, Panopticon), I think your conventions are wonderful and I can't wait for the next.

I'd like to pop another quick tangent in here and tell you how I came to be writing this second lot of pages in the first place. About a month ago my lovely publishers took me out to lunch in the pub next door to their offices in Chichester. We had a great time and happily chatted about this and that. I had a beautiful piece of very fresh cod – there's a superb wet fish shop in Chichester, I bet the pub buy their fish there – accompanied by an excellent salad. When we'd finished, and were sipping the second, or third of our favoured tipples, Stewart (Ferris), one of the founding partners of Summersdale and no mean author in his own right – *The Busker's Guide to Europe, Don't Lean Out of the Window* etc – said suddenly, 'Michael, *Yes, Mr Bronson* is going terribly well, what about giving us another?' I confess I was a wee bit taken off guard. Flattered of course, most certainly, but just a smidge gobsmacked. Imagine, *me* gobsmacked! Particularly as I was being asked to continue doing what I'd so enjoyed doing the first time round. But after a moment I found myself saying that I'd be delighted, but he did remember, didn't he, that *Yes, Mr B.* had taken quite a longish time to write, because I could only put finger to word processor between engagements, and that now I was also doing far more conventions.

'Don't worry,' Stewart cut in, 'you'll have bags of time, we don't want to bring the new book out until next year . . .'

Then the penny dropped. A publisher must find a hook on which to hang his author's work; that's why Bronson was chosen as the title of my first book, because of *Grange Hill.* Stewart figured that he had, with the resurgence of interest in Sci-Fi, an excellent hook whereon to hang the second. Fingers crossed, that by then I'll also be starring in the new Sci-Fi series I mentioned, *First Frontier.*

I told Stewart that I thought it was a great idea. 'You know masses of people connected with Science-Fiction,' he continued, 'try and find a theme you haven't covered before which will allow you to weave in as much Sci-Fi as possible and with your inimitable style we're bound to have another hit.' Inimitable style! How could I refuse such flattery, not that I had any intention of so doing of course. I already had the theme, indeed I think it had always been there, lurking, but I did ponder Stewart's suggestion for a couple of weeks and talked it over with Dearly B. For one thing, although Stewart had said I had bags of time, actually, I only had some fifteen months in which to write it.

But there was never really any doubt, on top of everything else, I love a challenge. I got back to Summersdale and told them I'd love to write *Yes, Admiral.* And an added bonus is that now, when I go to conventions and see my mates, I tell them they'd better watch out and mind their Ps and Qs, 'cos they're going to be in the new book. Everybody is, organisers too.

Ha, ha, ha! Read on . . .

Now then, where in the Galaxy was I? Ah, yes, Essex – Basildon to be exact. I did say a wee convention, didn't I? Well, yes, I did do a smallish trader's fair in Basildon later, but this one was, in fact, so gigantic that I don't think Paul Miley, the organiser, really knew what hit him!

At autograph signing sessions I always like to have space to chat to the appreciators, but here they were pushed through so quickly by the venue staff (not Paul, I hasten to add), that we didn't have a chance. It was utterly frantic. But it does illustrate the power of Sci-Fi. And long may it continue!

This escapade, for that's indeed what it was, also served to emphasise the advertising possibilities of the Internet. I didn't grow up with what is termed 'modern technology', and I've had to adapt to the wonders of the computer, walk-around phones, digitalised whatsits and fax machines. And as for the Internet . . . wow! I learn very quickly, I think, although I'm still amazed that I can pop a letter into a fax machine and the person at the other end can be reading it almost before the type is dry. I've got a word processor and I'm now very good with faxes. But the power of the Internet is awesome. Where is it going to end?

For the aforesaid Basildon convention, Paul had advertised through the normal channels – magazines, newspapers, hoardings, some of us did radio interviews, etc – but he'd also utilised the Internet to massive effect and updated the info every week.

Paul Miley, by the way, is a very nice chap who has a reputation for never being on time for anything. If you've any sense you'll turn up at least half an hour after the allotted time because you know he won't be there. He also appears to be very laid back about things, but on the morning of the Basildon convention, it has to be said that even he was ever so slightly, but justifiably, anxious. There were simply thousands of people descending on the venue – thousands. It was like the Cup Final and Grand National rolled into one.

Regrettably, in the end, huge numbers had to be turned away. Some who'd been queuing for hours were understandably something less than pleased, particularly as the venue staff had decreed that there should be only one queue, for both those who had booked in advance and had their tickets, and the ones who'd turned up on the day.

We, who were inside sitting at our tables, were not fully aware of what was going on outside of course, but we had an inkling. Walls of people (those who had managed to get in) kept heaving towards us. And they were being pushed at us by the venue staff who, in spite of all their bullying . . . 'Come on, for heaven's sake get a move on. And Mr Bronson (for the few who still don't know, that's me of course!), no talking, just sign. We must keep things moving' . . . their efforts didn't manage to get the last appreciator through until well into very late afternoon. Oh yes, we all ignored the orders and still found time for wee chats. But blimey, the power of the Internet. Dearly B. and I have just been connected so I know what I'm talking about – and I still don't understand it. WOW!

Now then, my chums. I will, as I've said, introduce one or two every so often. So here then, in no particular order – oh these actors, you've got to be so careful not to offend them – is the first. My very dear valued chum – Uncle Peter Mayhew.

Peter and I have a very special rapport, particularly at signing sessions. I do with all my mates – I think and hope – but Peter is very special. For example, I always like to sit next to him. OK, I know, it's because he's big and he can protect me, and he lends me his silver signing pen when I haven't got one, or mine's run out. But it's more than that. Peter and I have an easy-going relationship, which particularly lends itself to these occasions. We joke as we sign and can thus put the odd nervous app at their ease. And there's even something else. I've always been fortunate, or found it necessary, to have all my faculties about me when I'm thesping. I've never had to give a performance with one arm tied metaphorically behind my back. Imagine what it must be like, then, to make your mark, as Peter has, with your face completely obliterated by mask, make-up, or machine. There is one scene in *Empire*. Harrison Ford (Solo) is expecting Debbie Reynold's daughter (Princess Leia) – sorry Carrie, I trust you'll understand, I think your Mum was so completely wonderful in *Singing in the Rain*, still do – Harrison is expecting Carrie Fisher to kiss him and she kisses Mark Hamill (Luke) instead. There follows a great sequence in which Peter, without the benefit of his face remember, all but steals the scene with his knowing looks and raised eyebrows. Great.

I'll be coming back to my signing partner later . . . Often.

Imagine. My publishers have sent me on a book signing tour. 'Just up and down the south coast and around to begin with Michael, you'll love it. And just before Christmas, so you're bound to make masses of sales.'

Of course I loved it, and I'm going to pop a twist of these sessions into the pot as we go along. Don't by the way confuse shop book signings with convention book signings. Convention signings come later, and as often as not I've had to contend with and compete (albeit with affection), with the likes of Kenny Baker, Tom Baker, Colin Baker, Sophie Aldred, Gareth Thomas, Sylvester McCoy, Jeremy Bulloch, Dave Prowse, Robert Picardo, Peter, *et* many others, bless 'em every one!

My shop book signings are all mine. I'm on my own when I do them and they are (mostly) huge fun. Apart from anything else I'm the only guest there and if I don't do well, if I'm not bright eyed and bushy tailed, I don't sell. It's my fault and I might as well have stayed at home.

Let me give you a flavour. Two Saturdays before Christmas, I think it was, I arrived at Guildford station. It was eight in the very cold morning. As I girded up my spirits for the day ahead, I literally bumped into Mike Vardy, the distinguished TV director with whom I'd worked many times. He'd just seen his lovely vision-mixer wife, Sandra, off on the train to London Weekend TV.

'Michael,' he said, 'what on earth are you doing here at this hour?'

'I'm here to do a book signing at Smiths, Mike.'

'You've written a book? What is it, a thriller?'

'No, it's about me and my first thirty years in the business. It's doing very well, actually. You're in it.'

'Oh, I am?'

'Yep. Remember when we formed that production company that nearly made it? It's all there.'

'Oh, is it? Ah. Well, perhaps I'll drop down later and buy a copy. I hope you're nice about me.'

'Always am, Mike. You know me, I speak as I find.'

No, he never did drop down and thus missed the best book about the business he's ever missed. And he needn't have worried. Although I call a spade a shovel when I have to, Mike, I'm a pussy cat, me.

But, by Vardy, I can't go toddling off insinuating sillinesses from yesteryear; I must set the scene. First of all, forget Vardy. I'm sure he won't give a damn if I class him as a very small actor in this play. A walk-on, even!

I was due at Smiths at eight-thirty a.m. and I had 150 books to sell. Yes, that is a hell of a lot. I did however have two things in my favour. My youngest – Rupert – is a teacher at Guildford High School for Girls; and I had Southern Counties Radio on my side. Southern Counties had already asked me to do a phone-in the following weekend (more later) and when I told them that I was doing a book signing in Guildford which is their main base, they'd very kindly suggested that I do a wee chatette during my signing. A sort of boost for me and a trailer for them for the following Saturday.

Super, great. Only one problem. Have you ever been to the Smiths in Guildford's High Street? It's next door to Dillons, would you believe – a touch more of that later, too – and the only problem is that the ceilings are a trifle low and if you're at the back of the shop selling your wonderful biography you can't get a signal on your doctor daughter's mobile. (Those who have read *Yes, Mr Bronson* will know her as Susannah, my little girl, who became a doctor of medicine and who is now a mum in her own right.) Zanna had come over to Guildford this day to show off her new baby daughter Bethany. I must admit, by the way, that whereas Dearly Beloved is just about there, I can't certainly be advanced enough in years to be a Grandad. Can I? Oh, alright then. I'm a Grandad.

OK, I had Zanna's mobile, but I couldn't get through to Southern Counties and they were desperate to contact me. So, what the hell to do? The excellent teacher of A-level History and Politics at Guildford High School for Girls came to the rescue, as he has on many occasions. Rupert stood outside Smiths, in Guildford High Street, amid the seasonal carol singers, chestnut vendors – I had some later and they were gorgeous – and the clowns, and when at last Southern Counties were able to reach him, he vigorously waved a Guildford High School scarf. (A pre-arranged signal, the scarf had been loaned to us by his terrible four, The Four Musketeers – read on!) I then rushed out into the street, having first asked the next purchasers of my book, a couple of very tough looking chaps with shaved heads and rings all over the place, if they would mind waiting. Their reply had been,

'Yeah, 'course we will mate. You go an' talk on the radio. And don't you worry mate. We'll make sure nobody nicks your books, Mister BRON – SON!' (When the apps really get going it always comes out like that, as a two syllable chant.)

I was rather relieved to have two such excellent bodyguards.

I did my radio interview, out there, in the road. Actually the High Street in Guildford is a pedestrian precinct so there was no possibility of my being knocked down by a passing double-decker. Great stuff, we had a wonderful time. I loved it.

So did the all the appreciators. Dearly B. and I used to live near Guildford and a goodly number of old friends popped down to say hello. Our ex-next door neighbour, for example, and a lovely lady from Dearly B's baby-sitting circle days who didn't buy a book 'cos she had one already. And the Four Musketeers of course, mentioned above, Erika, Alexa, Lulu and Esther – the only girls from Rupert's form who are, well, let's say high spirited! Thanks for the loan of the scarf, by the way. The five of us – the four of them and me – bought a copy of my book between us. One pound each. Oh yes, didn't I say? Normally the book's great value at its shop price, but at book signings and conventions it sells for only a fiver. And you get it signed!

Hey ho. A great day. And when I'd finished and was on my way to Rupert's flat to see Bethany, I popped into Dillons, which was next door remember, and left a note for dear Tom (Baker) who was due to do a signing there the following week, of his book, *Who on Earth is Tom Baker?*. (I must watch this, that's the second time I've advertised someone else's work!)

> Dear Tom,
> As always, I've got in first. If you sell
> as many books as I've sold today, you'll be
> doing very well!
> See you at the next convention.
> Yours Aye, with love . . .

I've liked T. Baker Esq., immensely, ever since I first met him at the start of rehearsals for director Paddy Russell's *Dr Who*, 'The Pyramids of Mars'. 'Pyramids' was a great four-parter, as was 'The Invisible Enemy', which I of course also did with Tom. Two very nice contrasting parts in fact. Scarman, in 'Pyramids', was a rather meek man, terribly concerned for his brother, who hid in a very small cupboard with Elizabeth Sladen and actually got to enter the Tardis. For one scene at least I became a *Dr Who* companion.

I was also in a very small space in 'Enemy'. As Lowe, who, once he'd been taken over by the virus was a very evil man, I had a fight with the delectable Louise Jameson, inside the Doctor's head. Work that one out!

But what I'd like to tell you about here, is the *Dr Who* movie which never happened – yep, another one.

Tom and I were sitting in the restaurant at the top of the Acton Hilton (Beeb rehearsal block) having a cup of tea. It was a rather cold day and I certainly wished it could have been something a trifle warmer. (But remember, never, ever let a drop of the hard stuff pass your lips until the day's work is done, and if you're driving, not till you get home.) Anyway, 'What about a *Dr Who* movie?' says I for want of something to say.

'Yes,' says Tom, 'funny you should say that. I've been sent this script. Rather good as it happens. Trouble is how. How to get the OKs, how to get the money. How . . .'

Now my bonce is just a touch hazy for once on the exciting programme of events which took place over the following weeks (apart from anything we had 'The Invisible Enemy' to rehearse and record), but Tom and I were both increasingly enthused as the days all but bounced forward.

Perhaps it had been done before, I don't know, but we'd certainly never heard of it, and I suggested that the fans (I hadn't come up with 'Appreciators' then) might be interested in investing in a *Dr Who* movie. My Bank manager, Wilfred, introduced me to some city chaps and yes, they thought it could be done. We'd need some set-up money, but the idea was to form a PLC (Public Limited Company) from which shares could be bought – grandad might buy some as a Christmas present for his grandchildren, an uncle or aunt for their niece or nephew, even wife for husband, still addicted. Oh, there were many permutations. Market research suggested that scores of people would buy them for themselves, and companies were also interested. It seemed a sure-fire certainty. In an interview on TV, or was it radio, Tom mentioned the project and was all but flooded with fivers. It was a super time. And to top it all there was of course a very nice part in the script for me!

But, oh dear, you've got to take the rough with the smooth haven't you? But this rough was not easy.

Another reason, probably the main one, why I can't recall events with as much clarity as usual is that things very quickly slipped from our grasp. Others became involved. Nothing wrong with that, certainly, the project was far too big for us, and anyway we didn't have the time. But Tom and I had done a might of planning and suddenly our tune was being played by others on their piano. And in addition some unacceptable cadenzas were introduced.

All of a sudden it all went wrong and we were left with what I still think is a great and worthy idea for raising finance, if it's handled properly. The film of course never happened, those fivers were returned, and we withdrew. But by gum it was exciting whilst it lasted. Mind you, I'm very glad it fell before we had put our houses on the line to form that PLC!

Chapter 3

As I've just written about Guildford I thought I might go straight on and tell you about the following Saturday and the Southern Counties Radio interview, 'cos it's fresh in me mind.

Radio interviews can take several forms. There's the recorded/live type, in a pukka studio where everything is done in the gallery by a producer and all you have to do is talk. There's the drive-your-own, and there's recorded/live on location. All of these I'll address as we go (Anthony Minghella at the Flamingo Park instantly springs to mind), but the Southern Counties interview was yet another – the phone-in from your own home radio interview.

This is how it went. I'm due on air at two-fifteen on the Saturday afternoon. The idea is that the chap who's doing 'Saturday Sport' will interview me between the races, football and anything else that's on.

First, I had my lunch and poured myself a wee dram. The time is now one forty-five. I turn on 'Grandstand' and try to gen up on the sport which will be about the land this afternoon. All the while I'm waiting for 'the call', and at five minutes past two, not long after I've said to Dearly B. that something has obviously gone wrong and that they've had to cancel, and she's told me to stop being a twit and that I know they don't usually call half an hour before, it arrives.

The idea is that the studio has you standing by on the line a goodly time before you're needed.

'Hello, Michael?'

'Yes. Good afternoon.'

'Afternoon, are you ready?'

'Yes.'

'OK we'll be coming to you after the next record. The presenter's name is Fred. Stand by . . .'

'Fine, I'm standing by . . .'

At this point you're patched through to the studio and now you are really standing by and waiting. You hear the next record in your ear and it seems to go on forever. Finally, just as you're wondering if it will never end, the disc jockey – no sorry, this is after all a sports programme – the presenter (Fred) comes on the line. 'Hi, Michael, we'll be with you in a minute, after I've given the info on this afternoon's games. Nice to have you with us. Just a couple of minutes. Alright?'

'Yes, fine, can't wait . . .'

And that's the one frustrating thing about live radio, and telly come to that, it's either too quick and over before you've started, or it's too flippin' slow.

So you wait. Now there's more modern pop ringing in your ear, yep, they've popped another one in. Your glass is empty; so you pour another wee one – why not? You're only just about to speak, live, to thousands! (Actually no, oddly enough I don't get nervous or butterflies before live interviews, funny that.)

And at last . . . 'And now, I'm delighted and privileged to be joined this afternoon by my special guest, Michael Sheard – the creator of the infamous Mr Bronson from *Grange Hill*. He also played in *Star Wars*, and *Indiana Jones* and has been in literally hundreds of other wonderful productions playing a host of marvellous parts. Michael, it's a pleasure to have you here, thank you very much for joining us.'

'Thank you for asking me. Good afternoon Fred, good afternoon everyone.'

'Great, we'll talk in a minute. But first . . .'

And so it goes on. And it's great fun, I love it. On this Saturday they had footie reporters at both Brighton and Woking – it was Southern Counties Radio, remember – and Brighton and Woking happen to be very dear to me. My last school, after I left Aberdeen, was near Brighton, and Woking was our local team when we lived in Surrey.

For almost the rest of the afternoon Fred and I chatted, in between the sport and music, about my career and what was happening next for me. I must confess that I did ask how my teams were doing now and then, and at one point, whilst a record was playing, they let me speak direct to the reporter who was actually at the Brighton match. And when, after the interview had finished and I'd hung up, the phone rang again and it was Fred saying that we'd forgotten to mention what part I'd played in *Star Wars* and they'd had lots of calls and could I come back on the show, now, quickly, before they went off the air. I said, 'Delighted, but before I tell you that I played Admiral Ozzel, please tell me how Brighton and Woking are doing!'

Deary me, why I've decided to put the Bulloch next I simply don't know. Maybe 'cos he's a nice chap.

Boba Fett. I really can't get my head around what dear old Jeremy Bulloch has done with this character, it's wonderful.

I'd better start at the start. Do you recall a Cliff Richard film – I beg his pardon, he's now Sir Cliff of course – a Sir Cliff film called *Summer Holiday*? I most certainly do, and if you do, you'll remember a very young red-headed youngster – the one who didn't dance! Yep, that was Jeremy. He must be all of twenty-eight now (that's a year older than me, by the way, I often call him dad), he's a bloody good thesp, a superb conventioner, and my chum, I'm delighted to say.

Actually, I'll not be dwelling too long on his early career here, it started when he was nought and would take forever. And anyway, this is my book, let him write his own. Thereby, in fact, hangs a super tale I'll tell you somewhere.

In the summer of 1971 (Jeremy and I were discussing it recently and he confirmed the date), I arrived at Euston station in London on my way to Douglas Bader's wartime airfield. I had a contract to appear in a documentary film about an aeroplane that for some reason had fallen out of the sky. I've said before that an actor's life should always encompass every facet of our business and apart from that, this was damn good work for a jobbing thesp. I strolled up the platform and there was a face I recognised, from Auntie Beeb's 'The Newcomers'.

'Hello, you're Michael Sheard aren't you?' he said. 'My name's Jeremy Bulloch.' Our first meeting was as simple as that, and it's lasted . . . well, thus far anyway!

It is true you know, you meet someone in this lovely business of ours and you're mates for life. Even though you might not see each other again for years, it makes no difference, you pick up where you left off as though it were yesterday.

Well, would you flippin' believe it, I hardly do. I'm completely gobsmacked. I promise you that what I'm about to report next is absolutely true – ask Jeremy. The phone has just rung, this very minute, as I write. My Dearly B. answered and it was J.B. asking if I'd heard from Doug Murray in America about a convention in Oklahoma which he, Jeremy, had instigated. Dammit, I was going to ask him to write one of the forewords to these remembrances next time I saw him. Now he's already typing – I trust!

(I stopped after the previous paragraph and it's now the next day – or rather the following week, I can only tap when I'm free, remember – and I'm still a wee bit nonplussed by that call. Why should I have decided to write J.B. in when I did? There are something like seventy other chum headings on my list and I've not long been writing so there were masses to choose from. OK, coincidence, or maybe even telepathy, but certainly eerie!)

Right, let's continue. I mentioned above that I call Jeremy my dad. I'll come clean right away, he's not really older than me I'm older than him by about four months, but it makes for good copy at conventions.

I'll be talking of course in much greater detail of our convention enjoyment as I go. The time, for example, when Jeremy and Kenny Baker feigned sleep during a Q&A (question and answer) session at an Aberdeen con. I turn round, see them, put on my best Mr Bronson voice and bellow, 'You Boys, Pay Attention'! The three of us are doing a convention in America shortly; I wonder what they'll make of us. Another time I pretended to forget Jeremy's name, and on another occasion – in fact on many, this one works particularly well for some reason – I tell everyone that I gave J.B. my worst Mr Bronson wig. (In case you didn't know, Jeremy has a splendid head of hair, I don't.) All silly perhaps, but fun. And as I always say, if you don't enjoy conventions, if you don't have fun, *don't* do them. You'll have a bad time and it's not fair on the appreciators. I'll also talk more about that . . . later!

Suffice it for now to affirm that Bulloch is a very nice man and I look forward to doing many more gigs with him.

Heavens, I've just remembered a really daft one. We were flying to Scotland to do the aforementioned Aberdeen con, and Jeremy, who is a very seasoned professional of course and always arrives for appointments early, wasn't there when we were called. He'd rung the airport and been told that the flight had been badly delayed and he needn't get to the airport for at least an hour. Not so, and anyway we didn't know that. ('We', by the way, were Mike and Darren, two faithful apps who go to every convention possible and are great mates, and me.) Mike, Darren and I were greatly concerned at Bulloch's non-appearance and I showed it thus, 'Where is he? My Father's never late . . .' etc, and when J.B. finally rushed up, just as we were about to board, I continued in similar vain, 'Daddy. Where have you been?' Yes, OK, I know. Silly again, but still fun I think. No, dammit, I'm sure. The passengers certainly enjoyed it. That day the convention started early, at London's Heathrow!

If I don't move on Jeremy B. will get big headed. I shall return, I promise. But for now, let's see. How about a dollop of Penguin and Anthony Minghella?

The first thing to do, as always, is to set the scene. The phone rings, Dearly B. answers. (Somewhere in a book gone by, but assuredly not forgotten and still selling like there's no tomorrow, I explain how Beloved will always try to answer the phone if she can, as this gives me a moment to collect my thoughts.) Ros hands me the receiver.

'It's the Flamingo Park.'

'The what?'

'The Flamingo Park, you know, and Tony Minghella.'

Actually I didn't know. I was vaguely aware that there was a Flamingo Park somewhere near us, but what Anthony Minghella, who'd recently won Oscars galore for his latest film *The English Patient* and who'd been script editor on *Grange Hill* when I was creating Mr Bronson, had to do with it I definitely couldn't fathom. 'Hello,' I therefore said somewhat tentatively into the receiver.

'Afternoon, Mr Sheard. My name's Peter Adams. We've recently set up a penguin pool here at Flamingo Park and we wondered if you'd honour us by opening it.'

You know me, always honest. After, therefore, I'd pushed down the thought that they wanted me to pull the plug, I hastened to say as I always try to, filming commitments permitting, 'Yes, love to. When and where?' And if the answers to those questions are OK with my diary, 'Could you please check with me a week before the event? Thanks.' I've found over the years that it's simply not possible to keep all the reins in your own hands. There are not enough days in the week or hours in the day to have time to ring everyone and ask if this or that supermarket opening, or whatever, is still on. That's why I always put the onus on those who ask, and they always prefer it that way, too. This time, however, I did add a supplementary question:

'Why Anthony Minghella? I thought he was in Hollywood.'

'No, no. He's coming. He was born on the Isle of Wight you know.' (My ears pricked up. The Isle is, of course, my home island.) 'But please be assured Mr Sheard and have no fears,' he continued, 'he's just a guest, you are the celebrity.'

I told him, just a wee bit tongue-in-cheek, that of course I had no fears, I knew I was the star, and said that I looked forward to meeting him and re-acquainting myself with Tony.

The great day arrived. Dearly B. and I drove to the venue and were greeted by the gorgeous Lorraine (Peter's daughter) who was in charge of the penguins. And there were masses of people gathered, including the Island's MP, Dr Peter Brand, Gil Taylor (cinematographer on *Star Wars*) and of course that great director, writer and script editor extraordinaire, Mister Anthony Minghella.

This time he'd added yet another string to his bow. He was doing a sort of *Down Your Way*, without the music. There was a rather fetching radio sound lady with him and we did an interview for the Beeb about me, and why my main base was now on the Island of Wight.

'It's a wonderful place to re-charge your batteries, Tony. And there's so much to do. There really aren't enough hours in the day. There are wonderful walks along deserted (in the winter anyway) beaches, Ros is painting more than ever, then there's the garden . . .'

(Remember? I said I'd mention this one – the 'live on location' – when I was talking of the different types of radio interview!)

When it was time to open the penguin pool I duly gave my speech and then, just before I cut the ribbon surrounding said pool – in which I should add there were a great number of penguins already swimming happily about, wondering what all the fuss was about – I called on Tony to join me, wasn't that nice of me! What I actually said was that perhaps, if we all clapped loud enough, Tony might come up and cut the tape with me and added that if everyone clapped even more thunderously and maybe popped in the odd cheer, he might give me a part in his next movie. (Well, you can't let any opportunity slip by, you never know where the next job might come from!) It was all done in fun of course, Tony's a good friend and he's passionately in love with the Island. Aren't we all.

We cut the tape together and proceeded to feed the penguins, which clustered eagerly around us, once Lorraine arrived with a bucket of assorted fish – anything will do, herring, whitebait, mackerel, *et* anything else.

But the fun wasn't over. Two tiny little baby penguins, just arrived, were brought from a hiding place somewhere to be introduced to the pool and we were asked to name them. It was suggested that there was no question as to what mine should be called, it just had to be Bronson. Then it was Tony's turn. Very quietly and with much modesty he said, 'Well, I suppose mine had better be named Oscar.' There was certainly no answer to that!

It was a super day. Gil, his lovely wife Dionne, Dearly Beloved and I went down to the shore and had a great seafood lunch, and afterwards I returned to the penguins and repeated my duties at their afternoon feed. Then Dearly B. and I were invited to join Peter, his wife Margaret, and Lorraine, for dinner, and we finally trotted home not much before midnight. I'm delighted to report by the way that Bronson and Oscar are still chums!

Chapter 4

Oscar, hm . . . Philadelphia . . . How about a trip to the USA?

I've mentioned Doug Murray already, but not his wife Pam, I think, and I introduce her now. These two organise guests for conventions in America. It's hard work and the time difference plays havoc with your senses, but it's enormous fun.

Because I live where I do I learned very early on that if you don't want to be stressed about being late you should always try to catch the train before the train you should get, or if driving, endeavour to leave half an hour before you need to. I therefore arrived at London's Heathrow Airport really quite early on departure day. I checked in, one of the first, had a dram – I'm still not the best flyer in the world, far from it in fact, but needs must – and I couldn't see a soul I knew.

Kenny Baker, Mike Carter, and Peter Mayhew, were all due on the flight, but nothing – no sign of them. So I thought, blow it, if they're late and I have to carry the convention on my own I will. I'm the resourceful sort, me!

The flight was called and I boarded. I found my seat, which was nicely halfway down the aircraft, not too far from the screen so I could watch the movies. I find it best not to sleep on the way out if you can possibly manage it, then when you arrive, and it's evening again, five hours earlier, you can go to bed and hopefully have a good night's sleep.

I put my bag in the overhead locker, sat down, heaved a sigh and was just putting my fate in the hands of whatever it is that looks after those who are silly enough to jump into the air in a large metal can, when I heard a voice which I thought I recognised.

'Hello Michael, remember me?' Remember Johnny Hollis – how could I forget him?

We've appeared in countless productions together over the years, but never actually met, if you see what I mean. If you don't, then that's a reason for giving John his own personal paragraph later.

John and I chatted away like – like thesps who last chatted only yesterday, or who haven't seen each other for ages. We covered golf, agents, the state of the business, everything. And after a good meal and a couple of large ones I watched one of the in-flight movies and finally – but not for too long – had a wee kip.

Then we arrived, and suddenly there were Peter and Mike. They'd been with us all the time. OK, I know these aeroplanes carry a very goodly number of passengers but how could anyone miss Peter? There was, however, no Kenny, so he had missed the flight and I'd miss him. Ken's a particularly good egg and a great sport, and I'd been looking forward to seeing him again. (Kenny will never forgive me if I don't tell you now that his connecting flight from Manchester had been delayed, so it was no fault of his that he'd missed our Philly flight.) But my mate Kenny wasn't beaten yet. Not by a very long chalk!

Hell, but it takes ages to get through immigration and customs, doesn't it? The world over. Quite right, mind you, for all the obvious reasons. But in the States, I don't know, it does seem to take a trifle longer. Mike Carter in particular was held up for yonks. His mother-in-law lives in America and immigration wanted to know why he seemed to have been in and out of the country like a yo-yo. But eventually we were asked to have a nice day, and were met by one of the convention organisers who courteously bundled us into a large American eight-seater and proceeded to propel us towards our motel.

Now, Dearly B. will tell you that my memory is awful, but it's not true, how else could I be in the middle of my second book of memories? My memory is damn good, but selective, and D.B. knows it. However, I will make an admission here. Try as I may, I cannot remember the name of the motel. I've asked the others and they can't remember either. Neither can we name the restaurant on the other side of the six-lane motorway, which we had to cross in order to get anything, and I mean anything, to eat or drink. Maybe that's it. The restaurant was fine, once you got there – more later, eh Ken? But the motel! In spite of the fact that the bedrooms were clean and the man at reception bellowed, 'Have A Nice Day' every time you went anywhere near him, the motel had absolutely no ambience. This was mainly due to the fact, I'm sure, that there was no restaurant and no bar. We didn't really mind. After all, it was simply somewhere to rest our weary feet. But I felt very sorry for Pam (Doug wasn't on this trip. If I remember he was in Canada with Jeremy). Pam, too, had only recently flown in and had had to arrange everything by phone from her home in Florida. Perhaps a question or three might well have been asked of the Philadelphia organisers about accommodation, as it was they who would have made the sleeping arrangements. I don't know, maybe they didn't know their home city. Don't misunderstand me (he adds quickly, wanting to go back), it was fine. I slept like a baby. And the following morning, before we set off for the convention venue, we took our lives in our hands, crossed the motorway and had a super American breakfast, sunny side up.

And guess who led us fearlessly across those six lanes? Yeah, my chum Kenny B! He'd taken an alternative flight to New York and an internal connection and finally joined us just in time for those eggs.

It was now Saturday of course and I had great difficulty believing that I would be back home on Monday morning, the day after tomorrow, doing a book signing in li'l ol' Portsmouth, UK.

It's true, you know, everything in the USA is large. Or certainly seems to be. The venue, when we arrived for this toy fair – yes, actually this was not a convention in the ordinary sense of the word – was absolutely *ginormous*. Vast is far too small a description. The aircraft hangar-like structure seemed to go on for miles, with rows and rows and rows of stalls, selling everything you could ever imagine connected with Science-Fiction and then some. At one end, mounted on rostra in front of blue curtains, was a line of tables which also appeared to go on forever, but which in fact only stretched as far as the refreshment area, about halfway across. This was where we were going to sit and autograph, and talk to the appreciators. Being a fair, as opposed to a convention, there were no walkabouts and certainly no question and answer sessions planned. In truth, this somewhat disappointed me for, as you surely know by now, I look upon conventions as a chance to meet people, to wander around. No matter, Kenny and I did manage to promenade on both days and made lots of new friends among the stall holders who couldn't come to meet us, 'cos they were working. And there were tons of apps who came up to our tables. Hundreds of them.

And now, here speaks that wee lad frae Aberdeen who used to go to the flicks at every opportunity. We were not the only guests. There were American thesps there as well. All loosely connected with Sci-Fi. Adam West and Burt Ward, for example – Batman and Robin of course – and Pat Priest, the Munsters' daughter, who is now a grandmother herself, *et* many others.

And, Richard Anderson was also present, the American character actor, with more films and TVs to his credit than even he'd had hot dinners. *Forbidden Planet* was one of his early movies and I'd admired Richard for countless years. It's not often you get a truly supporting, jobbing, excellently damned good thespian, on that side of the water. Indeed it's been said many times that Britain produces the character actors and America makes the stars. Not strictly true of course, not by a long chalk in fact, but it illustrates the point.

Richard was great. I introduced myself, and we talked for ages about everything – did you know that his film idol and inspiration was none other than Gary Cooper? He asked to see *Yes, Mr Bronson*, and I gave him an autographed copy. When he came in on the following morning he told me that I'd kept him up most of the night because he couldn't put it down. He also mentioned that he was now producing and had a new *Million Dollar Man* script in preparation – he played Lee Major's boss, Oscar, of course – and that he'd like to find me something in it!

But I'm getting ahead of myself. Back to our arrival at the venue. Actually, I think I've given you a good scent of that morning. What I'd really like to do now is to have a Kenny Baker section, which will also continue this American story. But before I do, I must indeed return to our arrival, just for a mo. After our breakfast, across that motorway, we bundled into the eight-seater again and arrived quite early at the hangar. But the traders were already there – had been for hours it seemed: let no one say the Yanks don't catch the worm – and there was also another early bird. Mr David Prowse had not been expected, but there Dave was, already sitting at a table, and already signing away like there was no tomorrow. It was nice to see him again, we had a good blether and he bought my book; after asking to see it and giving it his seal of approval! More Dave later . . .

Now to Kenny. Kenny Baker has a wonderful car, of which he is very rightly very proud. It was, however, quite some time before I got a ride in the Roller. It's not always possible for him to take it to conventions, certainly not when we're in

America. But at last I got the chance at the aforementioned Basildon extravaganza – at the hotel, mind, not the venue itself where we were swamped. Kenny's Rolls Royce is completely unique. It has been adapted so expertly that you really would think that it was custom made. Everything blends in. The seat, which has been made smaller and higher, the controls – the pedals for instance have been lengthened – even the radio, which he operates by remote control. And it hums; yes Kenny's car actually hums quietly as it glides along. He's a very good driver, is Ken, and he took me for a trip around the hotel. It was like floating on air.

What a lovely man – and what a great performer. Kenny had a superb double act with his partner, the late Jack Purvis, and they played virtually every theatre in the land.

Let me give you a flavour of Kenny's personality. You remember the restaurant across the road from the motel in Philadelphia? Well, that evening, at the end of the first convention day, we returned first for a wee libation then for dinner. There were some enormously high stools round the bar, but in no time Kenny, John Hollis and I were perched up on top, talking to a young USA chap of thirty-odd who was a millionaire already and about to retire. They make 'em young in them thar hills!

Later, after we'd been joined by the others, Pam, Peter, and Mike *et al*, we had a super meal: gigantic T-bone steaks as big as dinner plates, salad and French fries, followed by mulberry pie. And every twenty minutes or so, when a particular piece of music sounded, the nubile waitresses – eight to ten lovely lasses, dressed in traditional, if rather short, black dresses and little white aprons – would stop whatever they were doing and give us a line-dance. Don't please ask me exactly what it is but there were a lot of high kicks involved. After the second time they'd performed, Kenny, who was sitting at the far end of the table, caught my eye. 'When they do that again, Michael, I'm going to join them.' In a flash of bravado I replied,

'Kenny, mate, if you do I'm with you!'

And I was, high kicks and all, and we have 'Served with Texas Pride' badges which they gave us afterwards to prove it.

Before I leave my chum for the moment, I must tell you about our return from Philly. A long but enjoyable second day – during which we were even asked to sign the sun-visor of a huge six-wheeler truck which was standing in the centre of the hall – finally came to an end. Once more we were whisked into the eight-seater and beautifully transported to the airport to await the evening flight which would land us in the UK at something like eight the following morning – pushing us forward the extra five hours this time.

We were all tired after a happy weekend, and when we'd checked in, we found a convenient watering hole on the way to our gate of departure. But, would you believe it, once again no Kenny! There's a great rapport twixt those who are on a convention together and we were concerned about him. But there was no need. A few minutes later there was Ken, trundling his wheeled suitcase behind him, accompanied by the most lusciously sexy blonde you've ever seen. He's always doing that is Kenny, chatting up the birds. But this one was different, this one was something very special.

'Can I introduce you,' he said nonchalantly, 'to the wife of the Captain of our flight? She's come over with her husband for the trip and wonders if we'd like to watch the take-off and landing. You see, there are two spare seats, Michael (I must have looked particularly dumb-struck), in the cockpit behind the pilot.'

In no time at all we'd arranged that Kenny and I – I knew I'd have to cross everything, because of my fear of flying, but it was a chance not to be missed – would see the take-off, and

Peter and John would watch the landing. (Mike C. had gone on to his Mum's.) We duly thanked the lovely lady, who said she'd arrange everything and have the stewardesses call us, and we plied her with at least a triple thank you vodka each. I for one had never even been in an aeroplane cockpit, let alone watched an actual take-off. Perhaps this was what I'd been waiting for. If I was actually there, as it happened, and could see how expertly the pilots handled everything, I might be cured of my fear of flying.

When our flight was called, we boarded with excited anticipation for the adventure ahead, settled back in our seats and waited. Then . . . nothing, not a bloody thing. No one came to invite us to anything.

It wasn't Kenny's fault. There were two flights due to take off for London at almost the same time that day and the lovely sexy blonde was the wife of the other Captain!

A short digression. I've always enjoyed thespian 'in' jokes, provided they are harmless and don't detract from the action, and Dr Martin Rogerson (Edinburgh *Dr Who* Appreciation Society) reminded me of a great Gareth Thomas story the other day. Gareth had been up to Edinburgh to join the Society for a Claremont Bar evening. (He's almost as good a storyteller as I am!)

Gareth's idea was that Blake (Gareth, of course) should be walking swiftly down a *Blake's 7* futuristic street, and meet Dr Who – in Gareth's time it would have been Tom – coming the other way. Gareth would say 'Hello Doctor,' to which Tom would reply 'Morning Blake' then they'd pass and go their separate ways.

If you think about it there's no reason why this shouldn't happen. The Tardis of course can go anywhere, backwards and forwards in time.

Gareth, I believe, suggested it to Auntie BBC, but the bit of fun got no further. Pity, really, I think it would have been great. I feel sure that Tom would have agreed. I wonder if he knew. I must remember to ask him at the next *Who* convention.

These harmless little jokes, between hard-working dedicated professionals, happen quite frequently. (See *Yes, Mr B.* for the time William Holden came to visit the set of *Escape to Athena* – I was delighted to be involved with that one. And the time – at the Richmond Theatre – when a certain actress, who was supposed to have no clothes on under her fur coat, turned upstage, opened it, and really *was* starkers.) I don't know, perhaps they help to relieve tensions; anyway it's great to have a damn good laugh – after the take or scene is over of course!

Incidentally, although my *Blake's 7* was later (after Gareth had left and Paul Darrow had taken over as boss), I work a lot with Gareth at cons, and as he has a similar sense of humour to mine we always get on like a house on fire. Mind you, my tipple is of course the heather, while Gareth's is the barley!

A small footnote, I saw my episode of *B's 7* recently – 'Powerplay'. I was bloody good! *Section Leader Clegg* . . .

Chapter 5

OK . . . the Isle of Man. I was invited to be the surprise guest at Andy's twenty-first remember? I mentioned it at the start. In order to recount this nosegay, however, I must also include 'The Saturday Aardvark', and the first time I did 'The Phill Jupitas Show' (both live shows of course), because, God help me, they all three took place on the same flippin' day! It went like this:

On the Friday evening I came up to London and had dinner with Simon (son number one, the chartered accountant, soon to become a film producer and keep his old man in work). I stayed the night at his sumptuous flat – these accountants don't 'alf do well thank goodness – and the following morning he drove me to Auntie BBC's Children's studio at the Television Centre. And waited for me. Thing was, you see, that I'd also agreed, long before the Aardvark had contacted my agent, to do the Phill Jupitas BBC Greater London Radio Show that morning. Reluctantly ('cos I'm such a splendid guest!), Phill's producer had agreed to allow me to do Aardvark, provided I could be with Phill by nine-thirty a.m., instead of nine, when *both* programmes were due to start. Oh dear!

In order to keep you with me I'd better explain that the TV Centre is of course in Wood Lane, and BBC Greater London Radio is right down the other end of Westway, in the Baker Street area. Quite a fairish way on a busy Saturday morning.

But it all worked out very splendidly in the end. Phill had the (TV) Aardvark Show on a monitor in his (radio) studio, and did a running commentary: 'No, Mr Bronson hasn't appeared yet – hang on, yes, here he is' . . . etc.

I have huge respect for the super thesp who spends his Saturday mornings leaning backwards on a wee trolley with his hand shoved up an Aardvark's arse.

Otis, or 'Fuzzy-Face' as he signs his photographs, dedicated a photo to Lucy, daughter of Ian Rolfe a producer friend of mine, and he mentioned her by name – and her broken arm – on the show that morning. He has my undying admiration. He really does spend the whole time lying on his back. He has a small monitor at his beck, so that he can see what's going on, and he does the voice of the creature as well. He, and the equally talented Kirsten O'Brien, rehearse their bits whilst the filmed inserts are transmitting. That's the only time they have. Great stuff, I'm glad it's not me. Well, not every week anyway!

Back to Phill. By now I'd finished saying, 'You Boy – Now Pay Attention', in a Bronsonish voice to Otis, who had been suitably terrified, and Simon (my Simon) was hurtling me down Westway in his BMW.

'Alright, he's on his way,' Phill said (we had the car's radio tuned in), 'Mr Bronson will be here soon, if he gets through the traffic at Marylebone. Don't go away . . .'

I got to 'The Phill Jupitas' studio at nine-forty-three a.m. Yes, I know, thirteen minutes late. But how Simon managed it I just don't know. The Saturday traffic was absolutely terrible. He dropped me off at the rear of the studio, which was nearer, and I was thus able to rush straight on to the airwaves.

'Good . . . (pant, pant) morning. Sorry I'm late Phill . . . (pant)'

'That's fine, Michael, we've been charting your progress. Delighted you made it. Pull up a chair, I'll ask one of the nice young ladies to get you a cup of coffee and we can have a chat. I hear you've written a book . . .'

All very relaxed. I settled down, the coffee arrived, and we talked, in between the records. Phill had read *Yes, Mr B.* from cover to cover and was very complimentary, which was exceedingly kind of him and I told him so.

'You don't have to thank me, I mean it. I always say what I mean. Did you know I was born on the Isle of Wight . . . Just a minute, there appears to be someone trying to attract our attention. Do you know him?' It was Simon waving at me through the window, which divides the control room from the studio. He'd finally found a parking space and had brought my bag.

'That's my son, Simon,' says I.

'Your son? Well, let's have him in. Come on Simon. Come and join your famous father.'

Simon did join us and was great. After Phill had had a chat with him about the Prince's Youth Business Trust, that Simon was working for at the time, and we'd all said how nice it was to have a Superstar (me, of course) on the show, Simon went off to get on with his day. I'm sorry he did actually, because Phill and I continued to have a great, no, a wonderful show.

(That's why I was asked back a few weeks later when Michael Cronin – Mr Baxter from *Grange Hill* – was a guest.)

Phill is a huge Sci-Fi appreciator and he said that we must do a scene. And we did. I played the lead of course and Phill played all the other characters, apart that is, from the baddie. We had to get a baddie. Enter Phill's producer, who gave a superb rendition, in the strongest Welsh accent you have ever heard. You could literally have cut it with a knife. It – we – were superb! After the show – it was something like twelve-fifteen p.m. by this time – I was asked to join them all for a dram at the local hostelry, but I had to decline. I had a flippin' train to catch for Liverpool and the Isle of Man, hadn't I?

It had been a great morning with Auntie Beeb, both TV and Radio. But I had to move on. Once I'd got to King's Cross station and had caught the Liverpool train, I had, on paper at least, masses of time. I was due to arrive (in Liverpool) almost two hours before the catamaran departed for Douglas. No problem. No?

The train belted along, until we reached Wavertree. Those of you who have read t'other book of mine will remember that Karen, my number one fan, hails from Wavertree. Wavertree is just outside Liverpool, isn't it Karen?

Perhaps Karen wanted to say hello. Whatever, we stopped and we didn't move. They gave us complimentary cold wet things with which to wipe our hands and face. But we still didn't budge. Eventually we were told that it was something to do with a massive electrical failure in the Liverpool region. But I blame Karen, and the woman sitting next to me who'd said we were making such good time that we'd surely arrive early!

I wasn't the only one anxious. I'd already asked the very accommodating guard if he could suggest a solution and he'd radioed ahead and had taxis standing by to run eight of us to the catamaran. In the end I think they must have put a torch battery in the engine. We literally crawled into the station just in time and bundled into those taxis. I had but a fleeting view of Liverpool – never been there before, looks nice – as we raced through the city, down to the quay, and scrambled aboard the last cat for the Isle of Man that day.

Hey ho. But I had a very peaceful two hourish passage over to this lovely island. I met my super hosts – not Andy of course – and was swiftly transported to my hotel. I then had three minutes to change before I was rushed on to Andy's party, which was being held in another hostelry, fairly nearby.

Let me tell you how things unfolded. But hang on, just a party minute . . . there's something I must say before another word is tapped. Throughout these pages I'm going to be mentioning hundreds of lovely people, from all walks of life. People like 'Peterhead' Craig who refused to buy my book, but I'll get him next time, and 'Edinburgh' Craig who loves *Rocky Horror* and who eventually did buy, after we'd played the gag for virtually the whole weekend. But I can't, I simply can't mention everyone I've ever met along the way, it's just not possible. Apart from anything else it would end up as nothing more than a book of names, and useful though the telephone directory is it can get just a smidge monotonous. So may I please say right now a very big Thank You to everyone. I continue to enjoy meeting new friends and old, and I appreciate tremendously all the great chats we've had. But if by chance you don't find your name in these pages, please, it doesn't suggest for one second that you've been forgotten or that you are not appreciated. Pay Attention! Is that understood?

Back to Douglas. Rob Craine, my driver, got me to the party on time and I was smuggled down the back stairs to the basement of the hotel where the gig was already in full swing . . . Oh heck! I've not told you how I came to be with Anorax Anonymous, have I? Shite, I'd better put that straight right now.

Something like six weeks previously I'd had a letter via my agent from Steve Hall – he's the sort of leader, the organiser-cum-spokesperson – asking if I'd be willing to pop over to meet 'The Isle of Man *Dr Who* Appreciation Society', and that they'd be particularly pleased if I could manage the weekend of Andy Byrne's twenty-first, because he was a massive app of mine. Not only of my umpteen *Who* appearances, but of all my work, and in very particular, dear old Maurice Bronson.

Right, scene set, reason given. I'm in the basement remember. I'm hiding behind a pillar, and I've now been handed a radio mike. Andy is at the other side of the dance floor and they've managed to seat him with his back to me. He's opening presents and when he gets to a 10 x 8 photo of me – which I'd signed a couple of weeks previously and the Anorax had had framed – and he's saying something like, 'Oh Great', and I bellowed, 'You Boy. Now Pay Attention! You don't need to look at a photograph when the real thing is here, in person!' and the Birthday Boy all but flipped. Sorry Andy but you really nearly did.

'Oh, that's great,' he said again. 'Who did the imitation? I know, he recorded it didn't he? Did he record it? Umm . . . ?'

'No,' says I coming out from my hiding place, 'I'm here alright, bow tie and all!'

Oh Gordon B. what a night. What a *morning* – the party didn't finish until nearly four a.m. And what a day to follow. The food, I must give mention to Andy's Mum's food. It was gorgeous and went on forever. I danced right up to and including the last dance. Well, I do tend to you know. Wait till I tell you about the Klingon sword dance at that convention in Aberdeen.

The next day – in fact the same day, we hadn't finished until the Sunday small hours remember – these lovely lads gave me the most wonderful tour round their Island. This included a visit to Castle Rushen in Castletown, where you all but jump out of your skin when you enter under the portcullis, and a replica guard, bow at the ready, shouts 'Halt! Who goes there?'. There's also another very life-like chap from yesteryear who growls most effectively as he sits on the loo! We also took a turn round part of the TT race circuit, something I've always wanted to see. (I can't resist telling you – there *will* be more to follow later.) I was in my element!

Before I leave the Isle of Man (for the moment at least, yep, I am due back there shortly), a wee snippet more. On the Sunday morning, after I'd had about four hours sleep, I went for a little walk, before I was due to be picked up by the lads, to clear my head as much as anything. And I decided to give Dearly Beloved a call to tell her of the great night we'd had. As I peered down the narrow Douglas High Street, I was miffed to see that there were two people waiting to use the phone. When I reached the box I found that it was Norman Wisdom and George Formby! Both have a strong connection with the Isle of Man. Or rather I'm afraid, in Formby's case, had. George Formby, who made a film on the island about the TT race, has been gone for a long time (I saw him once in panto a short time before he died. He was old certainly, but bloody marvellous). Dear Mr Wisdom still lives on the Man of course.

I was looking now at two excellent bronze statues, made in their likeness and honour, with one tiny flaw. Formby's statue stands, or rather leans – on a lamppost, naturally – Norman's likeness sits on a bench, legs crossed, and every time it rains a little puddle collects in his lap!

Drewe Henley and Angus MacInnis. I've done them alphabetically, so as not to offend. But it should I suppose be t'other way around – MacInnis/Henley – because I know Angus so much better. But what the alphabet, I'll stick to it this way.

Actually I'd wanted to meet Drewe for ages, and I only finally managed it last year at a wee convention in Honiton organised by Mr Steve Parsons (christened Paul Miley the Second by me, after the convention organiser Paul Miley who is never on time because Steve is never on time either)! What I'd like to say here is that Drewe – once married to Felicity Kendal and Jacqueline Pearce – is a most personable guy. He was a very superb thesp and now lives in the West Country with his lovely new wife, Lynn. He's not been too well lately, and we all wish him a very speedy recovery. Come on, mate, we need you back under the lights. He was a great and handsome Red Leader wasn't he?

Now it's on to Gold. Agnes – oops – Angus! (Sorry chum – you do know, don't you, that you only take the piss out of people you like?) The first time I worked with the star of the new Sci-Fi series, *Space Island One*, he killed me. Actually we killed each other, in Yugoslavia. It was of course a movie and

a damn good one in fact, considering it was a sequel. Angus
and I both fell off the *Force 10 from Navarone* cast list at the
same time. And we did it wonderfully. He shot me and I shot
him, or perhaps I shot him and he shot me, or perhaps
Harrison Ford, who was also in the film, had a shot in there
somewhere. Whichever is the bravest, for me, that's how it
happened!

Strange isn't it, that however good the memory is there are
certain moments which are so crystal clear that they really
could have happened this morning. *Force 10* was made in 1977,
that's well over twenty years ago, but on the particular evening
I'm recalling I was wearing jeans, a greenish shirt, anorak, and
light brown leather slip-on shoes. OK, I know they were leather
'cos I've always hated smelly trainers. But if I tell you that
Harrison was also in denims, with a brown shirt and a casual
sort of tweedy jacket, and that Angus wore grey trews, red
shirt and quite a strikingly blue donkey jacket, you'll appreciate
that even my superb recall is in overdrive for this one.

We were all staying in the same hotel in Opatija. It was a
Saturday and I was popping out to call Dearly B. – from the
Post Office, never make calls from the hotel, it's far too
expensive – and there coming in were the two American
thespians (actually Angus is Canadian but no matter).

'Michael, where the hell are you going in such a hurry?'
said Harrison.

'Oh, I'm just off to phone my wife, she likes me to keep in
touch if I can.'

'Hell, I'm not surprised,' said Angus, 'a handsome guy like
you.'

'Oh shucks,' says I, 'you do say the sweetest things.'

'No, I mean it!'

'Yeah,' Harrison put in, 'hey, we'll be back out in a minute
and we're going for a meal at that place at the far end of the

street, where we were the other night. Come join us for a meal when you've done.'

I did, and we had a great evening – yes, I do still remember. I had pork, a great speciality in that part of Europe.

A final note on Angus for the moment, I mentioned that I'm returning to the Isle of Man in a few weeks. This time I'm going (principally) to do an Anorax *Dr Who* convention with the lovely Katy Manning, but there's a possibility that I might stay on to appear in an episode of *Space Island One* – if my agent extracts the digit and gets things organised. That'll be great, perhaps I'll get to be killed by my chum Angus again!

Having said what I've just said about memory, I have to add something that occurred to me last weekend when I was lying in the en-suite bath next to my hotel bedroom in Paisley, after a great ceilidh at the ConeXion convention that was held in the University. I have now to confess that if there's one thing I really find it extremely hard to do, it's to differentiate between one hotel bedroom/bathroom and another. I can recall special, exceptional ones, indeed the Paisley room was magnificent, huge and with two tellies, but they are mostly all the same – a room, a bathroom (there's never a window in the bathroom of course, just a thing which goes buzz every time you turn on the light), and a trouser press. So no reflection on me for not remembering them, eh?

That said I'd like to take you to . . .

. . . Peterhead. I want to do Peterhead now because I've just received a fax – a copy of a letter regarding books, which was received by my publishers from the 'USS Wallace' (a *Star Trek* appreciation society based in my home city of Aberdeen), and it's reminded me. So why not mention them now? I am their Honorary Admiral after all. I first met the Wallace at a glorious convention organised by the super Scott McMillan –

he and it will come later. The Wallace, Captain Jamie Kelly, Commander Clark Bowie, Ian, *et al*, arranged to get me to Peterhead for what was a truly wonderful weekend. I know I seem to say this a lot, but it was, and a great con too.

Oh, but I haven't finished. I must tell you of the excellent time I had with the Matson twins, who organised, with Mr McMillan the Supercalaf (sorry I can't spell it) the *Star Trek* weekend at the Palace Hotel in Peterhead.

No, I can't remember my room, but everything else was great and I'm sure it was too. To start with, I sold a mass of books, in spite of the fact that we were snowed in (or is it under?) for the whole of the first day. Even Aberdeen airport was shut – yep, in fact it happened only about two hours after I'd landed. But mine hosts were . . . wait till I tell you!

I – we – really did have a fabulous two and a half days and on the Sunday there was a small gap, between the end of the main event and the start of the disco. Mr McMillan and I were invited to the Matson house for dinner. We arrived and were immediately invited into the front room. And before I could sit down, David (Matson), father of the twins, said, 'Here, Michael, try this. Scott?'

Well, Scott had first taste of the brew proffered, and it all but blew his head off. Don't please misunderstand me, it was the most wonderful whiskey we had ever experienced. It was as smooth as velvet, as dark as a peat stream, and as warming as Christmas round a log fire. The only problem was that it stood, very proud, at 120 per cent proof!

I don't actually think that even I can top that. Let's leave Peterhead with the memory of that wonderful dinner at the Matsons'. The meal, cooked by Mum (Helen) was also out of this world – the most excellent beef I've ever tasted, beautiful vegetables, done perfectly, the most exquisite trifle. And so we pass on to . . . Dave. I have a special rapport with this guy.

It was Dave Prowse after all who almost single-handedly blazed the *Star Wars* convention trail. Let no one forget that.

When I first met him we were both, well, a wee bit younger than we are today. I arrived at Elstree studios on a rather cold, drizzly autumn morning to begin what I thought would be just another job. A nice one. But still a journeyman acting role. In fact I was particularly pleased that the part wasn't too lengthy because it fitted neatly between two other far more important engagements (or so I thought) – *Enemy at the Door* and *Jukes of Piccadilly* with Nigel Hawthorn. Little did I know!

I must stop doing this, patting myself on the back. If you've read *Yes, Mr Bronson* you'll know what a super career has been enjoyed by me – thus far. There are some great things already completed and exciting possibilities in the pipeline. I had a fax last evening for example, asking if I'd be interested in playing Dr Who. Perhaps by the time this little collection of words reaches the bookstalls, you'll know if I did.

But back to mate Dave. And I do consider him a friend, a mate – I hope he does me! We've been through a lot together, haven't we Dave? Again, by the time you read this, I'll have done his convention (Multicon '98) in Blackpool and told you about it I'm sure.

OK, that cold autumn morning. My chums, Ken Colley, Michael Culver, and Julian Glover, were with me, and we were asked to 'stand by' . . . Dave was super and tremendously helpful that day because he'd done it all before and could show us the ropes.

Many years later I met him for a second time, in America, Houston airport. He was dashing one way, I another – on my way to *Green Ice* and the killing of Omar Sharif. But we're now meeting lots of times, conventioning, and I must just mention one meeting we had recently which in fact redounds to his credit. I'm sure he won't mind my recounting it.

A couple of weeks ago I was invited, along with Jacqueline Pearce and Michael Keating (*Blake's 7*, Michael was with my agent) to a signing gathering at Dave Phillips' house in Biggin Hill. Dave (Phillips) is a good egg, by the way, and if you ever need a genuine signed photo of anyone – anyone from Gloria Swanson to Alan Ladd and Harrison Ford – get on to him. I'll give you the address.

Back to Biggin. We had been there all morning and into the afternoon when Dave (Prowse) suddenly arrived. Dave lives quite close to Dave Phillips and he'd come along to boost the guest profile. (He didn't know that I was going to be there!) The only trouble was that there was nowhere for him to sign. We who had been there from the dot of morning and had indeed had an excellent dinner with Dave (Phillips) and his lovely wife Debs the evening before, had been allocated all the available space. So Dave Prowse had no alternative but to set up a table in Dave Phillips' garage!

Nice man. As I mentioned, I'm doing his Blackpool convention later. It's going to be flippin' gigantic!

I enjoyed that remembrance, and I'll come back to both the Daves later. But now what? I know, let's pop along to Honiton and then nip down the road to Bristol. Although both these smallish conventions were some time apart, I did both of them with Warwick Davis – Wicket in *Star Wars* – just the two of us, so they fit together quite nicely.

(No, Warwick, I'm not going to be so un-gallant. You are far too important not to have a section all to yourself in my book. You chum will feature, same as all the others. In fact more so because you'll also play a leading part here!)

Now, I love big movie sets, large agencies, whacking parties, *et al*, and I adore vast conventions. But if you press me, I would be bound to say that I think small is best of all. At a small convention for instance you're able to spend more time getting to know people. The same is true, of course, of the small versions of the other examples I've cited, indeed of everything that's small I guess.

Let's start with Honiton then, Honiton in Devon. A small convention fronted by a smashing chap called Steve Parsons. Steve was very ill not that long ago and spent months in hospital. I don't know if that's where he caught the Sci-Fi bug, but when he came out he decided that he would put on a charity convention as a thank you to the hospital.

The one Warwick and I did was in fact his second, the first had been even smaller, so that Steve could test the con water. I feel sure his actual words were 'test the beer' as both his 'do's were held in the bar and restaurant area of the Dolphin Hotel. Mind you, a lot of conventions are held in like establishments!

Oh . . . Merde. Do you know what I've done? I've omitted to mention another guest who appeared with us at Steve's convention. How could I have forgotten Drewe Henley? It's only because in my enthusiasm to get it all down, I've got ahead of myself. Drewe, I'm very sorry chum. I feel sure, however, that Drewe would be the first to add that he was in fact only able to be with us at Honiton for a very short while. But as I've said previously, it gave me the chance to meet him, and I'm very grateful for that. Drewe, by the way, had been the only guest at Steve's first – test the beer – convention.

And now hangs a wee bit longish tale. I've just had a call, again, actually as I'm writing (and if you don't believe me ask him) from that superb convention entrepreneur the great Mr Steve Parsons. Honestly. I told him I was in the middle of jotting Honiton and he said, and I quote:

'Michael, that's great, but please don't leave anything out. Tell them that it was leukaemia I had and tell them how you came down here a day early so you could visit Caroline. (Caroline Edgecumbe is a super lass and *Star Wars* app who'd had a fall from her wheelchair and was in the same hospital – Exeter General – which had treated Steve.) And you be sure to tell them,' Steve continued, 'that our convention here in Honiton was the best convention ever because of y. . .'

Modesty forbids me from completing Steve's remark!

Shucks. There's only one thing to do now and that's to move on swiftly to Bristol with Mike and Tara. What a lovely couple.

But just before I do, I must drop in a couple more thoughts, Honiton-wise. I've just got back from Steve's next – his number three – convention. Yep, today it's a whole year later (doesn't time fly) and I'm popping these remembrances of last year into the pot because this – my number two book – is off to my publishers in the morning. OK here we go . . .

> Here's to Andy and Andy, Bruce Smith and Dear
> Parsons,
> Jeremy, Karyn, Doris Parsons and John,
> And, didst know there are ghosts at
> The hotel called Dolphin?
> And a small room at back of reception which when
> I opened the door to collect my stored luggage . . .

. . . there – staring me slap in my face – was the most luscious bum I have seen in a long time. A curvaceous waitress was changing her pants!

Right, back to yesteryear proper. Mike Parker in fact was a dealer at Honiton so that makes the connection even stronger. A dealer is of course he, or she, who has a table in the dealers' room and sells his or her wares. Everything Sci-Fi. Models, photos (Dave Phillips for example does lots of these fairs), comics, playing cards, and costumes. There's a lovely lady I've met at these functions, on several occasions, who does the most exquisite glass paintings, and there is Danny.

Danny Flynn is a remarkable man I'll tell you about later. But for the moment, can I tantalise you by saying that Danny has – could – have given a new slant to my career?

Mike had asked both Warwick and me if we'd join him in Bristol for his company, Twisted Toys' fair, whilst we were in Honiton. And Twisted Ts was super. Large – one third of an indoor basketball pitch hall in fact – venue, with the dealers ranged round the sides and Warwick and me in the middle. I did suggest to Mike that this did perhaps make us a wee bit too high profile, but he insisted – honest!

This was not a charity event you understand, and although I'll go to that studio in the sky saying that selling is not the most important element for me at conventions, by far it's not, I'd sold out of Bronson books by midday and the show had only started at ten in the morning.

So that's all for the mo, I think, about Bristol and Honiton. Except to say that I'm delighted that Steve (Parsons) is looking to the future – when he phoned just now he gave me the date of his next convention, Feb. 21st – and that I had a superb dinner in Bristol after the show with Mike, Tara and Mike's parents, and I've promised to return there very soon, with my Father, Jeremy B.

Chapter 6

See. I told you, Warwick, that I'd give you a section all to yourself.

Actually, chum Warwick Davis alights here by pure chance, and if you believe that you'll believe anything! Fact is, I thought they – Honiton, Bristol and Warwick – went naturally together.

Did you know that Warwick was only eleven when he first appeared in *Return of the Jedi*? Yep, and it was his Mum who sent off his details. He was first cast as one of the crowd, but was very soon promoted to a leading character. Since then he's done masses, *Time Bandits* with Kenny B. for example.

I first met his lovely wife Samantha and their delightful baby daughter, Annabelle, who is the spitting image of her Dad, at Honiton. Warwick is a great chap to convention with, he's so – shite, for once I'm stuck for a word – he's so . . . honourable.

Yes, I think that's the cap that fits. If Warwick agrees to appear at a convention for example, he'll be there. At Honiton he was the first to commit himself to return the following year.

We get on famously. Let me give you a flavour:

At Bristol, as I've said, the dealers were ranged around the sides of what had indeed been a World War Two aircraft hangar – before its expert conversion into a sports complex – with Warwick and me in the middle.

Warwick had to ring our pal Kenny (B.) about another convention, and when he got through – on his mobile – we were still in the 'middle' of things. He said that I sent my regards –

'Oh no, I don't,' says I in a loud Bronsonish voice from the other side of our square (of tables in the middle), 'I send my *love!*' The lovely company of people in the hall stopped almost dead in their tracks and looked at us, so Warwick and I continued the repartee.

'Yes, that's right, his love,' Warwick continued. 'No of course he's not like that, he just likes you . . .' and so the double act continued, quite spontaneously. It was a huge laugh for all of us and that's what conventions are all about. Enjoying oneself. Sometimes in a rather daft manner it's true, for both attendees, and very surely for guests. But why the convention not?

I don't know what Kenny thought that day, I must remember to ask him next time I see him. Now let me see, will that be Oklahoma, or Barry's wee Plymouth 'do' . . .

Right, now I'm going to relate a quick couple of book signings that I did in the land of my birth – my beloved Scotland. By the way, those who are under age had better get their parents to read these mementoes first, because the tag in both cases is a wee tad naughty!

Those who've read *Yes, Mr Bronson* will know that by pure fluke – nothing to do with my being born in Scotland or that my Dad had got me a job working back stage during the panto when I was still a weeish lad – I actually started my professional career with the Perth Repertory Theatre.

I hadn't been back to Perth for years, and when I found myself working in Scotland I thought it would be grand if I could do a book signing actually in the theatre. Happily my publishers agreed with me, and the upshot was that I stayed on in Scotland for an extra week and not only did a signing in Perth, but in my home city of Aberdeen as well.

It was fantastic to see the old Perth theatre again, much changed since my day but still recognisable in places, and to visit landmarks of yesteryear, like the house which Dearly B. and I (we met in Perth) had shared with Donald Sutherland and his wife. But my main purpose in telling you about Perth this time is to describe my meeting with the sweet lady who in my day had been a very junior junior, but who was now in charge of everything to do with the front of house box office.

'It's Michael! Hello Michael, nice to see you after all this time. So you've come to do a wee signing of your book, then. You'll find it awful hard. You ken the people of Perth, it's all fur coats and nae knickers up here.' I sold out, 'course I did!

Bruce Miller's bookshop is now in Aberdeen's Union Street, but when I was a tot it was round the corner at the top, not far from the Odeon cinema. I normally do signings with the WHSmiths chain, which in Scotland are known as Waterstone's (same firm). But there was only one shop for me in my home city. Bruce Miller's has always been privately owned and today it stands proud amongst all the multiples. Indeed I like the fact, and I have a sneaking feeling they do too, that it's now almost bang opposite Waterstone's.

I'd been royally entertained the previous evening and given a bed for the night by David Angus (*Grange Hill* scriptwriter), and his wife Sheila, who are lucky enough to live in my city, and on the day of the signing David gave me a lift to the shop. And there was a queue, a lovely queue of appreciators waiting for me. I've had queues before, but this queue was very special. I was grateful and touched that I, a prodigal son, was remembered. Thank you Aberdeen, I'll be back soon.

OK, now the tag. I think it was the sixth copy I signed that day. As I was writing, the chap and I chatted, and he told me this story of the day he went to the Aberdeen première of the new, re-jigged *Star Wars*.

'The cinema was packed,' he said, 'and I settled back in my seat as the opening credits for *The Empire Strikes Back* began, anticipating your excellent performance and death. When you made your first entrance, a chap at the back of the auditorium stood up and shouted, "Fuck me, it's Mr Bronson!" and everyone in the cinema cheered!'

In another book I've already set the record straight. Nicholas Courtney has worked with more Doctors than I have. All of them. I won't even state here (oh yes I will!) that he had it easy, for apart from the story he did with Billy Hartnell he, Nick, played the same part every time, the super Brigadier Lethbridge Stewart. It really is an excellent characterisation. And the way he's been able to gel with each Doctor is masterly. I was delighted that he (sort of) got a story to himself when Andrew Beech made *Downtime*. The Beeb should have done that, you know, given him a story to himself. All the Doctors were smashing, but so was the Brigadier, and he surely earned it.

How long have I known Nick Courtney? If I say too long, you'll get the wrong idea. We're not old, are we mate? But one has chums, and one has super, best friend chums. Chums who last a lifetime. I love all my friends in this super business, but inevitably there are special mates, stands to reason. Pete, Kenny, Father Jeremy, and my old singing 'pardner' Nick C., to name but four, belong here. There are many more, thank the stars.

I spoke to Nick on the phone today, 'Dear old darlin' where's that foreword you promised for the new book?' says I.

'Ah, well now, Michael, it's on its way, by this very weekend at the latest . . .' Can't you hear Nick talking? I most certainly can.

We shared agents for a time and I'll finish by saying that I've never seen him working better than when he was playing a transvestite! See you soon mate.

I must give the *Star Wars* gang a word. Without assistant directors, no movie or TV would ever get made. No, they did not pay me to say that! Fact is, of course, that everybody in their own field is indispensable, but the assistants are more high profile and it is they who are responsible for getting the day's work done.

Oh yes, the director will determine what we put in the can, but it is his assistants who must make sure that all is ready for the next set up. And they deserve praise, lots of it.

David Tomblin is a director of TV films in his own right, and Steve Lanning has gone on to produce for Lynda la Plante. (Now there's a thought. I first met Steve on *Space 1999*, so I've known him a long time, and he hasn't used me on any of Lynda's great series – yet!) Roy Button, I admit my memory is somewhat hazy here, but I seem to recall that he, too, has established an enviable production career.

It's odd. I find I can only recall snippets of memories about these three. I'm sure it's because they were so good at their jobs and had to be everywhere, at all times. I distinctly remember Steve, on a very cold early spring morning during the filming of *Space* greeting me with a heartily upbeat, 'Good morning Michael. You're very early' and Roy very kindly steering me around Elstree studios when, on the first morning of *Empire* filming, I'd completely lost my bearings. And I think it was on *The New Avengers* that I bumped into David. He was directing the next episode to the one I was doing. 'I wanted you in mine,' he said, 'and the casting people told me you were here already.' (I'd have loved to have done David's episode.)

Anyway, nice to recall some truly very nice professionals.

Now, if you don't mind, I'd like to go back to Scotland. No, it's not that I'm feeling homesick having just written about it, that was penned on a different date. So let me take you quickly to: Dundee Radio; The Fred MacAulay Show for Auntie Beeb in Glasgow; The Art Sutter Show for Grampian TV; and Scott McMillan's wonderful convention at the Stakis Hotel in Market

Street, Aberdeen, which was one of the very best we've done, ever.

I might just as well take them in order, as above. So . . .

Dundee Radio. Actually, this one was great fun, but silly. You remember 'fur coats nae knickers' of course. Well, on the previous day, when I'd been given that excellent tour of the revamped Perth Theatre by the lovely Lizzie, the theatre's press agent, guest liaison, etc, person (as of old, everybody does everything in rep), she asked if I'd be willing to do a radio interview the following morning, before I started my book signing. I said that of course I'd be delighted, but what I didn't realise was that it entailed a sixty mile car dash from Perth to Dundee and back. The whole expedition was completed, and I was back in Perth ready to sign by coffee time. Lizzie was a very fast, expert driver, and we talked football all the way there and back. The interview went well, too!

Fred MacAulay's BBC Scotland radio show I did, not in fact from Glasgow, but from the Isle of Wight. I don't think I've mentioned the small BBC studio in Newport where you have to mastermind the operations yourself. You arrive at Culvert's hotel, yes, hotel, and ask for the key at reception. You're given said key and you proceed down the road to a rather small Alice in Wonderlandish door. The key opens the door and you enter. There's another door ahead of you. (No, it's not smaller still!) The same key opens this door and you enter the radio studio. There are notices everywhere – do this . . . don't do that . . . be sure to turn the power off before you leave . . . dial this number (there's a telephone beside the mike) so that you can be patched through to the switching centre . . . do not, on any account, hang up the phone until you have been linked through by landline to the station which will be conducting the interview . . . position yourself ten inches from the mike and turn on . . . speak, and if the needle goes above the red mark turn down the fader . . .

They're perfectly nice instructions, actually, but precise and concise. A bit daunting perhaps when you first encounter them. And there is a problem that can occur. What happens when the switching centre in London can't switch you through to the station you've asked for – in my case, on this occasion, BBC Glasgow? They did try and I'm sure it wasn't their fault. I have to admit though that at one stage the guy said there was a telephone number on the Isle of Wight he could try for assistance. He did and said it was engaged. I quietly pointed out that the reason it was engaged was because the number he'd quoted was for the phone we were using! Time was running out so I suggested that he phone Glasgow and get them to phone me, after of course I'd disobeyed instructions and put my phone down.

In the end I did the whole interview with Fred over that phone. The quality was not quite so good as it would have been had we been able to make a landline connection, but it was perfectly adequate. I could as well have been sitting comfortably in my sitting room at home.

The Art Sutter Show was something else. Grampian TV who are based in Aberdeen of course – indeed in the converted tram depot which I used to visit when I was a tiddler – flew me up, put me into a scrumptious hotel, and looked after me as though I were a star. OK, on this occasion I'll allow that perhaps I was. I was top of the bill anyway, above even Sian Phillips who happened to be at His Majesty's Theatre that week, gracing Aberdeen with her wonderful tribute to Marlene Dietrich.

I got a great plug in for my book. It went like this:

Art: Nice to meet you Michael, I've been a fan of yours for ages. (What a nice man.)

Me: Thank you. I'll come and do your show any time if you pay me compliments like that. I'm delighted to meet you, too.

Art: OK. Let's talk about some of your eight hundred television appearances and, what is it, thirty-eight feature films?

Me: (Glowing by this time – these occasions are awfully good for the ego.) That's right, Art. Have you read my book?

Art: Oh yes, and it's excellent. But I want to talk about what's not in the book.

Me: Great. But in that case, I'd better give the book a plug now, hadn't I?

And I did. It was live TV of course and we had a super time. When I mentioned The Capitol (cinema and now also a pop venue, which was about to be closed), and how it had been such an enormous source of filmic enjoyment to me in my early years and what a dreadful mistake was being made turning it into yet another pub, the audience clapped and cheered in agreement.

And that's it for now. I'll come back to Scott McMillan and my chums, later. Today is Cup Final day. Dearly Beloved is away in London and I'm going to sit down with Sophie, our dog, and watch the match. Well, most of it, I'm due to present the prizes to the local marathon runners later on. They must be bonkers running in this heat.

Oh, one other snippet before I depart. I've just had a call from Anthony (Tony) Keetch, great thespian and writer. He's just sold a film script which centres on, and I promise this is true, conventions. It's called *Moonquake*, or as re-named by the producers, *Day of the Anorak*. Tony doesn't like this title but I think it fits the bill perfectly. It's a bloody great script and there's a bloody super part for me. Nice one Tony!

Tony also reminded me that I'd promised to set the record straight. He's right; I did, and here goes. In *Yes, Mr Bronson*, when I was talking about my time at RADA and the fact that I'd done nicely and won the Tennents contract for 'All Round Progress and Ability', or something equally nice, I said that the Gold and Silver Cups had been won by the likes of Sarah Miles, Tom Courtney and John Thaw. Some of that is indeed very much so, but I left out lovely Eileen Helsby who was also a winner that year. Eileen was great. I did a *Dr Who* with her a few years after we graduated: 'The Ark'. I actually remember her as terribly English but she married a great American chap, Ted Teichgraeber, who was also with us at the Academy, and they've lived for a long time now in the States, in Connecticut. Perhaps that's why it slipped my mind. Nevertheless it's no excuse. I'm sorry Eileen.

I'm off to the footie!

I'm back. Not a very good match, I'm afraid. I'm going to have to fax my chum Pam Clarke in Gateshead and say Sorry. Pam's a wonderful lady, a chartered accountant and superb convention organiser who adores Newcastle United. More anon.

Now, do you remember Mike, Darren, my Dad Jeremy Bulloch and the convention that started early at Heathrow Airport, when Jeremy all but missed the flight? Well, now we'll continue, for that was the beginning of Scott McMillan's Aberdeen con.

It does continue to catch me unawares you know. The simple fact that one never actually knows where that very extra special TV, or movie, or whatever will turn up. And it's certainly also true of conventions. We've done lots, and between us hundreds, and I've enjoyed them all enormously, never had a bad one – well, there was just one which wasn't the equal of the others, but I'll tell you about that some other time.

Here I'm dealing with the tops. For some reason Scott's Aberdeen convention at the Stakis Hotel in Market Street clicked in a very big way. I wonder why?

First and foremost it was Scott. He's a smashing chap who loves Sci-Fi. A great organiser, he worked tirelessly the whole weekend to make it a success. He's a superb musician, is Scott. As I write, he's just returned from conducting the Los Angeles Symphony Orchestra in the Hollywood Bowl.

The venue was great. There was a large, spacious room for the Q&A sessions, which also doubled as an excellent dance venue in the evenings. It was there that 'School's Out' was first evolved by the appreciators, because of *Grange Hill* of course. Performed to the Alice Cooper hit record, I stand on a chair in the centre of the floor and everyone circles me. I conduct, they point fingers. 'You can't catch us . . . School's out for Summer!' It's been a favourite at conventions ever since – always called for at the dances, and I'm very flattered. I also did the Sword Dance here for the first time. No, not the Scottish Sword Dance, the *Klingon* Sword Dance. You'll note of course that a Klingon's sword is somewhat broader!

Nice comfortably sized rooms were at Scott's disposal for signing sessions and the dealers. Our own rooms were great, too. (No, I can't remember them, but I'm sure they were, because I visited several parties, held in various room locations and I do remember that there were over fifty of us at one of these, so at least the rooms must have been spacious!) The dining room was friendly and there was a rather nice bar. What more could anyone desire?

Well, above all you do need appreciators. Without friends you've had it, and this time we were particularly blessed with some really smashingly great folk. I made masses of new chums that weekend.

There was a very nice clutch of guests, too. Jeremy, of course, Peter, Kenny, and Dave, plus Robert O'Reilly (*Star Trek* Klingon Leader) and Richard Arnold, who knows everything there is to know about the making of *Star Trek* and worked with Gene Roddenberry at one time. These two both hailed from the States of course. Oh heck, I've left one guest out, how could I have been so modest? Last, but I trust not necessarily least, there was me!

I've come to a conclusion. It wasn't one ingredient alone that made this convention a success it was quite simply everything and every blessed one of us.

I've already told you about Kenny and Jeremy feigning sleep at the Q&A, so I'll finish this remembrance with Jeremy's book, the book behind the bar, followed by Richard and the closing ceremony.

Both book stories pivot on Mr Bulloch in fact. I mentioned earlier that a super tale hung on my saying that Jeremy should write his own book. Well, it must have taken him hours, even with the help of his sons Robbie and Jamie, but he arrived at the convention with his book. 'Oh yes, didn't you know I'd written a book?' he said.

'No,' I replied in all innocence.

'Ah, well. We don't all shout it from the rooftops, like some!'

'May I see?' Then the penny started to drop slowly down. He held the book up and I could see that it had the most strikingly vivid dust cover, with a magnificent photo of Jeremy, looking at least two dozen years younger. He turned it round and there was an excellent résumé on the back.

The penny finally landed when he refused to pass it over. The gag could only have lasted a bare five minutes, but Jeremy, Robbie, and Jamie had taken ages perfecting this dust cover, which they'd then carefully wrapped round an old Agatha Christie or something. All this just to wind me up.

It was a great gag and I suggested he brought his book with him when we did the Q&A. He did and proceeded to tell the audience that I didn't believe he'd written a book, that I'd said he'd just got a cover. 'But here, I'll show you. Look.' As we were on the stage and thus further away, he could now open the book, and of course there was writing. I suggested he read us an excerpt, and he did. He made it up on the spot of course, but it was great. He 'read' in very great detail of our first meeting.

The bubble finally burst when he was asked if the book would be on sale at the convention, along with mine. 'Ah well now, this is in fact the only copy. But I'll have more soon.'

The last time I saw him, he really had started his book. I'm seeing him this weekend, in Spain, where I shall expect to hear that it's progressing. Nice one Father!

The Book Behind the Bar. This could almost be sub-titled 'Free Publicity'. The hotel buy my book and place it high up in the wine rack behind the bar, in front of some of their vintage bottles. Jeremy saunters in.

'Ah, excuse me. I'm interested in that bottle of wine. Yes, that one. The one hidden by . . . what is that? A grubby piece of paper? Would you mind removing it so that I can see? Thank you.'

The 'piece of paper' is taken down with great solemnity – everyone knows what's going on – Jeremy declines the vintage, and my book is returned to it's high position. And it's still there to this day. I had a call of verification from David (Angus) a couple of weeks ago.

Richard Arnold and the closing ceremony went as follows. We're up on the stage, in a line. Jeremy, Kenny, Dave, Peter, me, Richard, and finally Robert. The idea is that each of us says a few words by way of thank you and goodbye. So Jeremy starts, and says what we all feel, that it had been a smashing weekend. The next three echoed these sentiments and then it was my turn. Well, you know me, I thought it was all going a wee bit serious and anyway I was the only one qualified, because I was born in the city. I called for a note from Scott, and then asked the audience to join me in a chorus of 'The Northern Lights of Old Aberdeen'. And they did, lustily. We swayed from side to side, arms held aloft Mexican Wave style, singing our hearts out.

When we'd finished it was Richard's turn, 'cos he was next to me. Richard turned, looked at me for a moment, smiled, and then with impeccable timing said, 'How the hell do I follow that?'

As I say, a very great convention, right up to the very end.

Chapter 7

I can't remember how long I've known Leslie Scofield. I've worked with him lots of times. Let's see, I remember *Softly, Softly,* I think that was the first, then there was *Force 10 from Navarone, Murder Not Proven* etc. We didn't in fact meet on the *Star Wars* trilogy because, I think I'm correct and correct me if I'm wrong Leslie, but you were in the first *Star Wars,* which of course is number four in the cycle. What is very clear in my slightly middle-aged bonce is that Leslie is a bloody good actor/golfer.

Now then, Shakespeare for Schools at the Shaftesbury Theatre, the last time I set foot on a stage. That's where I met this next gentleman, and the only reason he gets into my story is that he started me off on golf and introduced me to Leslie. Anthony Dutton (and where the hell are you? We once had some very great days on numerous golf courses. Get in touch you silly twit), phoned me one day and asked if a chap he'd met on a film set somewhere could join us for a game. Leslie beat the pants off both of us.

I once spent the night with Leslie. We travelled back on the overnight train together from Glasgow, after recording *Murder Not Proven* (BBC TV), in which I played the prosecuting council and he was one of my witnesses. And I once tried to get with his agent but they were full, probably with Leslie.

Back to radio again. Simon Bates this time. Been all over, has Simon, but when I joined him he was the mainstay of 'Liberty Radio'. I was invited to join his show to publicise the book – modesty prevents me from naming it!

I arrived early and was greeted warmly. I was offered a coffee and asked to wait.

'Simon is in the middle of his cinema rundown, but he'll be free soon.'

I gladly accepted the coffee and sat down in the small reception area. I could hear Simon's show coming over speakers. He was saying that he had that famous actor Michael Sheard coming in soon. And in the end he did and I was invited to join him in the studio.

A record was playing, so we could chat without what we said going out over the airwaves. Simon Bates is a lovely man.

'Michael,' he began, 'very nice to meet you, you old bugger.'

'Erm . . . nice to meet you, too, Simon.'

'No, no. I say old bugger because of what you've done with your book. I don't usually review books on my programme you know, but my producer said that yours was worth a look, so I took it home yesterday. I thought I'd give it a glance and read a couple of pages. But I didn't get to bed till after three in the morning, because I couldn't put it down. You old bugger.' (Echoes of Richard Anderson, and many others, before him!)

'Thanks Simon, I appreciate it. You old – very nice man!'

Sometimes, very seldom, it's true, I put both feet right in it, up to the armpits and further! I was very, very young and very, very new to TV, when I did my first *Dr Who*, with William Hartnell. For those who can remember, I played a chap called Rhos. But, sorry *Who* chums, I don't remember much else about it, except that on the first day of rehearsal, I bounded up to the leading actor and greeted him thus:

'Good morning, Billy, my name's Michael Sheard. Nice to meet you.'

WRO–ONG! *Mr* William Hartnell may have been known as Billy when he was a child actor, but by then he was a true blue thespian of great standing.

Apart from saying his lines, Billy didn't speak to me again for the whole of the engagement!

Am I allowed a wee toot on my trumpet? I really am terribly chuffed and tremendously gratified that *Yes, Mr Bronson* has proved so popular. If I promise not to laud it again, can I give you now a wee flavour of the gobsmacking reception my first book has received?

The written critiques have been wonderful. Every flippin' one, from 'Loaded' to 'The Big Issue', and all the others in between.

Let me take 'Loaded' first. Dearly Beloved and I had been out for dinner at one of our local hostelries – hey, the owners will buy a copy of this book if I mention the restaurant by name. Burdens Restaurant on the Isle of Wight. Roz – note the spelling, not like my Ros – and Keith Burden are chums and they serve damn good nosh, try them.

When we returned home that evening there was a message on the answerphone from Jonathan – Danny Kendall from *Grange Hill*. Jon ordered me to buy a copy of 'Loaded' magazine post haste, before they sold out. Dearly B. very kindly offered to get me a copy the next day as she was going out to the shops. She didn't mind. She was the one who'd bought *Fanny Hill* in the early sixties, when it was still bound in brown paper. There certainly was an excellent review of *Yes, Mr B.* by 'The Loafer' in a great, but wee bit naughty magazine. Thank you very much 'Loaded', I enjoyed them both!

'The Big Issue'. I've huge admiration for the people who stand out in all weathers selling this paper, but I confess that I'd no idea what a bloody good and informative paper it was until I was sent a copy, which also included a wonderful review of my book by Cameron Robertson. Thank you, 'Big Issue', too.

I've a postscript. The latest paper to do a piece on me is 'The Sunday Sport'. My agent had a fax from them a couple of weeks ago asking if I'd answer all manner of innuendo questions. I don't think they can have liked my jokey replies because they haven't used them. I've just seen the article by Debbie Manley and they've treated me fairly fairly – bearing in mind that there is a definite slant to this weekly. What they've done is taken the funny sexy voice-over sequence and the naughty film story from *Yes, Mr B.* and quoted them out of context – 'Red-hot Porn Secret of TV's Mr Bronson'. Fine, there's no such thing as bad publicity and I've certainly nothing to hide. Only trouble is they didn't give my book a plug. I'm dropping them a line and asking them to rectify their oversight.

Here's a list of chums. Oliver Maguire, *Star Wars* Imperial Officer and understudy to my last stage appearance in *The Merchant of Venice* at London's Shaftesbury Theatre. Robin Scoby, also an Imperial Officer, who was with my agent at the time we did *Star Wars* and was married to Barbara Kellerman (a lovely lass who was in *Space 1999* with me). Brigitte Kahn, a Rebel Officer who also played my secretary in *Auf Wiedersehen Pet.* And Burnell Tucker, another Rebel and a friend of a friend who I met lots of times a long time ago. Oh yes, no question, I know 'em all. Every one but one, actually, but I'll include him later anyway.

Oliver. In fact this was so long ago that even Richard Price, who was a walk-on in the production and subsequently became head of casting at London Weekend TV (and gave me lots of work) has now retired. But in those far off days Ollie did understudy me in both *The Merchant of Venice*, where I played a very young, handsome and sexy Bassanio, and in the unmentionable Scottish play – for some reason it does bode ill if you mention it – in which I was a superb and caring Ross. I did apologise to Ollie at the time but no, he never had to go on for me. Dear Kate O'Mara, by the way, my mate Kate, was also in the company.

Nah, I can't leave it there, can I? Kate has been a platonic friend for many years. She is a very sexy lady – see the poster for her company's production of *The Taming of the Shrew* where one of her bulges is in full view. If the world had been different, if I hadn't met my own very sexy lady . . . but I did, thank heavens, and Kate and I are happy with our platonic friendship. When we meet on the set we always have a huge and a great blether.

Robin. I'll be honest, apart from meeting him at our then agent's sumptuous parties, I can't really say a lot about Robin. Nice guy, who I believe has since left thesping and the industry, I certainly haven't heard from or of him for years. But please pal, if I'm wrong and you're still in our wonderful profession, don't sue, I can't afford it! Get in touch. Whatever, it does perhaps say a lot for our then joint agent who got both Robin and me into *Star Wars*. Mind you the lovely Irene Lamb, the *Star Wars* casting director, who'll be on later, might have had a wee something to do with it!

But do you know something? All through *Yes, Mr B.* and thus far in this one, I've never mentioned an agent by name. This is because agents change or are changed as the years go by. But perhaps now I have an opportunity to hail one with whom I stayed for something like seventeen years. June Epstein Associates represented me throughout all the years that my children were growing up and I kept working all the time. Indeed, not a month went by that I didn't thesp. The naughty movie mentioned above (re: 'The Sunday Sport') was not June, by the way. Ken Coles – Old King Ken – rang me direct. But only because he'd seen me in the film *England Made Me* with Peter Finch, Michael York, and Hildegard Neil, which June had got for me, and where I first met Ken.

We still exchange Christmas cards, June and I, and I'm delighted that my new book has developed in such a way that I can now, at last, say a very big thank you to a super and hard working friend.

God Bless June Epstein Associates!

OK, onwards. Brigitte. Oh my, what a lovely . . . nah blow it, I'll go the whole hog, what a truly sensuously sexy dish. Brigitte oozed it without being aware of the fact, which is tops, certainly in my book. Her great scenes in *Auf W.* with Tim Healey were smouldering. She was super to work with and very kindly complimented me on my German – I did all my own translation for that series you know!

Burnell Tucker. In fact Dearly B. knew him better that I did. I believe they first met around the time she was at the Webber Douglas Academy of Dramatic Art. I've been bumping into him over the years at various studios up and down the land.

Perhaps I should add here that there's always been a loving rivalry twixt Dearly B. and me regarding our starts, our acting colleges. In fact I don't think it matters a damn, RADA, Webber D., Central, or any other, it's what continues thereafter that counts. Anyway, Burnell Tucker was – is – a nice guy, I think in fact he's another Canadian, like D. Sutherland and Angus. Quietly spoken, evenly tempered.

Very nice colleagues. Now, how about a quick glance at my next producer? To do this, I'm going to take you back for a mo to Steve Parson's Honiton convention.

Andrew Dymond is a great, wonderful, sweet, loveable, clever, chap. (He is my producer after all!) He's invited me to play Makian in his forthcoming, superb, scintillating, out of this world, Science-Fiction series. (Lots of superlatives – and I mean them all.) *First Frontier*, has been co-written by the equally exquisite Jim Mortimer – *Cracker*, *Babylon 5* books, *Dr Who*, and masses of others.

When Warwick and I were at Honiton, Andrew and his delightful fiancée, Sue, came along to join us for a while to heighten the profile of *First Frontier*. They did, very successfully. I invited Andrew up to the mike during the Q&A session to chat about his series. (Not too much. The idea is to hype it, but at the same time to always keep everyone guessing. Then they'll be dying to see it when it comes out.) Andrew also gave a walk-on part to be auctioned for Steve's charity.

Now then, having said that my part of Makian is one of the best I've ever been offered – a seemingly evil man who sits in the middle of the Universe manipulating the planets and the rest of humanity – I'm not going to dwell overly long on *Frontier*. Watch the forthcoming series and the films, they'll be the best yet, I promise. But wait . . .

. . . Back to Andrew. Sorry mate, but you did give me your permission. What I would like to record, so I can elicit a blush from Andrew now, and remind him of it when we need a laugh in the future, is what happened later, that night in Honiton.

After the convention ended, those of us who were staying till morning gathered in the bar for a night-cap. A couple of hours passed during which Andy, one of Steve Parson's gang, but also manager of the hotel, insisted on plying the drinks on the house, the nice man.

When Andrew and Sue finally retired for the night, Andrew started preparing himself for bed . . . or so he thought. Sue, indeed, was getting quietly worried for he was a hell of a long time in the bathroom. Eventually she looked in on him.

'Are you all right?'

'Of course I am,' came the frantic reply. 'It's just that I can't get any lather out of this damn soap.'

'Darling,' Sue said as gently as she could, 'you'll never get a lather out of that, you're trying to wash your hands with the basin plug!'

Andrew had been plied very well that night!

I'd now like to pop back to Scotland again (*Dr Who*), and then invite you to a dance – The Dudley Bug Ball!

Andrew Beech (*Dr Who*, Panopticon) first drew my attention to the following which had, by pure chance, been trawled off the Internet by one of his Panopticon colleagues:

>From: Gerard Sweeney
>To: Multiple Recipients List.
>Subject: Michael Sheard.
>Can I just say that should anyone ever get the chance
>to go see Michael Sheard at a convention, they should do
>so with all haste.
>I went to a small informal gathering last Saturday
>organised by the Edinburgh *Dr Who* appreciation
>society.
>It started at 3 p.m. and was supposed to go on until 9 p.m.
>with a break at about 5.30 for a buffet . . .
>It went on till 1.30 a.m. when we were eventually kicked
>out by bar staff desperate to go home . . . It didn't feel
>like an hour!
>Michael was amazingly open and friendly to everyone,
>and you really got the feeling he genuinely wanted to be
>there, as opposed to a 'you've paid me – you've got me
>for a couple of hours' type of approach.
>If by some miracle Michael gets to read this, I'd just
>like to thank him again. A superb host, and someone who
>genuinely deserves the description of 'Gentleman'.
>I realise this might sound a bit gushy, but I make no
>apologies. I had an excellent time.

>Gerard.

I was very touched and terribly flattered. And the moment I'd read the above, I dashed round to our local library – we didn't have access to the Internet then – and told him so in my reply.

That *Who* 'do' really was one of the most joyful evenings I've ever spent. Everyone was magic. Dr Martin Rogerson – yes, he is a real doctor, of chemistry – Robin, Robert Dick (I have a nickname for Robert, 'Dick Head', and yes, he has given me permission to use it here), all the other members of the Edinburgh *Dr Who* cell, and those, like Gerard, who'd come over from Glasgow. We laughed a heck of a lot, chatted, had a great Q&A session which sort of went on all evening, and showed a super compilation of clips of my work, that Dick had expertly put together. There was a charity auction, and photographs. ('Have your photo taken with Michael, we'll get it developed and ready for you before you go home. Signed of course'.)

Maybe that's why the party went on so long, waiting for the chemist to develop the photo negatives. A great buffet was supplied by our hosts, Graeme and Robin. Oh yes, and I'll tell you something else, when you're a guest at a 'do' held in the Claremont Bar in Edinburgh, Graeme and Robin insist that you never pay for even one drink! Great evening, super people. Thank you very much.

The Dudley Bug Ball, that's an interesting name, is it not? Once upon a time there really was a plague of bugs in the beautiful city of Dudley which were decidedly unfriendly. But this is not where Sue and Steve Turner got the catchy title for their games convention, The Dudley Bug Ball. They borrowed it from the Burl Ives super song hit, 'Let's crawl, to the *Ugly Bug Ball*'. You must recall it.

The Turners are really nice, as is my namesake Michael, their wee son. But what I'd really like to tell you about my visit to Dudley is, tarra, my hotel! This time I certainly do remember it, and I particularly remember my room.

The Station Hotel in Dudley is nowhere near a station, not now anyway. But it still stands opposite what was, in its day (indeed until quite recently, it's now alas a bingo hall), a hugely successful variety venue, The Dudley Hippodrome. All the very famous played there and they stayed of course in the Station Hotel, just across the road.

I recently returned from a wonderful trip to the Isle of Man (more later) and have now actually met one of my idols, dear Norman Wisdom. Norman played The Hippodrome. So did his fellow bronze statue, George Formby. As did Laurel and Hardy, Max Miller, Tony Hancock, Max Wall, Tessie O'Shea, Harry Secombe *et al* and many hundreds more.

My room in the Station Hotel was huge, as was the adjoining bathroom. Rounded windows directly overlooked the theatre, and as I lay on the sumptuously gigantic bed – yes alright, it was probably new and was not the one actually occupied by somebody famous – I could easily imagine that I was a part of that great army of variety troupers waiting for my call: 'On stage please, Mr Sheard. On stage'. Wonderfully marvellous.

I had a superlatively lovely time in Dudley. Many thanks to Steve and Sue – see you next time. Of course I've been invited back!

Right, now let's talk to . . . Well, blow me. Again would you believe it? Again I hardly do and I'm the one who answered the phone just now, just as I was writing about him. That's the third time it's happened!

You remember Scott McMillan. I thought I'd be filming the weekend after next, but the dates were changed yesterday. And lo and behold, Scott has just rung to invite me to do the 'Continuum' convention in Glasgow with Robert Picardo and Rene Auberjonois. Same dates: 'Because you're free now, aren't you?' What a very nice man. I'll tell you how it goes.

In a golden book, entitled *Yes, Mr Bronson*, I talked about a great movie called *The McKenzie Break*. I'd like to pull from that great film the most superb Wardrobe Supervisor it has ever been my very great pleasure to work with. Tiny Nicholls is of course huge, and he's lovely. When I did *McKenzie* I was quite new to the movie game. Shortly after I'd arrived in Ireland I was due at the costume department bright and early to try on my uniform. If you've seen the truly super film *McKenzie B.*, directed by the equally excellent Lamont (Monty) Johnson, you'll recall that at least the first half is set in a prisoner of war camp, a barracks. And that's where we were, that was our location, a very muddy Irish army barracks in the middle of nowhere. And that's where the costume department was located, in one of those huts. And when I arrived, there was Tiny – he must have been up since very early dawn – with everything laid out.

'Morning, Michael. Did you have a nice flight over? (I enjoyed flying even less in those days than I do now but I didn't mention it.) Here it is then, your frock. Try it on and if you don't like anything, be sure to let me know.' Very relaxed, no fuss or frills.

It's difficult to give you a true picture of Tiny, he is – please heavens he's still with us, I've not heard from him for some years – one of the greatest unsung heroes of our profession. But when a slightly nervous thesp came to him at the costume hut in Ireland that morning he was simply bloody marvellous and put me at my ease in no time. And I'm sure he felt as I did when we met up again on the day I came to his domain at Elstree studios some ten years later for my costume fitting for *The Empire Strikes Back*. In fact, and I quote as near as I can, he greeted me thus: 'Michael, hello again, how are you? Quite a long time no see since *McKenzie*. I've been following your career since then. Well done, great work.'

Still laid back, still nonchalant. Tiny is a very nice man.

Sorry, I've got to stop, the World Cup is about to start and my Scotland are in the opening game. Here's hoping they make it. I'll see you after they've won!

Chapter 8

Confession time. I just took a break to watch the footie. I came back and checked my work – I knew I'd written more, but it wasn't there. I can only surmise that in the wake of my haste to get to the game I didn't save it. And now Scotland have lost as well. No matter, here goes again – I've a note of what was to have come next: Ian Liston, followed by Andrew Beech's Garden Party. Andrew as in Andrew, Panopticon, mentioned just now.

I'd not met Ian before there was a convention on my Island of Wight to which my chum Chris Gardner from the County Press made more than a small contribution – it was his idea. The con was organised by Mr Jason Joiner, and one of the other guests was Ian.

Since *Star Wars*, maybe even before then, Ian has been devoting himself to his 'Hiss and Boo' theatre production company. Great title, eh? 'Hiss and Boo' have put on many plays over the years, including several in London's West End, and they've been very successful. And that is, in a way, what makes it a pity, because it means that Ian hasn't been free to do more conventions, or thesping. Mind you, I'd be the very first to say it, if his productions are doing well, great. I'm delighted and I wouldn't want it any other way. But Ian, you're such good roly-poly value (Ian would be the first to admit that he's not small), can't you give yourself some more time off 'as you did last summer', and at least do some more cons? I really enjoyed our merry banter. Give me a call.

Great chap, Ian. Perhaps, after this, he'll give me a job!

Let's move quickly on to Andrew Beech's Garden Party at his lovely home in Putney.

His call to me went like this,

'Michael, are you free in three weekend's time? I'm having a *Dr Who* party. There'll be all sorts of people there who were connected with the show – producers, like John Nathan Turner, and Jon Pertwee's wife – but no other actors, is that alright?'

Twit! And I told him. To be the only thesp at such a superly great party was a heck of an honour. Mind you, I think an odd reprobate (Nick Courtney perhaps?) had had to pull out, but what the hell. I – we all – had a gigantically great time. The food – I can remember it like it was yesterday – was completely top drawer. Succulent meats of every type, beautiful salads – which are my particular favourites, and sweets like there's no tomorrow. And the wine! Dearly B. says that I should describe the table fare but I just can't go further on this occasion. There was so much, so varied, so damn good. I do hope I'm invited again.

I was in fact invited back very soon afterwards, to sign the masses of a superb book, which I'd sold out of at Panopticon and had to complete mail order. It took me all afternoon, after Andrew had provided a superb lunch.

What a nice chap. Mr Beech knows that I have a great photo of the two of us taken at that Panopticon, Andrew chum, you will feature further in these chapters. Apart from anything else he's promised me a super part in his forthcoming movie. Oh yes, his recent one, *Downtime* is doing very well, and Sophie (Aldred) and I are scheduled for the baddies in his next.

A spot more J.J. Jason Joiner is . . . another old chip off the old . . . chip. I first met him after he'd been writing to me for what seemed years, begging me, pleading for me to join him for one of his conventions. When I was finally free he invited me to his North London 'do' held in something like nineteen-eighty . . . heavens, I can't remember, it was long ago anyway.

Jason's in fact were the first. I am right in saying that, am I not Mr (Paul) Miley?! J.J.'s conventions were some of the first conventions in our land. Anyway, they were very early. And this one in North London was my first.

It went like this: I arrived at the station ('I'll get one of my drivers to pick you up, Michael, no problem') and there was nobody there.

When I finally sussed that I wasn't going to be picked up and had inquired of the local newsagent where I was due to be and had walked the fairly shortish distance and had arrived at the hall, there was Jason, apologising like there really was no tomorrow and telling me that I should have phoned.

In truth it was a fun day. Jeremy B. was there, with Declan Mulholland and Peter Diamond and we had an excellent time. And as this was my first foray into the wonderful world of conventioning, it can also be cited as the beginning of my convention relationship with Jeremy, my (con) Dad. So there's another first for Jason. You saw it first at J.J.'s North London convention!

Do you remember Declan Mulholland? Of course you do. He's the extremely nice, great-value-at-conventions chap, who did not in the end play Jabba the Hutt. And how Declan milks it at convention Q&As, 'I've never been more famous for not doing a part in me dear ol' Oirish life!'

Declan's a darling. With his umbrella, 'This is my trademark Michael. Some will say that it's in case I fall down, because I'm not as good on my pins as I used to be. Bollocks, it's my fucking trademark,' and his wonderfully very, very merry banter, 'What, only one bottle? I didn't come here for water!'

Let's have some more wine soon, matey, I want to hear much more. Come to think of it, you'll be in Plymouth won't you? See you there chum.

Right, let us trot over to Central London, a few years after the above. This time we're somewhere just off the Edgware Road in a large recreation centre that doubles for everything else. It seems it was apparently always being double booked.

Ladies first of course. Shelagh Fraser, followed by Ken Colley, John Hollis, Gary Kurtz, Peter Diamond and me. Not a bad line-up of guests I feel sure you'll agree.

Do you know what? Apart from saying that I took Jeremy B.'s place and chaired the Q&A sessions (extremely well of course), and that I sold lots of books and there was a mix-up on the second day – the venue had indeed been double booked and we couldn't start until midday, after a basketball game had finished – I'm going to go straight on to thumbnails of my friends who were there that weekend, then you'll get a flavour of both pals and the con. Right, it's ladies first, remember, so . . .

Shelagh, what a lovely great gal. I've completely no idea what age this super lady is and even if I did I wouldn't tell 'cos it makes no flippin' odds. Shelagh is wonderful and I'll be seeing her soon at the Rebellion con in Northampton – yes OK, more after that's happened too!

(I've just heard, in fact this minute – the fax again – that Shelagh was the belle of the ball at another Jason convention yesterday. North London again.)

When I arrived, last Easter, at the Regeneration venue near London's Heathrow Airport, Pam (Pam Clarke) the superbly wonderful organiser of that super event, asked if I'd sit next to Shelagh at the signing sessions because I would give her confidence, seeing as she was new to the convention game and I was an old hand. I did of course but there was no need. Shelagh may be newish to conventions but she's a very experienced performer.

We were old chums and we'd sat next to each other at the J.J. Central London convention, both at the signings and during the Q&A. You'll remember that I chaired that particular Q&A, because Jeremy was not in evidence. (He was probably in America.)

A question came up. I don't recall exactly what it was, but it went something like this. 'Shelagh, what was it like being part of the greatest movie of all time?'

'Well, dear,' was her immediate reply. 'I did go to Tunisia and it was all rather splendid you know. The hotel was divine and that lovely man, George, you know dear, George Lucas, he was such a darling. So was everyone. Harrison and Mark. I did enjoy playing Luke's aunt. What a very nice young man. Do you know, he was so polite . . .'

And so this lovely girl went on, ever so slightly tongue-in-cheek. As chairperson it's a miracle that I eventually got her to take a breath! The others needed a turn and I was finally able to divert the questioning.

This is all said with very much affection, but there were other guests present and it was my job to push things forward. Heavens I'd still got to announce Peter Diamond – who when he finally did come on didn't half bang his head during his excellent demonstration!

Shelagh, you will feature in further chapters I promise. But if you'll forgive me, it's now the turn of . . .

Before I continue however, I digress again. This, my book, is not really about my thesping career of course, but life still goes on that side of the fence and if you're writing a sequel and something happens which embroiders an entry in the previous book, then it's worth including. Actually it's delightful to have the opportunity. Okay then . . .

By the time you read these pages you may have heard of (or possibly seen) a feature film called *Je m'appelle Crawford*. It's perfectly possible that the title will have changed, I certainly don't think it's terribly compelling. Anyway, look for a middle-aged, bewhiskered character called Uncle Airdrie Dunbar. Great description and name, eh? Well, yes. And when I was told a couple of days ago that there was a wonderful part in the movie for me – that it was me to a T, I was very excited and waited with bated breath for the script to arrive.

It plopped on to my mat this morning and if you've seen the film I need say no more. Except to add a question. Why do people think that all they have to do is say that a part is wonderful and the poor bloody actor will jump at it? I'm a character, journeyman thesp and I'll play anything, large, small, or cameo, but Uncle Airdrie in *Je m'appelle* is a pathetic part and no amount of hype will alter that. I'm not using these pages to vent my anger at those who think that a thespian will grab at anything. And I'm certainly not against cameo parts. But this one – all he said right the way through the piece was that all the men in LA were poofs – no fucking way. That's it, off my chest. Thank you.

Now it's Ken's turn . . .

Ken Colley started of course as my subordinate, a mere Captain.

It's difficult to say how long I've known Kenneth. It's a hell of a long time. Don't misunderstand me, we're not old, it's just that we've been around for a couple plus years, haven't we Ken? If I say without humility that I've given some decently good performances down those years, then Ken has certainly matched me. His King Edward, for example, was superb.

When we came to *The Empire Strikes Back*, we were pretty well established. We were sitting next to each other in the make-up room on the first day.

'Well, Michael,' he said, 'what do you make of this?'

'Mmmm,' I mused. 'Well, you've read the script, I get killed off and you take over. I bet you anything you like you'll be in the next *Star Wars* film.' Ken was in the next film of course, because he was so damn good in *Empire*.

When George (and Paramount) gave that superly wonderful great party at Olympia after the première of the new special edition *Star Wars*, Ken and I were having a chat. We'd not met for some time and were blethering away catching up on our news. After we'd reached the present, Ken suddenly looked wistfully at the sky (and it was the sky, too, Olympia had been transformed into the universe). 'Michael,' he said. 'You know they're doing these *Star Wars* sequels-prequels? Well, do you think they might ask us to play our fathers?'

Ken, I love your great dry sense of humour. Please let's thesp and con together again soon.

(Added whilst I'm doing the edit. Ken and I are off to a convention in America, Dallas, next month. Just the two of us. A brace of Admirals!)

OK, I admit it, I'm mortified. John Hollis is above me on the cast list. Just below Jeremy in fact. Mind you, that's only because the Imperial Officers have a section all to themselves.

John, what more can I say about John? I've told you about that most enjoyable several hours we spent flying to America. Did I tell you that John's a great golfer? No, I don't think I did. I mentioned that we discussed golf but not that John is damn good at the game. And I didn't tell you that Roy Purcell is a chum of his.

Roy is one of the mainstays of the Stage Golfing Society, which operates out of Richmond Golf Club. I worked with him on *Dr Who* ('The Mind of Evil') and it was during that production that he got me into that illustrious collection of riffraff, the S.G.S. I think Roy must have been flummoxed, because when we played a round to establish my handicap I beat him. Mind you, the committee gave me a fifteen handicap as a result of that game and I've never been able to play to it!

Have I said that John and I first worked together on dear *Dixon of Dock Green* but that we've never met? Of course I have. That's why I said, if you remember that John would get a section to himself. What I'm on about is that we've never actually met – on screen. But off, at rehearsals, at conventions, in aeroplanes, in the bar, John and I have been able to continue the friendship we first forged in a drill hall, yonks ago, somewhere not far from Paddington Station actually, the 'Dixon' rehearsal room. And that is so long ago that the Acton Hilton, as we affectionately call the purpose built BBC rehearsal block, hadn't even been built.

I'm delighted to say that we seem, nay, we are, as young and optimistic about the future as ever. Indeed, I'll tell you a wee tale I've not even told John. Some few years back I was looking for a new agent and I went to meet a certain chap, who was just starting out, and foolishly I turned him down. I wish I hadn't, because not only has this agent gone on to great things, he also represents Johnny Hollis!

I've always thought of Gary Kurtz as a man who is sad about something. His body language and his expression both tell me that he's sad. Perhaps he is, I don't know, or perhaps it's simply the fact that he's one of those very nice laid back Americans.

I'd not seen him for quite a number of years when we did Jason Joiner's London con, but he didn't seem to have changed at all. Mind you, we all said it: 'Great to see you, you haven't changed a bit'. In truth I suppose we have, a little. But I still look exactly as I did – not like our Dads, Ken, ourselves!

It has been a pleasure to continue to know Gary.

I've known Peter Diamond – stunt co-ordinator extraordinaire – for yonks. From way, way back in the long distant past when we were both very young and new to TV and movies. There were a lot of filmed series for TV around in those days, *Space 1999*, *The Persuaders*, *Man in a Suitcase*, *Jason King*, etc, usually with an American in the leading role. Not always, I'm the first to agree, *The Prisoner* and of course *The Avengers* spring instantly to mind, but a lot of the time there was, and Peter and I cut our film teeth on these TV movies.

We're always looking out for jobs for each other. Stunt co-ordinators are usually in place on a movie before the featured actors (the likes of me) are cast, and Peter's often got on the blower and said, 'Get on to your agent, there's a great part for you on this one.' I've got him invites to conventions, but he's not been free yet (apart from J.J.'s) because he's always in demand and working. And he's just been invited to join the Dymond gang on *First Frontier*. I wonder who suggested him!

Before I leave the guests of that day, I'd like to tell you the wee Peter story I've hinted at already. As you know, I was driving the Q&A on this occasion and we arranged that Peter would, on his entrance, give a simple demonstration of his skills.

At one end of the hall, steps led up to a line of highish rostra that made a sort of stage. On this makeshift arena there were tables at which we were to be seated. Long before the attendees arrived Peter had carefully taped several pieces of padding, one on the steps, another on the rostra and a further one on the underside of the table. These of course could not be seen from the audience, and the idea was that, when announced, Peter would bound up the steps, slip and bang his knee, then fall heavily on the top of rostra/stage, and finally, pretending that he'd lost a cuff-link or somesuch under the table, on a prearranged signal from me, 'Are you alright Peter?' he would jerk upwards and vigorously bang his head, only to emerge completely unharmed. 'There you are,' he'd say, 'that's how a stuntman does it.'

We were all sitting in our places, Peter was the last to arrive, for obvious reasons. All went exactly to plan, the audience were visibly cringing at the sight of this renowned stuntman falling all over the place and seemingly hurting himself. We on the stage knew of course that he was fine, until that is it came time for that cuff-link to roll. Peter dived under the table, which was open at the front and he could thus be seen from the body of the hall. I called out the cue and Peter's head came viciously upwards and he banged his (balding, like me) pate with such an almighty crash that I knew something was wrong. It was. He'd missed the pad. Now my line took on a new significance. 'Are you alright' really meant just that.

Peter, trouper that he is, never flinched. Certainly somewhat more than dazed, he clambered out from under, said, 'That's how a stuntman does it' and sat down to recover. But he never let on. Trouper Pete!

Chapter 9

What to do? I'd like to pop back again to the Isle of Man but I've just had an SOS from my accountant. Dear me, he is miffed, and I can't afford to incur his wrath! Oh blow it, this is a dip in sort of book after all, I'll digress again, just for a line or six. Right, SOS from accountant it is.

> 'In *Yes, Mr Bronson* you talked about accountants and mentioned that you'd not been too pleased with the ones you'd experienced thus far. What you should have gone on to say is something along these lines . . .'

Fair dos, Neil most certainly deserves it. So I'd like to record, verbatim, what Neil Robert Welch, my chum and accountant went on to say in his letter today. I have his consent, and these are his words:

> '. . . But I now have a really <u>super</u> chap, perhaps even underlining the word super. *(OK!)* I hope Vol. Two is progressing satisfactorily. Suggested further wording: Forget what I said about accountants in Vol. One, my current accountant is not only an absolute whizz at the old accounts and tax stuff, he is also one of the nicest blokes I've ever met (even nicer than Harrison Ford) and a superbly talented actor. What a pity he turned to the boards so late in life, he would have given me a run for my money!'

(I recently suggested Neil for a semi-pro production of Dickens' *Hard Times* and he's going to be great.)

OK, deed done. Now, before I even take you back to Andy Byrne's Isle . . .

You remember the Dudley Bug of course. Well, I'm popping back home to Aberdeen next week to another gaming convention (I've just picked up the ticket – flying again, I think I'm getting better!), and it reminded me that I meant to explain a wee bit more about Games Conventions, as opposed to t'others, or whatever ones. I'll tell you about Sandy Douglas' Aberdeen DrakCon later, after I've been, but I can't think of a better way to illustrate the 'game' convention as opposed to the 'other' than by quickly mentioning PolyCon and Meachelle and Gordon Hudson.

I've a sort of canvas shoulder-bag dangling from my desk light which reads 'Wizards of the Coast'. Wizards are an American company, also established in Europe, who hold a huge convention each year on the Loughborough University campus. Here are held the UK finals of all the many Sci-Fi card games – *Wars*, *Trek*, *Who*, etc, together with 'Magic', 'Dungeons and Dragons', and, oh dear, a myriad of others. In some cases the winners go on to compete in the world finals in America.

Table-top role-playing, where players are given characters and situations and roll dice to determine their moves and then act out the story, are also part of the proceedings here.

As is total role-playing. This time the participants dress up to perform the stories in some of the most exquisite costumes I've seen, mostly made by themselves. The fancy dress top prize is very fiercely contested.

OK, I think that sets the scene. I'll relate GenCon and how I was a guinea pig in the fullness of time. For now, let me just explain that there are other smaller games gatherings which, although they stand justifiably as game shows in their own right, also feed the main central meeting in Loughborough. Dudley Bug is one of these of course, DrakCon another. UK Games Fest in Harlow is a third – I'm due at that one next month with Mike Edmonds – and PolyCon a fourth.

A 'feisty lady' is how I'd describe Meachelle, and Gordon is a nice chap too! They've held PolyCon at different locations over a goodly number of years and this time it was Welwyn Garden City. These dos are superb fun. Welwyn Garden City very certainly was.

My involvement in all these role-playing, card playing, Wizard conventions came about as a direct result of my surprise appearance at my *first* GenCon in Loughborough (hence my guinea pig label) with the exception, that is, of Sandy's DrakCon. Sandy and I met at a superbly enjoyable but, I'm afraid, doomed 'do' in Edinburgh (doomed because it was held during the Edinburgh Festival and shouldn't have been). We are both Aberdonians. In fact Sandy's father was something very high up in the Scottish Kirk, and mine was of course also a minister. We're still trying to locate exactly where my father's church used to be. So many have been turned back into family houses since those long ago days just after the war. My date next week with Sandy is the longest standing convention date I have, even longer than Meachelle's.

Where in Hades was I? Yes, that's it, describing a GenCon satellite convention. The doors at the Monks Walk School in Welwyn Garden City open at ten a.m. and for the first hour all is hectic, with clamours of 'Can I buy a copy of your book?' 'Can I have a photo of you and me together?' 'A kiss?' Then, for the next three or so hours nothing, absolutely flippin' not a thing happens whilst they all go off to various locations within the building to play their deadly serious games. I think it's great. I couldn't do it, but I understand it – I love the excitement of a game of poker. During this time of feverish preoccupation I consider it my brief to go around the various tables and encourage, or sympathise, or congratulate as the occasion demands.

Then comes the change over, and the dealers' room (trade hall) is once more awash with appreciators. So it goes on: nothing, awash, nothing . . . I'm sure you get the idea. At the end of a hard but hugely enjoyable day, we pack up and transfer to the hotel for a very well earned meal and a bottle of wine. Nice one Meachelle, ask me back.

Before leaving role-playing for the while, let me tell you quickly about an incident that happened at GenCon. I know, I've not talked in detail of GenCon yet, but I will mention that I was so successful as a guinea pig that Wizards have agreed that there should be more guests, and I'm taking a number of my chums with me next time. But this is just a foretaste and more about that will come later. Just before the finals of the British *Star Wars* card game last year, one of the competitors asked me to sign all six of my cards (the cards in the pack with pictures of Admiral Ozzel on them). I did and he won. The prize was a trip to the finals in America!

'K . . K . . K . . KATY, beautiful Katy, you're the only, only one that I adore . . .'

I'd like now to introduce you to a wonderfully effervescent, superbly charming, sweet, witty, marvellous girl. Let's ask Katy Manning to take centre stage and tell everyone of that great *Dr Who* convention weekend we did on the Isle of Man – Andy's Isle. No blow it, she can write her own book. I'll tell it, starting with Mark Owen.

OK. He knew this was coming. I did warn him. Let's talk about Peel Castle and Mary Queen of Scots for a moment. Shall we, Mark?

If you walk round the perimeter of ruined Peel Castle which is situated on St Patrick's Isle on one of the western-most tips, you'll see a weather-beaten, grizzly, criss-crossed, barred opening in the wall. 'This,' quoth Mark, who is a renowned I.O.M. historical authority, 'is where Mary Queen of Scots was imprisoned by Elizabeth I. Mary was rescued by her loyal followers, who very bravely, and without a thought for their safety, came over from Scotland to free her. See here, these two bars are where they cut, you'll notice that the replacements are far newer . . .'

Nice tale Mark, but sorry chum . . . horse shit! The custodians of the castle told me that Mary Q. of Scots never even set foot on the Isle of Man. That trellis of bars was a gate to let the castle archers out so that they could fire their arrows along the ramparts and thus, hopefully, evade capture. And indeed they did, for the castle was never taken from the sea. But it's a great story nevertheless.

Katy and I had a wonderful time, along with all the chums I'd made on my last trip to my other Isle. If you remember, on that occasion I was a guest at Andy's birthday party, so this was my first Isle of Man convention.

We stayed at the Stakis Hotel and Casino, where anorak Ian Parker took me for a little flutter round the tables. I won five quid!

We had a another superb trip round the Island. This time visiting Lady Isabella, The Great Wheel of Laxey. A gigantic structure with a diameter of seventy-two feet. It used to pump water from the nearby mine, but now is a most impressive tourist attraction which can be seen for miles around.

They were about to hold the TT races and Ian and Rob Craine gave me a special preview of the TT course. The whole of it this time. There were masses of bikes out practising, and we went the wrong way round the (road) circuit so that we could see them zooming towards us at colossal speed. Breathtaking.

I did a radio interview with David, 'The Rollicking Rev', for his Sunday morning show. Very interesting. David (another anorak) always looks for a new angle on things, and he'd picked up on the fact, from reading the book, that my Dad was also a Rev. David has a great sense of humour. His car numberplate reads MAN 4 GOD!

Along the way there was also a lovely convention. Yes, lovely describes it perfectly. It was beautifully relaxed. For example, when I'd finished my chat to the press, I went into the main hall where Katy was giving her solo chat – we did one Q&A on our own on this occasion and several together – and there they were, the apps, gathered informally around Katy. Katy was not sitting on the sofa provided, but had perched herself on the edge of the stage.

As I say, a great, lovely convention, which culminated in the very special guest who arrived to accept the charity auction cheque . . .

We'd just finished the auction and whilst the chaps were totting up the figures, Katy and I were asked to draw the raffle.

'But before you start,' said Mark (Mary Queen of S.), 'a special guest has just arrived to accept the cheque for the monies raised at the auction. He might even lend a hand with the raffle, Michael. If you ask him nicely. Would you please step this way Sir?'

And in walked, with that jaunty air I remember so vividly from many countless happy hours spent in the cinema and later watching TV and videos, one of my all time heroes. A truly unique talent, a one-off if ever there was one, Mr Norman Wisdom. I of course rushed up to greet him and escorted him to the rostra stage.

He's eighty-five years old now, but on our way there Norman did the most superb pratfall, and when I asked if he'd be kind enough to help with the raffle he looked at me with a twinkle in his eye,

'Help you? HELP YOU! You will help me!' He already had us all in the palm of his hand.

It was magic. I assisted. *I* was Norman Wisdom's feed whilst he proceeded to pick every single raffle ticket – there were something like thirty of them – and he found a witty remark to make about each one. 'What would you like then?' he said, having spied the winning ticket held by a pretty young lady in the front row. 'I've got a pink one here. It's one, four, something. What would you like? A three? No, you want another four don't you? 144. It's yours!'

When we'd finished the raffle, the three of us sat on the sofa and had an informal chat. Mind you, Norman was more interested in chatting up Katy! He sang her a song from his as-yet-unmade new movie. (Alas, it's nigh impossible to get insurance on an actor of his age.) He stroked her knee, told me he was busy when I asked him a question, and we all loved him.

People will know, because I've written it elsewhere, how much I've loved this man's work over the years. Believe me when I say that next to working with him in the studios which I fear now may never happen, meeting him that day was the very best I could ever have wished for. Thank you very much, Anoraks.

Remember that I said I was due at UK Games Fest in Harlow with Mike Edmonds next month, a few pages back? Well, it's now been and gone.

The film studios have claimed my time recently, I'm delighted to say, and I haven't picked up the keyboard in some time. I've missed it though, my relaxation. Writing is one of the best ways I know to recharge one's batteries, apart from living where I live of course.

I think I'll wait a small while before telling you the saga of the three (yes Karl), the *three* missing roundabouts, and confine myself for the while to my friend Mr Edmonds.

I've never known Mike to be anything but the most courteous of chaps. Mind, he does have a great sense of humour. In fact he's always laughing.

When did we first meet? Let me think. Well, of course it must have been at that time, almost long, long ago, when the *Star Wars* movies were made. But my first con remembrance of Mike goes back to that famous, some might say infamous, convention in Basildon. Mike took it all in his stride, in fact he always does. I was trying to get hold of him recently for a convention in Holland and I kept getting his answerphone. When I eventually nailed him, he was on the loo.

'Where the hell have you been?' quoth I. 'I've been trying to get you for ages.'

'Oh sorry Michael. I've just been over in Belgium doing a nice play in Flemish,' came the reply.

'Do you speak the language?'

'Not a bloody word, mate. I had to do it phonetically.'

Mr Mike Edmonds is a super guy and excellent actor. We're bound to bump into him again during this literary stroll. Indeed, Iain Lowson, who is going to be looking after us at this year's GenCon, our guest liaison, said when he phoned yesterday,

'You'll make sure the other guests know what to do, won't you? You'll make sure that they circulate, like you did last year?' I think he may have a job getting Mike to sit down!

OK. The biggest most gigantic UK convention ever. This was where I was asked to blaze a trail and establish a precedent for future guest involvement and participation. I'm delighted therefore to name myself, the GenCon Guinea Pig!

> John Brown, John Brown, lend me your long hair,
> All along, out along, down along lea,
> For I want to go to Loughborough fair,
> With Steve Turner, Sandy Douglas, Gordon Hudson,
> Chris Baylis, Steven Consdale, Karl Eldridge,
> Old Uncle Ratty an' all, Oh Old Uncle Ratty an' all.

I promised Ratty that I'd enter him thus. By the way, there are masses included in the an' alls and I love you all. In fact I've just noticed that there's not one lady included in the re-written ditty. Very unlike me that. Mind you, the original text of Widdecombe Fair is all fellas. But fear not, I'll redress the balance. You wait till I get to Fiona.

Nah, I want to get to her now, and as it's my book, I will! Fiona Kyle is a super, sexy, lovely lady who works for Wizards. She doesn't have to attend, but she's always present at all the satellite Wizard conventions. All of them – Poly, Dudley, Drak, U.K. Fest, etc. And I've never not seen her wearing anything but the most exquisite leather trousers. Wooo-Wow!

Until, that is, this year's GenCon, which has just finished. (A huge success and it will appear here in full in due course.) But when I arrived, Fiona was not wearing said leather trews, she had on a pair of ordinary jeans. I said that I was devastated and told her that my lads were only coming because I'd told them about her trousers. Fiona quite rightly replied that it wasn't practical, with all the running around she had to do, organising things. But on the last morning, when we were sitting at our long line of tables in the dealers' room, signing away, Fiona suddenly appeared dressed in those leathers. We all stood up and cheered as she slowly walked the full length of those tables!

Fiona is in charge of, oh masses of things, including making sure that our contracts are in order – I told you this was a biggy. For GenCon we receive proper letters of agreement.

It all started when I went to Edinburgh to do a convention called Capsicon, organised by Miss Karen Newns and Mr Iain Lowson (already mentioned). It has to be said that although we all had a great time at Capsicon and it was a success as far as the enjoyment factor was concerned, I'm afraid it was not a huge success, financially.

Oh, for a number of reasons. Mainly because of the fact that it was held during the Edinburgh Festival. I think both Karen and Iain would agree that that was a mistake. There were far too many other distractions.

But we had enormous fun. At my suggestion we dragged a Dalek all over the cobbled streets of Edinburgh to drum up business. This Dalek had been superbly built by Dr Martin Rogerson, remember him – Edinburgh *Dr Who*? It nearly broke us physically, but please, don't tell Karen and Iain.

I christened Karen 'the Second Mrs McClusky' (of *Grange Hill* fame), 'cos she can't half boss people about! On the first morning, before things really got started, I happened to wander into the hall/dealers' room and there were my chums, the Edinburgh *Dr Who*s. I started blethering away as is my wont, but was almost immediately very firmly rapped over the knuckles by Mrs McC. the Second, who was in the middle of her 'This Is How It's Going to Be' talk to her minions. I hadn't even seen her!

We're very great friends, mind. Dearly B. and I have been invited to her ceilidh, on the occasion of her wedding to the super artist, Colin. She'll be a MacNeil 'ere long.

We even invented a new dance, Karen and I. It's called The McClusky Stomp. You stamp up and down the dance floor, from one far end to another, and you get more stompy as the music progresses. I wonder what my very dear chum, the other Mrs McClusky, Gwyneth (Powell) will say when she hears about it. Karen's also a damn good organiser of conventions and of anything else come to that. She used to work for

Wizards when they were based in Scotland. In fact, Fiona took over her job when the company transferred to Maidenhead.

Perhaps because of Karen's past connection with Wizards, I had a call from Iain a couple of weeks after the Edinburgh Dalek haul asking if I'd be interested in joining an experiment. Be a guinea pig. Wizards of the Coast had been thinking of broadening their base and having a celebrity guest at their card/role-playing convention at Loughborough University.

At this stage of course I knew nothing. I wasn't even aware that there were conventions where you played cards and role-played. Or that GenCon was the tops. And that if you won at GenCon you would as likely as not be on your way to the world finals in America.

And they wanted *me* to be a guinea pig! Of course I accepted with alacrity and I loved every darn minute of my time there.

It's a very vast venue. The campus seems to go on forever. I'm told indeed that it's the largest campus in the world. But I considered it my brief to visit all the gaming groups, even the far-flung ones, and show a bright eye and a bushy tail.

I made so many new friends that I can't possibly hope to list them all here. But if I tell you that my appearances at Dudley, Poly, UK Fest, *et al* (DrakCon had been arranged earlier if you remember), were as a direct consequence of GenCon, and that here was my first meeting with Ratty, Fiona, Chris Baylis and John, I trust you'll get a feel of how much GenCon meant to me.

I'll relate a couple more anecdotes in a line or two, but I must mention, before I forget (as if I could!) that as a result of my visit I was asked if I could bring along some chums to next year's GenCon. The guinea pig had earned his lettuce!

The line-up that week was as follows: Messrs Kenneth Baker, Peter Mayhew, Jeremy Bulloch, Michael Edmonds, Angus MacInnis and Femi Taylor. Plus Claudia Christian, my co-star on *First Frontier*, together with Andrew Dymond, our *F.F.* producer, of course, and Jim Mortimer, our writer. Watch this space . . .

Now for the anecdotes from my first GenCon.

The furthest outpost used for games at GenCon were reserved for the youngsters, the idea perhaps being that they could hike the distance more easily. Anyway it really was quite a step, and on my second visit there, one of the lads must have thought I needed reviving. 'Would you like a sweetie, Mr Bronson?' Well, I was supposed to be losing half a stone for my next part, so I thanked him but asked if I could keep it for later.

After I'd finished my rounds and was on my way back to the main building, I bumped into a little Scotsman, David, who actually looks a bit like a vampire, all teeth and pointed hair. No, this is not derogatory, the vampires have a huge following at GenCon, their role-playing evening is one of the week's highlights.

'Hello mate,' says I, 'would you like this sweet?'

He replied that yes he would provided I'd sign the wrapper. Needless to say, I willingly obliged.

The Charity auctions at GenCon are famous the world over and are always hugely enjoyable occasions. A lot of money is raised for many very worthy causes. People really dig very deep into their pockets, some even save up all year. I'm delighted to tell you that the auction on this occasion went far beyond all expectations and made thousands. Included amongst the goodies on offer were a couple of copies of an excellent book by a certain bum actor which went for £125 each, and a solitary signed sweetie which was knocked down for £35. One wee, tiny sweet!

Ratty, super Ratty. He's sure to have one, but most of us don't know his real name. Ratty's value cannot be overstated at these conventions. His main role is to gather the score sheets, collate them and declare the winners. A mammoth task when you bear in mind the number of games going on at any one time over the five days of the convention. There are numerous others involved too of course but it is Ratty who can constantly be found at the computers, beavering away.

To be honest I'm sure he enjoys it. Indeed he never seems to miss a card/role-playing con. He's certainly always been there at the ones I've attended. Even Aberdeen, when he had to fly back to England on the Sunday night, as soon as the convention finished, because he had some important conference (his day job as opposed to convention) to prepare for on the following morning. As often as not Ratty supplies the computers, too.

I haven't forgotten you Uncle Ratty, and I'll see you soon. Apart from anything I've got to tell them about your hats!

Chapter 10

If I have any regrets, career-wise, they are very few and very small. I'd love to have done a swashbuckler, for example (how many times have I said that?) and maybe I will. I know I'd have enjoyed a *Carry On*, and a musical – a fifties one, please, with Debbie Reynolds! It would have been a pleasure to work with the likes of Rita Hayworth, Ingrid Bergman, John Wayne, Claude Rains, Humphrey Bogart and Stewart Granger. And it would have been delightful to have worked on *Worzel Gummidge* with many people's favourite Dr Who, Jon Pertwee. I did do a *Who* with him of course, and that was not the next best thing, it was a very great pleasure.

My Halliwell, after listing Jon's movies credits, such as *Mr Drake's Duck* with Douglas Fairbanks Jr (almost swashbuckling), and two *Carry On*s (there, I could have killed a couple of my small regrets in one bound), and about half a dozen others, tells us that Jon also played the Doctor and Worzel, and then says . . . etc.

And that means that he did one hell of a lot. Masses. Did you know for instance that he doubled for Danny Kaye? I've got a wee feeling of déjà vu (see t'other book, I may have told this before), but Danny never came to the UK for the film *Knock on Wood*, even though it was set in England. Jon did all the long and back-to-camera shots in and around London for him. And damn convincing he was too.

I know I've told you of the trip round all the other rehearsal rooms when we were doing 'The Mind of Evil' – it was shortly before Christmas and we took the morning off and sang carols for charity. I've told you that although I love 'em all, Jon has to be my favourite Doctor; I've mentioned, too, how he used to take the piss, mercilessly, 'You're sunburned, you've obviously not been working, poor old thing' etc. What I've not perhaps emphasised enough is his professionalism, and above all his kindness, both on the set and off.

Let me give you an on the set taste. Picture if you will a rather splendid thespian, who didn't have a great deal in the bank at the time, nothing in fact, and who had just been told by his Dearly Beloved that offspring number three was on the way. This splendid actor had an excellent scene with Jon and Katy, the super Katy Manning. It could have been because of the news he'd just had, I honestly don't know, but this superb thespian dried, not once, but three times, and was crestfallen that the shot had to be done again. (You should understand that up to this point in my career I had been known as 'One Take Mike'.)

Jon, as leading player, could have been annoyed or even blown his top, and quite rightly. I'd let the side down. But instead, he was very patient and supportive and when at last I did get the lines in the correct order, he called the floor manager over and said, 'Please tell the director (Timothy Coombe) that I'd like to do it again. Michael was great, but I wasn't as good as I was in rehearsal.'

We did the scene again and I was as good as I'd been in rehearsal!

Thank you, Jon. Katy and I were talking of you and that scene only recently when I sort of stood in for you at the Anorax Anonymous' *Who* weekend on the Isle of Man.

This is very hot off the press, or perhaps I should say waves. Let me quickly explain because I'm away to the studios in a couple of minutes. I've just done another phoned radio interview standing in my sitting room, you know how it works by now. This one was for a local Northampton station. Thing is, I caught a cold at Infinity (Cardiff) the weekend before last – the hotel was unbearably hot and dry and I took to rushing out of the place to obtain some much needed oxygen. Anyway,

I really caught a whopper and all the way through the radio chat just now I kept thinking that my voice wasn't up to scratch and that I could hear the cold. Inevitable I know, but I never like being less that one hundred per cent. But never underestimate the power of Doctor Theatre. At the end of the interview I apologised to the guy for sounding like I was two paces from the knacker's yard. He told me that he hadn't noticed a thing! I'm coughing and sputtering like mad now, but during the time I was on air I sounded perfectly normal, even if I thought I didn't.

A wee postscript. Remember, I was just off to the studios? Well, it's now the following day and I have to add that I'm still hacking away. But last evening I was recording a piece for *Gatecrash*, a new TV programme for BBC digital, and again no cold showed. In fact the producer commented on my wonderfully powerful voice! Dear Doc Theatre.

Right, I'm off on some more book signings. Picture, if you will, a very tired Sheard arriving in the very early morning at London's Heathrow airport, having just spent eight hours in the air. He is jet-lagged, but somehow he finds his way to the Woking coach link. He arrives in Woking, not really knowing how he got there, and manages to board a Portsmouth train. He sits himself down in a corner seat, shuts his eyes, and falls very fast asleep.

'Portsmouth and Southsea. Portsmouth and Southsea is your next station stop,' the ticket inspector's voice blasts through the intercom. Sheard stumbles into wakefulness and just manages to remove himself from the train. *What's the time? Oh, only nine-thirty a.m. OK, I've got half an hour.* Into the gents, quick shave, splash of cold water, change of shirt. Then a cup of coffee in the station buffet and up the road to HMV – good job it wasn't too far!

When I arrived there was a small poster in the window, it's true, announcing the fact that I was due there that day to sign copies of my book. This to coincide with the release of the new gold and silver boxed videos of the special edition *Star Wars* trilogy. But as to an indication of where in the building this momentous event was to happen there was not a clue.

I stepped inside. The record/CD department on the ground floor didn't even know I was expected, 'No, no idea, Sir. Not here anyway.'

I was about to give up hope and go home for what I knew would be a most blissful sleep, when a rather nice looking young lady came bobbing down from the floor above.

'Ah, Mr Sheard,' she said, 'I didn't know you were here yet. If you'd like to follow me. We're ready for you upstairs.'

Upstairs, the video department was in fact nicely set out. They showed *Empire* all day, and gave me a beautiful baguette for lunch. I also sold lots of books, in spite of the fact that I was bog tired and that nobody knew I was there until they reached the first floor – and I do mean bog tired, very nearly asleep on my feet after that disorientating flight. And there was even another 'in spite of' reason. HMV would not let me sell the books at the convention book signing price, but insisted, very nicely, that I sell for the price one would normally pay in a high street book shop.

Ah well, a good day, once I'd finally got home to my bed. (Please NB. *Yes, Mr B.* at its high street shop price is still excellent value for money, you understand. It's just that when I'm doing a signing session I like to make it even more of a bargain. Why not come and see me when I'm next in your neck of the woods?)

Before I continue I thought I'd string together a few more book signings – I'd like to go sideways again. I've said before that this book is even more of a 'dipper-inner' than the last one, haven't I? OK, well, I've just returned from London, and as I came through the door, Dearly B. was on the phone. Nothing unusual in that, she often is. But this time she mouthed, 'It's for you, it's Pam.' I've not talked much of Pam yet, we'll meet her properly later. But as a result of the chat we've just had, I've been prompted into six words or a dozen right now, about David – David Scott – Pam's junior. Pam is a chartered accountant, remember, and terribly important.

Right then, Mr Scott is still a trainee accountant. Nothing wrong with that of course, it's a hell of a slog qualifying. Hell I should know, my eldest, Simon, went through the mill a few years back, those part one and part two exams were a pain. But it has to be said, Simon was twenty-three when he made it, David Scott is already thirty-one!

Why am I going on about an office junior? Well, it's because Mr Scott has been pontificating about my wonderful profession. His lunchtime pub blether goes thus. 'If you want to know about drugs then you should ask Michael, all actors are junkies.' When I pointed out (via Pam, during one of our earlier phone chats) that, yes, I'm in a high profile profession which can result in high profile cases getting the media hype, but that I personally have never even tried a joint, and that I'm confident neither have the bulk of my Equity chums, D. Scott came up with his next crack. 'Well, anyway, all actors are drunks.' OK David. I'm a Scot, I hail from the silver city, Aberdeen, and I do enjoy a twelve year old dram of the heather. But there is a vast difference between that and the gutter. Don't you like a pint, David? Let me put my record straight, which I assure you is par for most thespian courses. Tonight (Friday) I'll have a wee drop. The night before last I had two. But last night I was in the studio recording a show and not one sip passed my lips, at least until the job was done. I have to be on the ball, perhaps even more than you do!

And so we come to today, and my main reason for writing this digression now. Apparently this very day at lunch, in the pub probably, David had the presumption to say that all actors are neurotics and madmen. I have written a bestseller and been asked to do another. I have been married to the same lovely girl for thirty-odd years, who wouldn't have stayed with a drug-taking, drink-sodden maniac for five minutes. In my book, this doesn't make me either a junkie or a lush.

I could go on, but I'm running out of time. I have a production meeting in half an hour.

But thank you, David, for affording me this opportunity to state that there are as many hard-working, ordinary chaps in my neck of these lovely woods as I'm sure there are in yours.

This tangent has been fun and I trust we'll meet one day, but please, don't point fingers until you really can throw stones.

We shall now return to the previous topic!

If you remember, earlier on I told you how my publishers suggested that I do a book signing tour before Christmas. Claire Richardson, my very lovely new editor at Summersdale (Rob Bircher having moved on to publishers new), rang.

'It's just a little stroll up and down and around the south coast, Michael. You're not filming at the moment, are you?'

This is a flavour of how it went. WHSmiths in all cases . . .

I started, Guildford, Saturday, with Sue. (Sue being my WHS liaison.) I told you about that lovely day yonks ago, well, pages anyway.

Worthing was on Sunday. Manager Andy Davy wasn't even there. I don't blame him, Worthing is completely dead on Sundays. Don't do a signing in Worthing on a Sunday. I had to capture virtually every single plodder who came through the door in order to sell out. But I made it, just. Even the lady who said she never reads books bought one for her husband's stocking.

Brighton, Monday. With the lovely Jo and Sheila looking after me. Wow, now we're really picking up speed again. All the staff here were particularly nice. Cups of tea/coffee were on tap all the time and rushed to me. And I sold masses of books, very speedily. One was to a super chap, who mentioned that he'd recently turned professional (thesp), after retiring from his day job, teaching. Watch out for one of Arthur's (remember Bill Treacher?) allotment chums, the one with the dog, making a welcome return visit to *EastEnders*.

Tuesday. On my Island of Wight. I sold out before lunch, of course I did. And not only to all my old friends (even Peter Boffin, former top TV vision mixer at Thames television, turned up with his money in hand), there were many new ones, too. Sarah Ralph, for example. She's about to start training at the Central School of Speech and Drama. If she gets her A level grades. I'm sure she will. And I shall let you know later.

Wednesday was supposed to be Epsom. But I had to cry off and do a couple of voice-overs in London instead. But I'll be back.

Thursday I made the short trip to Fareham. I'd been there before in fact, at the height of the previous summer when it was bloody hot. I'd sold well then, in the long, rather narrow WHS shop, and John Woodis (the manager) had invited me back. I sold splendidly this time, too. John's staff were also great and very enthusiastic.

Friday. I got up early on Friday so that I could get to Bognor for opening time – Bognor's on a branch line so it takes longer to get there, what with having to change trains. Who said 'Bugger Bognor'? Some king or other wasn't it? Anyway, he got it very wrong. Bognor made a perfect end to a super week. I had a wonderful day with John (another one), and his Bognor gang. A great, nay, a fabulous time.

Thank you, everyone. I look forward to many more such trips.

(Since I wrote the above, the lovely Claire Richardson, editor superb, has in fact moved on to new manuscripts in London and the equally super Elizabeth Kershaw now looks after me, beautifully. Indeed, she it is who has put together that which you are now reading. Great job, eh?)

I'm sorry, I can't take too long on this thumbnail. Don Henderson – General Tagge in *Star Wars*, Gavrok in *Dr Who* etc – is gone now and not that long ago. He was a mate, a super friend and I miss him.

We first met on *Warship*, I played yet another Admiral – Admiral Forbes. How many years ago was that, for heaven's sake? And we finished our thesping duties together on Don's great series for Granada, *Bulman*. That wasn't the end of our meetings of course. The last time we chatted was at the last *Dr Who* Manopticon in Manchester.

Because of work commitments I only managed the last day and a bit of this convention, and when I arrived and presented myself in the green room, there, chatting to Michael Jayston, was Don.

'Michael,' he said standing up (rather shakily I'm afraid) and coming towards me. 'How are you son, me old darlin'?' He always called me son. I can't remember why now, something to do with our ranks in *Warship* I think. I was an Admiral, of course – and Don was a Chief Petty Officer.

Now that I mention it, I've got a good few foster fathers and uncles around the place – Jeremy B., Peter Mayhew – but let me, right now, make one thing abundantly clear. The only reason I call some of my chums dad, or daddy, or uncle, is as a term of harmless endearment. Maybe it's also my way of reassuring myself that there are some around who are a little bit older than me!

So, I put my arm round Daddy Don's shoulders – I remember he was wearing a plum coloured velvet jacket – and we chatted away like mad about how things were going. Don was very excited, he was off to Russia shortly to do a movie. But I, quite honestly, was horrified. There was no substance at all in his shoulders, just bone.

Don had had throat cancer some years before. I'm not sure of the exact details, but my chum died very shortly after this convention.

Dear Don was a trouper. I remember, for example, him telling me when we were doing *Bulman*, in which he played the named lead remember, that he'd just written off to over thirty directors. *Bulman* was coming to an end and he didn't trust agents to find him further employment.

I would not like to say that Don was like me, a working thespian who loved what he did. Rather, I am like Don. Don was a trouper. A thespian right down to his fingertips. He is very sorely missed by us all.

Where shall I go now, Don? Shall I chat about Manchester and the fabulous Fab Café? Manchester's where we made *Bulman* after all. OK, let's go.

This outing only took place last Monday, but what the Bulman, I've always said that these pages are not chronological. Almost, but not quite.

In fact, to tell you this particular saga, of which I'm really quite proud, I must go back three or so weeks. Paul Miley (remember Mr never, never-on-time), rang and asked if I'd like to join him on a trip to Blackpool. 'What for?' I asked, not unreasonably.

'Well, you know Dave (Prowse) and I are putting on Multicon, and you're coming.'

'Yes,' I said, wondering what the hell was coming next. 'Provided you put it in writing!'

'Yeah, yeah, we're doing all that,' Mr Miley continued. 'But I'm going to have a look at the convention venue, and on the way . . .' Here it comes, thought I. '. . . I'm stopping off in Manchester. They're opening a new themed bar. Gareth Thomas and Sophie Aldred will be there. Would you like to join them?'

Gareth's great, and how could I refuse the opportunity of seeing Sophie, one of my special chums.

So off we toddled. Paul and I arranged to meet on Euston station and he was on time for once. None of his doing though, his lovely lady, Tracy, was responsible for getting him there.

The evening went excellently. Particularly for me, I'm not ashamed to say. There were over two hundred people present, most of whom packed in around nine p.m. And at the end of this success, Steve Petricco, the partner (of three: himself, his brother Paul, and Mike Royce), who's in charge of liaison/media, came bounding up to me with a tumbler of whiskey and dry ginger and pushed it into my hand. 'Michael, everyone thinks you're great. Can you come back and bring copies of your book?'

'I'd be delighted, when?'

'Oh, any time. As soon as you're free.'

Three short weeks later I was once again hurrying down Euston's platform three and just managed to catch the eleven a.m. train for Manchester Piccadilly. I'd intended to go for the twelve a.m., but good connections across London had got me there early. Damn good job, as it happens!

I arrived in Manchester and grabbed a telephone. 'Hi, Steve, it's Michael. I've just got in.'

'Oh, great, I'll come and meet you. We can get started early. I just might be able to arrange another one.' Another one?

Steve is not the Fab Café's media man for nothing. Wow, I wish he was my agent. He explained where my hotel was, 'just next to the Café' but I didn't go anywhere near it until some three and a half hours later. What did I do during that time? I trundled around Manchester, my bag still on my back. First we went to Galaxy Radio and I did an interview with Neil. Then skipped down to the old docks and Piccadilly Radio. Jenny Cunliffe, who did this interview, seemed about twelve years old when we first met. But the moment she started, she grew in authority and her voice matured as if by magic.

That interview satisfactorily completed, we popped 'just round the corner, Michael' (actually miles) to Auntie BBC.

In fact, you know me, it was great fun and the interviews did go extremely well. Some, or parts of some of the chats were due to be broadcast later in the day and thus served to publicise the fact that I'd be at the Fab Café that evening. The other bits and the rest would be broadcast later in the week. All great publicity for the Fab Café of course. But never fear, I also got some super plugs in for the book!

And so we came to the evening. I'd finally registered at the hotel and deposited my bag, and after a quick wash to blow away the cobwebs of travel, I arrived back at the café. We were due to start at seven p.m., it was now a quarter past six and there was no one there. No, I tell a lie. There were the staff of course and Steve, who hurried over with a mouth-wateringly delicious chicken tikka ('Because you've not eaten all day Michael') and over in a corner were sat Emma and four of the nicest people I've ever met.

Before I tell you about them, I must just record Steve's reply to my question of 'Where is everyone?' He laughed as he put the plate of tikka down.

'You don't know the Mancunians do you? They don't start until late here. Don't you worry, they'll be along.'

Now, I know Maureen and David Davies, their son John and Chris Green, who were sitting in that corner, won't mind one bit if I talk of Emma first. Emma is fourteen years old and weighs almost as much as two bags of sugar. She's an absolute darling and just can't stop kissing everyone and loves having her tummy tickled. I could very happily have put her in my pocket and taken her home. Mind you, I'm not sure what Sophie – my Sophie, not to be confused with my mate *Who* Sophie – would say. (The names are quite coincidental by the way.) In fact I bet my Sophie would adore Emma just like everyone else.

Guessed yet? I'm sure you have. I am of course a huge dog lover. Our Sophie is a fifty-seven varieties, and Emma is the cutest Yorkie I've ever met.

The Davieses had been given special permission to bring her along, fourteen being a goodly age for a wee dog to be left alone, and she was as good as gold. She sat quietly on Maureen's lap until, that is, she was asked to do photographs. And there were lots of them. She was a little star. Check out her photo in the middle of this book.

Before I go on to later that evening, Emma, I must give more mention to the rest of your gang. They were all dressed as *Grange Hill* students. Maureen, David and Emma had come over from Sheffield and they'd been waiting there, in the café, since before five, when I was still radioing. John lives and works in Manchester and had recently written to me, via the Beeb. I didn't make the connection at first. He's a great chap and a tip-top appreciator.

Because all was quiet, Maureen was in fact somewhat concerned at the lack of punters, and was kind enough to tell me that it wasn't my fault and that it was no reflection on me. I told her what Steve had said about later. And later on she said she saw what he meant! Before that happened I had time to sign, in one go, all the goodies the Davieses had brought with them. Everything from *Dr Who* and *Empire* video covers, to books, *G.H.* and posters various.

Before I finally leave the Emma quintet, I must pop in a coincidence. I've mentioned already the last Manopticon which was held a few years back in the Manchester Piccadilly. Well, on the going-home Monday morning, after I'd said my goodbyes, I hitched my lovely leather bag on my back – bought in Greece (Rhodes market) when I was making *The Dark Side of the Sun* – and started off for the station.

Thing was that in spite of the fact that I knew, or thought I knew, Manchester pretty well – I'd been there many times doing *The Street* and *Crown Court* etc – I started striding out in completely the wrong direction. After ten minutes or so I began to wonder where the hell I was and decided to ask the chap who'd just turned the corner and was coming towards me.

'No, mate, you're going in the opposite direction, the station is behind you.' His name was Chris and it was the same Chris (Green) who was sat sitting in a corner of the Fab Café with Emma and the Davieses, waiting for me to arrive from my marathon of radio interviews. Until we got chatting, both of us had completely forgotten the earlier meeting. Small flippin' world.

Back to our Fab Café evening. It was great. As Steve had said, the place was bulging by nine-thirty, and I sold every book I had with me. We had a very good Q&A – more questions than ever – and amongst others, the Daily Sport took some (super?) snaps!

Steve, Paul, Mike and I, finally arrived at an excellent local Chinese restaurant at something like one-thirty a.m. the following morning. (Everything still happening late – or should it now be early? Last orders here were at breakfast time.) We had a lovely meal, we had a couple of jars, we relaxed, and I eventually got back to that excellent hotel at three-fifteen in the morning. And how I slept.

The Fab Café can be found, by the way, at 111, Portland Street, Manchester. Try it, it's great, even when I'm not there!

And you thought I'd forgotten, didn't you? Mr never-on-time Miley and I did pop over to Blackpool after my first visit to the Fab Café, and had a look round the Multicon venue, The Norbreck Castle Hotel. I'll be talking of that weekend soon. Thirty-six guests have been invited, would you believe. We shall see and I shall report.

Now, here's a little something. Having said that this small tome is about my life outside the studio and acting, I can't resist slipping in the odd nosegay.

I've just had a call from my agent, and I have agreed to do a commercial and, for two weeks only, to be plastered around bus stops. As . . . a headmaster. Advertising Nickelodeon.

As a headmaster? OK, hold on. This is not degrading my dear old friend Mr Bronson. If I thought for one moment that it would, I'd never have agreed to do it. I love Sir far too much. And there's one aspect that particularly appeals to my sense of fun. Although I did play a head teacher in 'Remembrance of the Daleks', not quite everyone saw that performance. Now there'll be no denying it, Sheard really has finally made it to headmaster!

Dearly Beloved is away today, painting the atmosphere of Cowes week, and I'm therefore on my own and waiting for Grandstand to begin. But before I go I'd like quickly to drop in that Harlow Games Fest, so that when I return I can go straight on to Regeneration with everyone, and Scott McMillan, Annie, and Pam.

Jan and Karl Eldridge will forgive me, I know, if I skate fairly swiftly over their excellent, and first, gaming convention.

Another satellite GenCon. Actually I don't mean 'just another', not for a moment I don't. Mike Edmonds and I thoroughly enjoyed ourselves in Harlow. Except for the 'arrangements'.

Mike was all right, he lives in the Harlow neck of the woods and left his home on the morning of the event and returned the same evening. But I had to be lodged in a hotel.

'You should get the train to Harlow Mill station, Michael, it's right next to the hotel,' Jan had said when she phoned. 'Would you like one of us to meet you?'

'No, please, you've got enough to do, I'll find it. And don't bother picking me up on the morning of the convention either. I've got Karl's excellent map. I'll make my own way to the Sports Centre (the venue), it can't be far . . .'

Can't be far my aching tired feet! It wouldn't have been far as Karl's map stood, but there were three, ever so slight omissions. He'd only left out three ruddy roundabouts! I seemed to trudge forever and I'm sure I only got to UK Games Fest because Steve and Sue Turner (Dudley Bug) came along in their car and took pity on me.

And there's more. This was a one day do, on a Saturday. When all was over and after a great day, after I'd been given a lift back to the hotel by a very kind Carl (another Carl, with a C not a K. Karl – with a K – was rightly far too busy), I slept very soundly. Not a sound. I should have known. When I came down for breakfast on the Sunday morning, I was innocently looking forward to at least being able to pop down to Harlow Mill and catching my train back to London – no long walks. But on inquiring from mine host, I was told that there were no trains that stopped at Harlow Mill station on a Sunday.

I had to go to Harlow Town Station, which was almost next door to the Sports Centre. This meant of course that I had to trudge round those three non-existent bloody roundabouts yet again!

Whew, I'm even exhausted just writing about it.

OK, I'm now off to watch Grandstand. But not before I state, categorically, that I bear no ill will towards the Eldridges. I said I didn't need a lift. And there was one very big consolation to all those roundabouts. The Old Cathay. An excellent Chinese restaurant was attached to the hotel. Yes, Chinese again. I love Chinese food.

I do hope I'm invited back to Harlow and its three non-existent roundabouts. And that marvellous restaurant!

Chapter 11

Right, Regeneration. The Radisson Edwardian Hotel, alongside Heathrow Airport. Here we go.

I arrived, Friday, at two in the afternoon. After, it has to be said, a pretty easy but bloody awful journey. Well, you get the train to Woking, then the bus to Heathrow Airport – that's not too bad. (I even did it, t'other way round, when I was asleep and on my way to HMV in Portsmouth.) But you then have to find the hotel bus, the one that links all the hotels surrounding the airport, and that's a ghastly nightmare.

But I did get to the Radisson eventually, and finally arrived at reception. 'Hello matey, you're on this one are you?'

I felt better already. I knew the voice. Peter Mayhew, my chum Pete. It was super to see him again. 'Hi, pal,' I replied. 'How the heck are you? Here, I'm hoping you'll pen a few lines by way of a foreword to my new book.' (This one of course.)

'Oh, I'm not sure about that. Chewys don't usually do that sort of thing.'

'Ah,' said I, realising that he was taking the piss, 'but if I tell you that Kenny, Nick Courtney, and Jeremy are jotting a couple of lines?'

'That's different. Chewys never like to be left out. Come and have a drink, you old – Grandfather. You look as though you need one!'

Excellent venue, The Radisson. Once, it has to be emphasised, you arrive. We were all there for this one. Peter I've already mentioned, Dave, Kenny, Jeremy. In addition, the lovely Shelagh (Fraser, of course) and Phil Brown, who'd come over from the States. And for Sunday and a bit of Monday, Colin Baker (Dr Who number six) arrived to liven things up even further. Simon Williams (*Upstairs, Downstairs* and *Who*) was also to have joined us, but in the end he couldn't make it because of work commitments.

What sort of a convention was this? Well, how about multi-media? But its main function was to raise funds for The Actors' Charitable Trust and The Authors' Foundation.

A great time was had by all. Well, as organised by that superlative chartered accountant, Pam Clarke, compèred by Mr Scott McMillan and the lovely Anne Page, how could it possibly fail? We danced (I did 'School's Out' twice), we had some great Q&As and played an assortment of excellent panel games. Andrew (*First Frontier*) Dymond turned up with the super Sue, as did 'never-on-time' Miley.

I'm sure everyone will agree that this was a happy convention. No, hang on, all cons are happy. Regeneration was a particularly happy one. With only one small fly . . .

. . . It was Easter, and because of the holiday, the distributors couldn't get my books delivered on time. I and a lot of people were disappointed. I'd only a very few copies with me and had to take mail orders. It's not the same. I prefer to dedicate my book in person at conventions, or book signings, or whatever, and I like to have a chat as I write. I like to think the apps prefer it too.

A wee postscript. Dearly B. and I have just been out for a spot of lunch. A chap came over to our table and asked if I indeed was M. Sheard. I answered that I was. He then went on to say what a marvellous job I'd done on *G.H.* with Mr B., and how could I possibly also play such a convincing German in *Randall and Hopkirk* (that really was yonks ago), and was he right, had I written a book? Yes, I said, I have. He then insisted that I send him a copy, without bothering to see it, or have me talk further of it, and thrust the lucre on the table. He wouldn't take no for an answer, the very nice man.

My book was delivered to him next day.

Garrick (Biggs) Hagon I don't understand. Why doesn't he do more conventions? He's a great guy and has an excellent Q&A presence.

It was in the spring that Chris Gardner (I.O.W. County Press reporter), rang me.

'What about a convention on the Island this summer?'

'Not too much preparation time,' said I, 'but go for it. I'll give you a contact number.'

And so it came to be. The first and possibly the last Isle of Wight Sci-Fi convention. Last, because although the apps were there in number, there were not enough of them – the Island is quite small after all. And the rest, the holidaymakers, didn't know that there was a convention happening. I've always said that you must publicise. Like mad you must. Then you have to do several years and get yourself established, before you know if you've made it as a convention organiser.

All this of course has nothing to do with Garrick. His star burns bright whatever the circumstances, and he always greets me in the same sort of fashion: 'Hello, Michael, how the hell are you?' I have a remembrance of Ernest Borgnine greeting me in the self same way when we did the remake of *All Quiet on the Western Front*. Mind you, Ernest is a smidge larger than Garrick and pumped my hand somewhat harder!

Garrick is the stuff that the true convention guest is made of. He's always smiling and has, as I say, a great stage presence. And some unique stories. Have a look at the CD Rom, 'Behind the Magic', where his missing scenes with Mark and Koo Stark (see later!) are on view.

(It happens to us all, you know – missing scenes – even me. The prologue for *Hitler, The Last Ten Days*, with Alec Guinness, Peter Sallis and Freddie Jones, in which I played Herr Doktor Schacht, vanished as if it had never been filmed. But it was. They simply decided that it was surplus to requirement. Mind you, *Last Ten Days* wasn't a very good film, so perhaps I was well out of it.)

If you get a chance to join Garrick at a convention, please come. I'll do my utmost to make sure he's there, and that he does many more. It looks, by the way, as if we'll be doing a movie together this summer. *Chaos*, great part for me: Duggan, a crusading vicar, and a super part for Garrick: Carter, a police inspector.

I'd now like to tell you of one of the strangest evenings of my life. It all began with a phone call.

'Mr Sheard?'

'Yes.'

'Good afternoon, my name is Polly. I was hoping I could ask you to do us a small favour.'

'If I can. What sort of favour?'

'Well, we need a judge for our beauty contest. There are two sections, one for the seniors and one for the juniors. We'd be so grateful if you could come along. We intend to appoint three or four other judges. Perhaps your wife might like to accompany you?'

'Er, yes, she might. When is this to be?'

Thus began the bizarre event. Talk about jungle. Hell, I've judged talent contests where the chosen, worthy, winner was not the choice of the girl who came second, and certainly not of number two's parents, who endeavoured to have the contest declared null and void. But this was gigantically worse.

Dearly B. did join me as a judge, thank heavens, and there were three others. One was a holiday camp entertainment's officer, who was going to offer the senior winner a summer season. Then there was a guy from the local radio station, and a rather toffee-nosed matronly type, who was connected with the company who were staging the event.

Before I continue, I really must mention that:

a) This contest was most certainly not Miss Great Britain.

b) If I seem chauvinistic, I'm sorry, I certainly don't mean to.

c) But blimey. You ain't heard nothing yet!

This was the grand final, and all the contestants had fought their way through regional heats, and I'm sure I do mean fought. There were a dozen juniors and for some reason, thirteen seniors. No doubt another panel of judges somewhere in the lower reaches just couldn't decide between the contenders. I wonder why!

OK, the stage is set, or rather, the auditorium. We judges were seated at tables in the body of the hall some twenty feet from the front of, and facing, the stage.

First it was the juniors' turn. The drums rolled, or rather the hi-fi crackled, and the compère danced camply on. He did a sort of act, full of double entendre jokes – it was very feeble and seemed to go on forever – and when he finally finished 'Humbert Humberting' he announced the first junior contestant.

The idea was that both juniors and seniors would make two entrances. First they would walk on to the stage in swimsuits, prance around a bit, and walk off. Then they'd reappear wearing evening dresses and come down to our line of tables for a chat.

I don't know about the other judges, but the fact that the cut-off age (junior to senior) was fifteen made absolutely no difference. If I had one under age teenager lean, ever so casually, towards me, I had twelve. The seniors were even worse, and one – I'm sure it was number thirteen mentioned above – actually winked at me. I don't know what she expected the outcome to be, but No Thank you. You could all but hear the mothers advice to their offspring . . . 'Go for it darling. Go for that actor, that Mr Bronson. Show 'im what you've got. Go on . . .' Oh, good heavens, no!

Deary me. We made our decision – the senior winner was not number thirteen – and Dearly B. and I beat as hasty a retreat as we diplomatically could.

Biggin Hill. And how I didn't get sunstroke I'll never know.

You remember Dave Phillips – his wife is Debbie and their lovely baby daughter is Charlotte Sophia. Well, Dave rang one day and asked if I'd ever thought of going to the Biggin Hill Air Display. I love aircraft – oh yes I do, just so long as they're not in the air – and my particular favourites are the aircraft from years gone by, the Spitfire and the Hurricane *et al.* So of course I said, 'Yes, but why?'

'Well,' Dave continued, 'I'm thinking of taking a stall at the air show and I wondered if you'd like to join me and bring along some of your books.'

'Oh I see,' quoth I, tongue firmly in cheek. 'I'm to be your, roll-up and meet the famous actor, buy his book and then have a look at my wonderful display of genuine guaranteed movie star autographs.'

'Yeah, that's it. But it could do us both some good. You can stay at our house.'

Dave picked me up at the station. We had a great evening and started to watch *Cromwell* – a particular favourite of Dave's – but we all went to bed early . . . because we had to rise at four flippin' thirty in the flippin' morning! This was not for the first day of the show you understand, but for the pre-day, the setting up day.

We got the marquees in place and decided how things should be. My table was placed at the front, out in the open, to catch the eye. Dave's were mostly in the tents. (That's why I got burnt to a frizzle and he didn't. The first day of the display was terribly hot.) When we'd done, we were free to stroll round the airport and admire at our leisure the many fascinating aeroplanes from around the world, which on the morrow and the day after would be completely swamped by punters.

I was one of the last to do National Service and am proud of the fact that I was a member of the RAF for two years. But I'd never been up close to a Spitfire or a Hurricane before, and I was surprised at how small they were, tiny in fact. I don't think I could have squeezed into the cockpit of either, even though I've recently lost over a stone.

A happy, very happy couple of days with the Phillips. And Dave's father George.

In the sitting room of his house, George has built his own private bar. It's beautifully constructed out of bits of wood he's either found, or been given, or scrounged. And on every horizontal surface in the room, including much of the floor, and hanging from the walls and the ceiling, and from the mantelpiece and over the backs of chairs, there are all manner of remembrances of yesteryear. It's wonderful. There's everything there. Everything from unopened packets of cigarettes and matches which still light, both circa 1920s, to army uniforms, tin hats and replica guns. And a Melody Maker 2000 juke-box, in full working order, with records going back way before the Beatles, stands in a corner. (In order to get it in, he had to take the sitting room door off. When his wife was out shopping!) Talk about Aladdin's cave. There's even the piece of shrapnel which almost did for him as he was hurrying home during the last war. It whistled down the street and all but scalped him before burying itself in the garden of the house next door.

The coldest location I've ever worked on, and that includes filming *High Road to China* in the mountains of Yugoslavia, was in the Yorkshire dales. It was in the deepest depths of winter and we were making an episode for a series, still fondly remembered, called *All Creatures Great and Small.*

The snow was piled high, the wind all but blew you over if you dared to step outside the barn where everything and everybody was clustered round upturned oil drums which, empty of oil, now contained fiercely burning fires.

This was where I first met Peter Davison, later to become – I'm sure he won't mind me labelling him thus – the cricketing Doctor. *Dr Who* lay some distance in the future, however, and Peter still had a goodly way to go playing Tristan, brother to Robert Hardy, and colleague to Christopher Timothy, another very old chum of mine.

In fact the scene we were shooting on this day concerned Chris rather than Peter. We dashed into an adjoining barn, which was very high with dung (almost frozen, there were no fires in here, hence our haste), to put James Herriot (Chris), newly arrived at the veterinary practice, through an initiation ceremony. Unbeknownst to him of course. I played the farmer who had called him out to a supposedly sick cow, and Peter and I were instructing Chris on how to put one's hand up a cow's bum. We explained that he had to wear protective waterproofs and sou'wester in case the animal needed to 'go'. Needless to say, Chris got covered, not with pee, but dung. He tripped, or slipped over countless times as he tried in vain to get the cow to behave herself!

It was a great scene, which still pops up sometimes on BBC compilation programmes, and we still laugh about it, as we did that day in the freezing cold.

Peter is a very good, hard-working, dedicated thespian, who's had a deservedly super career. We were due to do a movie together, but he's in *Chicago* in the London's West End and thus can't make it. But we'll be conventioning soon and I'm looking forward to seeing him again.

No, by the way, I still don't understand one word of 'Castrovalva', the *Dr Who* story I did with Peter – his first. I wonder if he does!

Continuum is next. If you recall, I have touched on it before. I'd had to cancel, then my filming dates were changed. But there's more!

There's Janet Stewart. She was at Scott McM.'s Aberdeen Con and she co-organised the Paisley convention (yet to be documented). At the Continuum fancy dress disco she appeared as Wonder Woman and just about managed to keep inside her costume. No bouncy-bouncy dances for her! She's a braw lass, a fine friend, and a very nice person.

Robert Picardo, and Rene Auberjonois (both *Star Trek* of course) were also a part of Continuum and had been flown over from America.

They did their Q&As and their signing sessions splendidly. But I can't agree with the guest who does their bit but then says, 'Now I'd like to take a look at Edinboro'.' I personally consider it my brief to stay at the convention. The whole time. If you want to sight-see, chaps, stay over after the con's finished.

A wee nosegay! We were being held up during the signing session because Robert and Rene were talking to each other about shopping in LA or somesuch. I was seated at the other end of the signing table, near the door. 'Watch this,' I said to the queue. 'Robert, Rene,' I called out. 'You've been nattering away about LA and California nineteen to the dozen. Do you speak Scotch?' (note the spelling) I continued, raising and indicating my glass of malt.

'Hey, no,' came the reply. 'Is there a language? Please speak some to us.'

'OK . . . Will you please stop your blethering, have a wee dram, and would you then ge' a bluidy move on!'

Lovely guys mind, of course they were. When we came to the closing ceremony, held early because Robert had to get back to LA for filming, I sang 'I Belong to Glasgow' (which is not quite true because I'm an Aberdonian), and they joined in.

But . . . I'm sorry (American) chums, I call the cards as they fall. I do think you should have been at this convention for the duration.

But what an excellent convention Scott and everyone gave us. I loved every minute. Especially the arrival of Pam (the wonderful chartered accountant) and her work colleagues/ friends Tina and June.

The three came all the way up to Glasgow from Newcastle, just to see me. They changed in the hotel's underground car park, popped up for a sniff of the convention, took me out for an excellent Chinese meal – it was my birthday – presented me with two wonderful bow ties, one was Mickey Mouse, the other Pooh Bear, came back with me to the ceilidh long enough to allow me to join Tina and June for the first of my Dashing White Sergeants, then dived down again to the car park. My eyes were averted as they changed back, Cinderella-like, to their travelling clothes. Then away they went, back to Newcastle and beyond. But it was super, the meal and everything, and I'm humbled by their trek. Thanks chums.

Oh, what the Sci-Fi, I'm tired and I'm hungry. Dearly B. is out, so I'm going to put a trout under the grill, make a little salad, and Sophie and I are going to settle down and watch a super movie, *The Lavender Hill Mob*, which stars, guess who? Plain mister he was then, Alec Guinness.

I never tire of that movie. The Ealing years. The golden age of British comedy. Marvellous. And Sir Alec Guinness was one of the main mainstays.

Take a look at his CV: From the late 1940s, *Kind Hearts and Coronets*, right through to the end of the fifties, *The Ladykillers*. Before that he'd made *Oliver Twist* and *Great Expectations*, and after Ealing he went on to even greater heights. An Oscar for

"Right chaps, are we ready to go?"

Who's for a Kenny Baker reel?

Uncle Peter and friend.

"Father" Jeremy Bulloch and I enjoy someone's merry quip.

Andrew Dymond, "First Frontier" producer.

Janette Dinse.
The Beast and the Beauty
– Unmasked.

"Now Michael, you do it like this . . ."
Anthony Minghella directs me on how to feed . . .

Oscar and Bronson.

*Dave Prowse and I really are
the best of friends.*

*"Buy us a drink, Earthman." Richard Allen at the
Stakis Hotel, Aberdeen.*

*My chum Pam Clarke, convention organiser,
accountant and proofreader extraordinaire.*

Mr and Mrs Warwick Davis and family.

*Nick (the Brigadier) Courtenay –
"Me and My Shadow".*

*"Strolling" with Sylvester
(Dr Who) McCoy.*

Andrew (Panopticon) Beech. Thanks for the invite, dear boy.

Well, I won't get to kiss Claudia Christian in "First Frontier" . . .

. . . even though I pleaded with Jim Mortimer, the writer. . .

. . . and with "Father" (JB) as Claudia's stand-in, demonstrated my superb technique.

Declan Mulholland at Neil Meadows' Rebellion: "There was this nun, so there was . . ."

Mike Edmonds, my mate.

I promised to get a pic of Fiona Templeton as Pinhead. Great, eh?

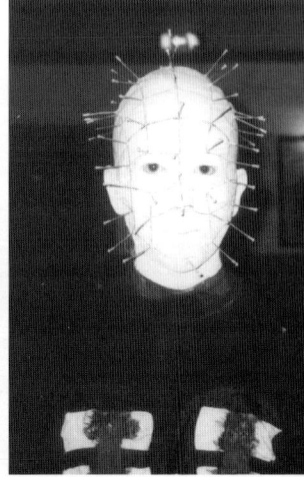

Will the real Norman Wisdom please stand up! Anorax Anonymous, I.O.M.

ConeXion, Paisley.
Sheila Knowler: 'Well, I like older men!'

Richard Allen calls "School's Out" at Cult TV.

Another kiss, this time with Melanie Hill.
The view from above was even better!

And now I'm ready for a signing.

Allan Pal . . .

Emma . . .

Dennis Taylor – The Former World Snooker Champion – and I hit it off in Newcastle.

And Paul Miley – Mr Never On Time.

"Neelix, I'd like a full English Breakfast please!" With Ethan Phillips – the cook in "Star Trek Voyager" – at the Starfleet Ball.

Kenneth Colley . . .

Escorting that Dalek around Edinburgh, with Rocky Horror help from Sue Weir and Craig Garvie. The Dalek was built by Dr Martin Rogerson.

Me and one of my classes at Musselburgh Grammar School, courtesy of Martin.

"Who's next?" – Martin built this Tardis too.

Here's to it!

Cheers m'dears!

And here's to Professor Nubrubble and his Manic Moonsters

The Bridge on the River Kwai and such memorables as *Lawrence of Arabia* and *Doctor Zhivago*.

Alec had been justly knighted by this time, (in 1959), and he continued to make some of the very best, *Cromwell* and *Scrooge* for instance. Right up to, including, and beyond, his next Oscar nomination for a movie which was going to take us all by storm. It was the fourth in a planned series of twelve, although it was the first to be made.

I first met Alec on the movie I mentioned a couple or six pages ago, *Hitler, The Last Ten Days*. It was not very good, I said that, too, and I feel sure Alec knew this even as it was being made and he was thus unhappy.

Alec's a perfectionist and cares very deeply about his work. And what a marvellous member of our profession. I do hope I have the chance to work with him again.

I've just had another wee remembrance. Do you recall a film, made about fifteen years ago, called *A Passage to India*? Alec played an Indian doctor called Godbole. The film was based on a novel by E.M. Forster and a play by Santha Rama Rau. Right at the start of my career I also played Godbole. In the theatre – Perth Repertory. I was damn good too!

> Please keep a welcome in the Hillside,
> Please keep a welcome in the Vale,
> This land of yours will still be singing,
> When I come home again to Wales.

No it's not a mistake. Thus I ended Infinity, the Cardiff convention. I'd penned the alterations to the song in my (hot) room the previous night, and I sang the above at the closing ceremony.

I'd really been looking forward to this convention and was only slightly disappointed.

The venue, from the outside, is superb. The hotel's on a corner, in fair and full view of everyone. Inside, at first glimpse, it also looks good – a long corridor, with large area adjoining, leads to a vastish ballroom/meeting room. The area next to the corridor will accommodate the dealers. The ballroom will serve Q&As and discos.

Jonathan Jones and his gang worked feverishly, frantically at times. I don't think Jonjo slept at all the whole weekend. But for some reason a few of the dealers were shoved upstairs, and the room set aside for signings and smaller gatherings was up there too.

In the end, the very hot hotel was the only real winner. Dammit, the only room in the entire place which had air conditioning was the ballroom. But as we used to say in our house when the kids were young, it's not of course my place to cast nasturtiums.

I, personally, had a grand time. I was so eager to get there that I missed Sharon, my meeter person, at the station and scampered up the road on my own to get there. I made lots of new chums and had merry banter with old ones. Anthony Pugh, a dealer who specialises in *Star Trek* replica uniforms, spent the whole time coming up with suggested titles for this book – 'Mr Bronson Strikes Back', 'The Star Adventures of Mr Bronson', 'The Brozzel Story', and even 'Toupee to the Stars'! (No, I think not Tony.) And Colin Baker turned up on the Sunday, having just finished his theatre tour (with Robert Powell, another old mate) of *Kind Hearts and Coronets*. Hey, we're back to Alec again. Alec of course did the movie, as if anyone could forget.

I was also filmed for *Gatecrash* the new BBC digital TV programme I mentioned (more later), and Mr never-on-time Miley suddenly appeared – indeed, with his knowledge of conventions he was of great help to Jonjo.

I'm completely delighted to report, by the way, that 'Jonjo' Jonathan, has picked himself up, dusted off, and has already agreed dates for his next convention. Only his second big one. The next is to be held in a different venue.

My next offering has to be *Gatecrash* hasn't it? Then I'll get back to a thumbnail of Phil Brown I think, I've left him long enough. Shelagh's entry was ages ago and they should really be together.

But first: I did that wee bitty insert for *Gatecrash* whilst I was in Cardiff. Little did I know that, five days after my return, the phone would ring. 'It's your agent,' Dearly B. mouthed. (Of course you remember that whenever possible Dearly B. answers the phone so that I can have a second or three to collect my thoughts.)

'Hi,' said I.

'Michael, the BBC have been on. They want you to do some more on their digital programme *Gatecrash*. As a special guest.'

The idea behind and indeed the point of the title *Gatecrash* is exactly that. A small gang – director, producer, presenter, cameraman, sound, vision mixer, make-up, secretaries, etc, etc – pop around the BBC TV Centre, and beyond, I guess, in times to come, and gatecrash any studio which happens to be empty. And they do a wee chat show. It might be the *Casualty* studio, after the *Casualty* lot have gone home for the day, or the reception area, the news room even. On the day I was summoned, they were in the children's Aardvark studio. I was back on home ground.

When I arrived, Kirsten O'Brien and Otis had just finished their show and Kirsten had stayed on and was the first interviewee. That's another great idea. Grab someone who's associated with the studio you happen to be in.

There is some forward planning of course. They've got to know which studios are free for a start, and who's available.

When she'd finished, Kirsten and I had a nice chat, whilst the camera looked round the studio and the *Blue Peter* garden which adjoins it. I asked her what plans she had for the future.

Then it was my turn to be interviewed – with my cold that didn't show.

Gatecrash is a great idea for a cheap, but interesting programme. The bit of filming, or rather videoing we did in Cardiff, for example, would not have been expensive. I hope it succeeds.

People do wonder how those of us who frequent the convention circuit frequently can go on so doing without running dry or becoming stale. 'Surely there can't be anyone left who hasn't read your book, or got your autograph?' they ask. The answer is simply, yes there are. I'm selling more books now than ever.

It's true though that one does tend to ring the changes a bit. Either from choice, so that you're never in any danger of overstaying your welcome, or because of work commitments. I'll not be at Panopticon this year, because I'll be away filming and then at MidCon. Next time though, watch out!

But suppose you were in *Star Wars* and had an important part, but you've been living in America ever since the film was made and haven't set foot in our neck of the woods . . . That was Phil. Until, that is, Regeneration. Pam Clarke suggested that he might like a little holiday.

As he'd not been back here, he was very hot. Appreciators swarmed round him at Regeneration and they literally deluged him at a Dealers' Fair a fortnight earlier. Oh yes, you can't keep a good organiser down. Mr never-on-time Miley heard that Phil was coming over early for Regeneration, to see old friends, and suggested that he might like to attend one of the little 'do's Mr Miley puts on in Basildon.

Paul had had a chat with Pam, explained that his was not a convention and therefore wouldn't clash, and Pam said fine go for it. Only thing was . . . It left the way clear for Mr Never to bill Phil thus: First Time Back in The Country!

But you see, it didn't matter. There was far more than enough cake for all. And Phil went home to the States a very happy chappie.

I should say a word about Phil himself. I've only met him the twice, at Regeneration, and again at Multicon. I did a Q&A with him and Shelagh at Regeneration and we had a very happy time. My memory of Phil is of a rather frail older man it's true, but one with the brightest of bright sparkles in his eye and the most wickedly dry sense of humour. He was far more with it than a great many of us and I very much hope he returns here soon.

I haven't forgotten DrakCon. Sandy and Anne and Mike and all. I've been saving them.

Sandy Douglas' DrakCon-vention is about the farthest north you can find a con. No, it *is* the farthest north. Unless of course someone knows differently . . . Yes, OK of course I know of one further north, the great Peterhead Snow Show. But apart from that wonderful and I fear one-off extravaganza, you tell me that there's a Sci-Fi convention on Shetland and I'll be there. And I'll correct these pages. OK?

But in the meantime. 'To my home, in Aberdeen'. I've said before that I'd give anything to live there, if it were possible. But Dearly B. says it's too cold. And anyway, the chap (oh help, what was his name?), who used to front *Pebble Mill at One* for the BBC, lived in Aberdeen and commuted each day to Birmingham by helicopter. He died of a heart attack not long ago. Aberdeen alas is simply too far away.

So it can't be. I can't live in the beautiful city of my birth. But I love returning. Particularly when I have the pleasure of Sandy's additions.

Let me explain. I've said that these table-top/card/role-playing conventions are always fully supported by those who hail from other parts of the country. The world even. DrakCon is very certainly no exception. The Aylesbury Bunch always attend. 'The Aylesbury Bunch' being the affectionate name given to everyone, from John Brown and Chris Baylis, to dear old Ratty, who hail from south of the border.

About four years previously I think it was, it had been discovered by the bunch that the self-service flat they took each year in Aberdeen, on these DrakCon occasions, cost just the same, whether they took it for the three nights of the convention – Friday, Saturday and Sunday – or a week.

So Sandy arranged something. And it's been taking place every year since. It goes like this: DrakCon lasts for two days, the Saturday and the Sunday. But everyone arrives, by various routes, on the Thursday. When I did Drak, the Aylesburies drove up (in two cars) overnight on the Wednesday, and I flew (yes I know), because of work commitments, on the Thursday morning. We all arrived at Anne and Sandy's lovely cottage at something like eleven a.m.

I was staying with the Douglases and I had in fact arrived last. When I'd landed, I'd finally discovered Sandy looking very worriedly at the arrivals board, wondering if I was coming from Stansted (that flight was due three hours later) rather than Gatwick as we'd agreed.

So, we were all foregathered. We had a cup of coffee and a biscuit and I deposited my bag. John Brown asked if I'd be interested in doing some themed weekends in hotels next year. His idea is to take over a hotel and hold a Robin Hood, or World War Two, or Wars of the Roses, or, you name it weekend, with history lectures etc and have a couple of celebrity guests to help things along. Super idea. Very exciting.

Then we set out for Sandy's, by now traditional and eagerly anticipated, 'The Thursday Before DrakCon Aberdeenshire Jaunt'.

Because I was part of the party on this occasion, the trip had been designed around my memories from childhood. Our first stop was the Shakin' Briggie, or what was left of the shaking suspension bridge over the river Dee, which I remembered with great fondness from years gone by. Trouble was that the Dee had decided, at some point in the years in between, to divert, and thus left the Shakin' Briggie going nowhere but to a small island in the middle of two arms of water. It had thus been decided to detach the briggie's wooden floor and disconnect its approaches. But the main supports are still standing proud, and the linking suspended cables, those which used to hold the floor, are also there. Forty-five odd years just slipped away and I was suddenly standing on the Shakin' Briggie with my Dad the Minister, shaking it like mad.

Our next stop was Banchory, where we had lunch. Then on to more wonderful childhood memories – Dess, where our family used to take our fishing summer holidays, and Aboyne. We never missed a Highland Games at Aboyne.

All along the A93 we went that day. What a wonderful trip it was. And when we arrived back in Aberdeen there was another traditional treat. Anne Douglas had prepared the most delicious chilli con carne.

It was the 'icing' (or the chilli) on a very great, super day. By the way, funny old world, Sandy is as Aberdonian as you can get, but Anne hails from Essex! It just happens that she attended Aberdeen University and that's where they met. Both are now teachers.

On the next day, Friday, we worked. Food had to be brought in from the wholesalers, tables had to be positioned and timetables checked. But we did it, and all was ready for the off.

We had a great DrakCon. I even autographed the eight remaining cheese and pickle sandwiches for the charity auction – perfectly easy, they were wrapped in cellophane and you use a felt tip – but the crowning moment of the weekend came at almost the very end. It was Sandy's fortieth birthday and I was invited to present him with a surprise 'This is Your Life', which had been prepared by Anne.

And at the very, very end, after the charity auction, after the attendees had all gone home, after we'd cleared up, there was one further DrakCon tradition. Happily I wasn't due to fly home until the following (Monday) morning, and it was therefore my huge pleasure to join the organisers and their helpers for a curry. It was the most delicious curry at a superb curry house, The Shish Mahal, at the top of Union Street, almost next to where Alexanders' fish shop used to be. My Auntie Dora was Mr Alexanders' right-hand man – lady!

Chapter 12

OK. I was going to stop here for a while, go back to the start, and do an edit. But it's hot today, I'm enjoying myself, and Chris Gardner (the newspaper man) is going to fax me some facts. So I've decided to continue. In fact . . . here comes Chris's info now – the fax machine is at my elbow.

Right then. I thought I'd give you a couple of further peeks at PAs – Personal Appearances.

I'll start with Brighstone and Disney, and follow it with Ryde High, Ryde School, and Edinburgh.

Lesley Cave is a very super lady. She's a teacher at Brighstone Primary on the Isle of Wight and she suffers from Parkinson's disease. One of Lesley's colleagues nominated her for the Disney channel's 'Teacher of the Year Award' and when she won the regional final it was my privilege to be asked by Disney to pop over to Brighstone and present her with her award. Dearly B. accompanied me and one of the teachers insisted on calling her Mrs Bronson! We both had an excellent day. The children sang songs and read poems they'd written about their truly exceptional teacher.

Ryde High, Ryde School, and indeed all the other schools and colleges I visit, are excellent. I have a compilation video of clips of some of my TV and movie credits which I show at these gatherings and we then have a Q&A which would put many a convention Q&A to shame.

Question: 'What has been your most embarrassing moment?'

Question: 'Would you like to do a scene in bed and who would you like it to be with?'

Question: 'What is it like to be killed and what do they use for blood?' And even,

Question: 'Are you ever tempted when you're away on location?'

Happily, to the above and any more of the same ilk, I'm able to reply: 'Buy my book!'

Edinburgh. Gosh, Edinburgh, I'll never forget it, not this one. Never. I've not told you of Conpulsion and the Teviot Row Union yet, but I will, somewhere. Here I'm concerned with the aftermath of that convention. The cold Monday morning when I'd arranged to meet Dr Martin Rogerson (yes, him again) outside the flat where I'd been excellently housed over the weekend. I'd agreed to visit Martin's school and give a wee chat to his class before I trotted off to the airport and home. But Martin, or rather one of his fellow teachers, a lovely lass who happened to have a car, had arranged to pick me up at the flat at seven bloody thirty in the morning.

Actually, thought I innocently, nothing wrong with that. Martin's school is in Musselburgh, which is not far from the airport. I'll get there early, do my wee stint, and be on a flight home in no time.

Ha! I did start with Martin's class at nine a.m., it's true. But from then on it was . . . 'Could you possibly just pop up to this class,' and, 'These children couldn't bear to be left out,' and 'The older boys and girls would love to meet Mr Bronson.'

Then the school gave me lunch.

What time do schools close in Scotland – three-forty-five p.m.? Whatever, I went on until the bell sounded. I loved it. But I'll be honest. After I'd completed my umpteenth classroom chat and was finally dashed to the airport by the lovely Scottish lass with the car, I was completely zombiefied with tiredness. I'd already done a difficult convention that weekend remember, and just for once and the moment, I really didn't care about the flight ahead. But, thanks Martin, more please!

Mike Carter is a very nice guy. Quiet. Quite unlike me. Maybe that's why we get on so well. And quite unlike the evil Bib Fortuna he plays in *Return of the Jedi*.

We know already that his mother-in-law lives in America and that he had difficulty getting through immigration on that flight to Philadelphia.

We talked a lot at that convention. About the state of the business, and agents – Mike and I were with the same agent for a while. On the second day Kenny and I walked round the place with him. And then, when Kenny turned up with the Captain's blonde wife at the airport on our return journey, Mike had quietly gone off to see his mum-in-law.

I think Mike is great. He's a very super actor. And when we met later, at the Plymouth convention, we picked up the threads of our friendship as if no time had passed, or quiet waters flowed under bridges.

I'm sure our paths will cross again soon. Indeed, we're due to do a convention together 'ere long. In Basildon!

Koo, I've seen her Starkers! It's true. I saw Koo Stark in the altogether. Well, almost in it!

But before I tell you that story, I should emphasise to those who are unaware, that Koo certainly does have a place in Sci-Fi. She was cast as Cammie, but – oh knickers! – that's another story.

Anyway, yes, OK, I'm sure that you chaps are dying to know how it is that I saw Koo in the nuddy.

A long time ago – not quite that long, but nearly – I arrived at the old Thames Television studios in Twickenham. They were making a TV series based on Graham Greene short stories. It was titled *Shades of Greene* and the one I was doing was to be directed by Philip Saville, son of Victor Saville, the very famous producer/director of *South Riding, Goodbye Mr Chips* and *The Citadel*.

The way it was to work was thus: two Graham Greene short stories were to be included in each programme. I was in the second of my batch and I played Detective Inspector Tweedie – I remember that because it was the first time I had my picture in the TV Times. The first tale in the two required the services of a stripper, for some reason that I'm sure was crucial but which I now can't recall.

No matter, we started rehearsals. The stripper story in the mornings, the detective yarn in the afternoons. But on the first day we had a read-through of both. And would you believe it, no stripper. Life was much more innocent in those days and we didn't like to ask who was going to play the part, we young red-blooded chaps from the other script. So we tended to arrive early for our afternoon rehearsals. 'Oh, hello. Just thought I'd have a spot of lunch before we start' . . . and we'd nonchalantly pop into the rehearsal room to drop off our coats. But there was still no sign of her. There were several odd rumours flying around. Someone even said that the daughter of a famous film producer was going to play the part. That only served to heighten the anticipated interest . . .

We had to wait until the day of the recording for the answer, and then they promptly closed the set!

But we young lads were not to be denied. We found our way into the studio through the scene dock door. And there we watched in awe as this sumptuously beautiful young lady – daughter indeed of Ray Stark, who had produced *Funny Girl* and *The Way We Were*, among many, many others – went through her routine.

Koo starkers was wonderful and I'm completely confident that our performances in front of the cameras that afternoon were more than exceptional.

I want now to go straight on to another beauty. But in fact, alas, I don't have a lot to say about Femi Taylor. I only met her a couple of weeks ago at GenCon – my second GenCon where I was asked to bring some chums.

The girls are very lucky Sci-Fi convention-wise, because there are not so many of them. Apart from Carrie, who as far as I am aware doesn't do cons, there's Shelagh; the *Dr Who* companions of course who include Sophie, Katy, Wendy, Deborah, Louise, and Nicola; *Blake's 7*'s Jacqueline Pearce; Caroline Blakiston; and Femi. And I think that's it. No, wait. I don't think she's done conventions yet, but Claire Davenport played the Fat Dancer. I've not seen Claire for ages, but at one time she played all the rotund parts going at the BBC.

But back to Femi. She made many friends at GenCon. Always smiling happily, full of vitality and chatting away, 'Hi, Michael, how are you? I've been wanting to meet you.'

She's a doll and I look forward to conventioning with her yet again 'ere long.

I would now like to introduce you to some new friends: Nero, Stephen Steppens, Al Samujh, Janette Dinse, Adrian Sherring, Richard Allen, Carina, Allan Green, and Walter Plinge (in fact Walter P. is decidedly not a friend, but he has to be included). And I'd like also to re-introduce you to a couple of old ones, and one I've already mentioned but only in passing: Karen, Sarah Ralph, and John Davies.

These super ladies and gentlemen will represent for me the many differing variations of the Appreciator. I've been wanting to write about the apps for some time.

The other day I had to remind someone that without appreciators we are nowhere. Nowhere at all. And that at conventions it's the appreciator, above all – organisers, friends, family – who is the most important ingredient. By far it is. Heavens, they've paid to get in for a start. But overriding everything is the simple fact that we lot, the so called celebrities, would not be where we are today without them. And anyway, much more than 99.99 per cent of them are also very, nay, they're bloody super nice people.

I got very cross once (unlike me) because someone said in my hearing that, 'Fans are just a load of smelly groupies who smoke pot, are out of their minds on drugs and drink and make celebrities' lives hell.' That was an outrageous thing to say and I said so. I have never seen a sign of drugs at any of the conventions I've attended. And I have never met a more generous, sensitive, appreciative, kindly crowd of people. Ever.

The small gang of chums I have with me here, then, are as different from each other as any bunch of individuals can be. But they have (with one exception) two things in common. They are very nice people and they are Appreciators. I hope that by telling you a wee bit about them that we'll quash, once and for all, any 'groupie' talk, and show that the Appreciator is Everyman. From any and all walks of life.

Richard Allen. Richard is first, simply because of A – for Allen.

Do you remember Mike and Darren who go to as many cons as they can? Richard does the same. But whereas Mike and Darren always travel together and have their own bunch of chums, Richard is a loner. He's always smiling, hails from Wales, and likes a chat, preferably in the bar. He also enjoys 'Pulling a bird, Michael.'

One of the reasons he's able to attend so many conventions is because he hardly ever takes a room in the hotel. No, wrong, his bird-pulling is not that successful. There is, inevitably, a mass of expensive video and audio equipment at conventions, and Richard is always on hand to volunteer to sleep in the room where this equipment is stored. He's then happy as he has a free place to rest his head. And the organisers are delighted as they have a guard.

A small footnote. Without Richard at the recent CultTV convention, I'd have had masses of egg on my face. They had 'Schools Out' at the disco, but none of the Cult lot knew of my version – it was my first time there. Enter Richard who'd been in at the birth of this bit of fun in Aberdeen. He took the mike and proceeded, American barn dance style, to educate the dancers into how it should be done. 'Make a circle around Mr B. Point your fingers so he'll see. Then shout out and he'll agree, 'School's Out for Summer'.'

Nice one, Richard. A very nice chap.

Carina. I'm very sorry, love, I don't even know your second name. I should have asked you, but you were gone so quickly!

Carina came all the way – at least over thirty miles – to Twisted Toys 2, which was held recently in Bristol. She was only there for about ten minutes. She didn't buy anything from the dealers, or a book from me. She came all that way, because she was very concerned that I'd made a dreadful mistake. She said that I was such a good actor she felt she just had to point out that when, as Hitler, I'd signed Harrison Ford's book in *Indiana Jones and the Last Crusade*, that I'd got it wrong. I'd signed Adol-ph instead, of course, of Adolf. I gently told her that in fact it wasn't me doing the writing. That cut away was done long after I'd left the movie. But I thanked her very much for bringing such a whopping error to my attention and said that I'd pass it on to Steven Spielberg.

But you know, I'm not sure. At the first opportunity I watched that bit again. I see what Carina means, but I think it's an F. See what you think. It was nevertheless very kind of her to take so much trouble.

Janette Dinse. I love Snoopy almost as much as Winnie the Pooh, and stuck to the top of my computer is a little picture of Snoopy reading a letter. It was sent to me by Janette.

Janette is a very talented artist herself. We first met at the poorly attended (because it was held in Edinburgh during the Festival) but excellent Capsicon, and she is one of the most beautiful girls I've ever seen. Not for a single moment does she permit the fact that she is profoundly deaf to inhibit her. She has a wonderfully outgoing personality and is completely unspoilt, fun loving and genuine. And her enthusiasm for all things Science-Fiction is unbounded. I look forward to the possibility of more Snoopies soon.

Karen. Karen Gillett. You'll have to read the other book to learn more about Karen. Suffice it to say here that I'm still receiving my calendar every Christmas; that she's now a grandmother at least another three times over; that I've not told her yet about being held up in Wavertree on my way to the Isle of Man; and that she is still and will remain my number one appreciator.

Walter Plinge. Is the exception that proves the rule. He's not a chum. And that's not his real name of course. Walter Plinge is the false name that provincial theatre managements put in the programme if they're not sure who is going to play the odd two line part, or if someone is doubling up. Here I use it to protect – me!

There is one type of app who can, frankly, be a very great pain in the arse. There are very few of them thank goodness, and they don't frequent conventions, at least I've certainly never met one there. But they are around. Indeed, now that I come to think of it, it must be this lot, I'm afraid, who at the very least, contribute to the groupie image I talked of just now.

The ladies suffer more that the men from these people – we've all read about the actress who is living in terror because of a stalker – but we chaps can experience them too. It's happened to me. Once. And that was enough.

I was doing a series. Whenever you do a series that's on TV every week, the fan mail shoots up. That's great, I'm terribly grateful and excited, and I always reply personally to each and every letter. Unbeknown to me, one of the letters that arrived during this time asking for a signed photo, was from Walter Plinge.

Within three days of receiving my reply another letter arrived, via my agent, thank heavens. It started off thanking me for the photo and saying again what a wonderful actor I was, and how he had, on tape, every possible performance of mine he could lay his hands on.

Then the mood of the letter changed. Would I like him to send me copies? If I gave him my address he'd be more than happy to bring them round – he lived up north somewhere. He then gave me his telephone number, again, and said that he would sit by his phone all evening, for the whole of next week, and wait for me to call.

I didn't call of course, and ten days later another letter arrived. This one whined and said I was horrid and that he had ways of finding out where I lived. And that he would see me soon. And in the meantime, could I send him a lock of my hair and some nail clippings.

I wasn't exactly worried. Well, yes I was a little, for Dearly B. Even if you have an agent who passes on your mail and even if you are ex-directory, if someone says, see you soon, you do begin to look over your shoulder. And there was something else. In one of his letters he said that he looked very like me, that he'd been brought up in an orphanage and thought he might be my son. He sent me a photo, and no, he did not look one bit like me. And anyway I'd never even set foot in his part of the country!

In the end, after a lot more correspondence and more lies along these lines, my agent wrote a very strict letter threatening legal action and I'm very pleased to say that it did the trick. I never heard from him again.

That is the only type of appreciator that we can all well do without.

Sarah Ralph. Although I've already told you that Sarah's off to drama college, I wanted to pop her in because she represents another type of app altogether. As far as I'm aware, Sarah's not the least bit interested in Sci-Fi and I don't think you're ever likely to find her at a convention.

I'm seldom asked by conventioning apps how they can get into the acting business. It's something that simply doesn't enter the equation. Even the role-players don't seem to harbour secret professional thesping ambitions. There are a few exceptions of course – Robin Craine on the Isle of Man for one – but very much in the main they are all happy with their hobby. It's a hobby which takes up a heck of a lot of time, which may also be the reason why few of the apps I've spoken to on the subject are members of even amateur theatrical societies.

I have to say that I'm glad, there's some bloody good talent out there in the role-playing neck of the woods who might nick my work. But I don't really know why none seem to want to venture further. One reason given a few conventions back when I was having a dram with Richard Allen, was that the app was in awe, and could never aspire to the heights we attain. My answer to that was straight to the point. 'Don't be daft. I probably fart louder than you!'

But Sarah and her ilk are different. They are fans of the business. This time I am using the word fan in its very proper context. Unless you are fanatical about your need to be an actor, then you must not do it. Hey, that could be it. The apps are happy being apps, they don't want to be fan-atics!

Sarah has really wanted, needed, to enter my profession since she was tiny. She's made it to drama college, she could make it to the stars! Watch her.

John Davies. John of Fab Café fame. What a genuinely nice guy. He's always chatty in his letters and talks with great authority about my performances. I've just been signing some photos for him which were taken on that Fab-ulous evening, and he's very kindly helped me with some of the pictures, displayed here, in my book.

My pal Allan Green – Allan Pal – is three years old. I'm sure he won't mind me saying that he's rather wee, particularly alongside his dad, Kevin, who is huge. Both have their own Klingon outfits. When Kevin's in his he looks terribly fierce. I'm sure he'd be extremely frightening too, if he wasn't such a nice man. Allan's costume is just like his dad's. Well, not just like, it's a tiny bit smaller!

These two, along with smashing, mum-to-Allan and wife-to-Kev, Fiona, hail frae Bishopbriggs, which is just outside Glasgow, and they attend every convention they can manage. Indeed, I had a little note from Allan the other day which he'd 'written' on his computer asking if he'd see me at this year's MidCon – alas I'm told it's the last. I popped back a photo saying that of course I'll see him there, and that photo is now on his bedroom wall. Let me tell you how it got there:

Until a short time ago Allan had a photo of Darth Vader on the wall above his bed. But after I, in my capacity as an Honorary *Star Trek* Admiral, officially welcomed him into the fold at the Landing Party's *Star Trek* ConeXion convention at Paisley University, things changed. The Darth Vader photo has now gone from the wall and has been replaced by the photo of me. And every night before he goes to sleep Allan says, 'Good night Michael pal.' Allan is a grand pal.

Al Samujh. In *Yes, Mr Bronson* I asked if anyone could help me with something. To recap, I asked whether Halfpenny Green, the airfield I guarded so courageously during my National Service, was the same Halfpenny Field airfield portrayed in that excellent 1945 film *The Way to the Stars*?

I'm going to be coming back to Al at the very end of the book. But I'd like, here, to quote a short extract from the first letter I received from him:

'. . . As a child, Sundays and Bank Holidays
were often spent near Wombourne, on
Highgate Common, and Highgate Common backs
on to a small aerodrome – Halfpenny Green.
Spurred on by your question, I went recently
to the town library's archive. And there
it was, written evidence that *The Way to the
Stars* was at least part filmed at
Halfpenny Green . . .'

Since that first letter, Al's unearthed much more, and next
time I'm in the Wombourne neck of the woods we're going
to revisit Halfpenny Green. I'll write of both in the postscript.

Like me, Al is a film buff and we've now gone on to other
investigations. The video tapes back and forth keep the post
office extremely busy. At present we're working on the small
part film actor whose only line – perfectly timed and thus
wonderfully memorable – in *Reach for the Sky* with Kenneth
More was, 'What's your name mate, Death?' His name was
Fred Griffiths. He sadly died in 1994 in his early eighties.

Adrian Sherring. Adrian is the quiet almost unassuming guy
who came up to me at a convention in London some time
ago and asked if I would mind if he formed the 'Official
Michael Sheard Fan Club'. I was very touched and flattered.
But I explained that I far prefer a 'hands on' approach to
appreciators and that when I've been asked in the past, I've
always declined the offer. That someone other than I should
reply to my letters has always seemed churlish and non-caring.
And anyway, I enjoy it.

Adrian understood I'm sure, but at the same time he was
very obviously disappointed. He explained that he'd been
wanting to do a newsletter that would also include items on

other actors, and it would only be sent to appreciators who had previously applied to go on a mailing list.

Having got his assurance that he would never write about anyone without first obtaining their written approval, and he'd said that he always intended to send the proofs for me to read first, 'You, Boy!' was born.

It's darn good, comes out four times a year, and this quarter's issue also includes a profile of Dave Prowse.

Stephen Steppens is blind, but it would be hard to find a happier guy. Or a more committed app. The first time we met he had a mini recorder with him. 'Let's have a chat, Michael,' he said. We had a chat and he asked some very astute questions about me, my career and ambitions. The next time our paths crossed was at the Biggin Hill Air show. I'd no idea he'd be there. But suddenly I heard: 'Ah, there's Michael. I recognise his voice. Let's go and see him.' And suddenly there was a nose snuffling my hand. No, not Stephen's, Nero's! Nero is Stephen's guide dog. He's a lovely Labrador who loves everyone. But most of all he loves Stephen. They're a great partnership.

It was Stephen who first suggested that I do an audio version of *Yes, Mr Bronson*. Here's hoping. There are already irons in fires. Kevin, Allan Pal's dad, already publishes an audio newspaper.

Chapter 13

Right, GenCon the Second was – marvellous.

You'll recall that I'd been invited to bring along some celebrity chums, because I'd done so well on my own as a guinea pig the year before.

'OK, let's see,' said I. 'How about Chewbacca, R2 D2, Boba Fett, Logray, Gold Leader and Oola Jabba's dancer?' Jaws dropped, there were gasps, and looks of disbelief.

'Can you really get them?' (This was Chris Baylis.)

'Of course I bloody can, if they're free!'

So it was that Peter, Kenny, Jeremy, Mike, Angus, and Femi arrived at GenCon – venue, Loughborough University. They came with some trepidation it must be said, because they'd never been to a gaming/role-playing con before and had no clue what was coming. I was a tiny bit apprehensive too. I'd brought them with me. They might hate it.

Did I need to worry? 'Course not. Let me tell you.

Jeremy always cites our digs as his first fond remembrance of that five day event. (Yes, five days, certainly the longest convention in the UK. Started Wednesday, finished Sunday.) We chaps were billeted in the University House. This is a house, certainly, but of rather unique design. It looks like a house from the outside and is situated in a leafy grove, on a fairly far flung point of the campus. It could be anywhere in up-market suburbia. Inside, though, it's a series of en suite, self-contained little flats, with a communal sitting/dining room.

It's normally used for visiting lecturers, and with the delightfully named Mrs Cook coming in each morning to cook our breakfast, it was completely ideal.

Imagine. Five of us are having breakfast, but there's no Kenny. He's late again. Shall we wake him? No, there's no hurry. Then we hear him coming downstairs. He strides into the room, an immaculately dressed figure and in his silk dressing-gown, he looks terribly Noel Coward. He saunters over to the kitchen door.

'Good morning, Mrs Cook, what's cooking?'

Then he comes back to the table, jumps up on his chair and grins very innocently at us,

'Right, what's up?' he asks. 'What are we going to do today?'

A lovely cheeky chap is our Ken.

We all had an excellent time. I did the midnight patrol with Peter, Wizards of the Coast American Director, the top man. Halfway through one of our tours I suddenly lost him. When I looked back, he was settling down to a *Star Wars* card game with the All Nighters . . . 'Just thought I'd have a game, Michael . . .'

The All Nighters are a group of (I say this with very much affection) complete nutters. They arrive at GenCon, settle down, start playing, and don't stop until the convention is over. OK, they pee and perhaps do the other. They certainly send out for grub and booze. But they never leave their pitch and they never, ever, sleep. That is their overriding rule. Arrive, set up, play, and never sleep. If you do you are out. These are great guys and I never left for my bed without saying goodnight.

But I've not finished with Peter, Boss. At the charity auction, after I'd sold a signed (by me) tiny chocolate bar for a total of ninety-five quid – fruit and nut this time it's true – which the younger players had given me that afternoon, Peter suggested that I auction a kiss between me and his lovely cuddly wife. I did. It was knocked down at £200. £250 – with tongues.

I'll leave you to guess how much Peter's wife and I raised for charity that night!

Somebody a long time ago – probably Frank Sinatra, he who has now justly been dubbed 'The Voice of the Century' – in a movie long forgotten, sang 'I Could Write a Book'.

Well, I could write one on this episode alone, my GenCon the Second. The super atmosphere, the Q&As (not, as far as I'm aware, ever before attempted at a gaming con), the Vampires – I raced between their role-playing evening and the charity auction and I now have a vampire black rose badge permanently linked to the lapel of my jacket. I've also been invited to a weekend of vampiring. I hope I leave there whole!

And as if all this wasn't enough, there was another first. This was the first time I met my *First Frontier* co-star, Miss, *Babylon 5* etc, Claudia Christian. I must tell you about Claudia!

Mr A. Dymond (*F.F.*'s producer), along with the rest of the gang and Claudia, had also been invited to GenCon. The aim was to publicise *First Frontier*. And boy, did it work. There were some excellent talks and great *First Frontier* flyers. As designed by *First Frontier*'s writer, Mr Jim Mortimer, they were, in fact, far more than mere flyers. They were superb pamphlets, on hard card, with the leading cast displayed thus:

JOE McGANN   CLAUDIA CHRISTIAN
MICHAEL SHEARD
in
FIRST FRONTIER

There are photos of 'er and 'im, and on the right hand side, and a sinister silhouette of the villain, moi, in a lighter, almost subliminal tone, on the left, but stretching all the way down the page.

OK, we're at a signing session. I, and Father – Mr J. Bulloch (did I tell you, he's in *F.F.* too?) quite rightly had decided that as we'd already filmed *Star Wars* and had yet to commence *F.F.*, we belonged on the other bench, and we were very busy signing. So when the attendees had been to Claudia's table and she'd signed one of the *First Frontier* cards, they came back over to us again so they could get our signatures as well.

And there was no room. Claudia had written right across my silhouette in large letters: CLAUDIA CHRISTIAN. So I crossed the floor to her side.

'Excuse me,' I said.

'Hi, Michael,' she chirruped. 'How are you? I'm looking forward to working with you on *First Frontier.*

'Well, that's great,' I countered, 'so am I, with you. But do you think you could sign just a little smaller so that I've got some room?' As she replied there was a definite twinkle in her eye.

'Oh no, that's not the way we do it in America. My name's above yours on the titles.'

'That's as may be,' said I, 'but I am on a line all by myself.'

'Nah, sorry, matey, too bad. See you on the set.' And she proceeded to sign her name even bigger, if that were possible.

OK my beauty, thought I, and the next time a F.F. card/ flyer came over to my table with a huge Claudia Christian written across it, I tucked my autograph within the C of Christian. Then I walked nonchalantly over to my co-star.

'There we are then, me darlin', there's no alternative. I've signed inside you!'

Claudia all but peed herself with laughter. She flung her arms around me.

'Michael,' she said, 'you've made me see how different film making is in England. I really am looking forward to our association.'

No fuss. No pretentiousness. Lovely lass.

I say this following with a smidgen of trepidation. As I write, the superb special effects for *First Frontier* are in the process of being completed. I saw a battle scene recently which was excellent. I dearly hope that all proceeds smoothly and that Claudia and I, and Joe, Jeremy and all the others, do get to work together on the best first draft pilot I've ever read. And the series and movies to follow.

But, it has to be said that there can be many a slip twixt script and screen. Normally we never discuss a project until contracts are in place for fear of breaking the spell. (This one is different of course as we've been cast and involved for ages.)

So please, by Thespis, I fervently hope (and feel sure) that by the time this volume hits the stands, F.F. will be in full production and that Claudia and I will have confirmed our friendship.

More about GenCon? Yes, 'course there's more. I'm delighted to report that John and Fiona (Brown and Kyle) are definitely in charge of next year's extravaganza and indeed for many years to come – there'd been a wee problem and they'd even thought about leaving, but Stephen Wilks (top UK man) invited the problem to leave and that's made everyone very happy.

I got masses more invites to future conventions. And I'm so relieved that not only did my chums enjoy themselves, but all very enthusiastically agreed to return next year. And, even before that, some of us are off (for Wizards' cons) to Barcelona, Antwerp and Germany. It really is a super life that we lead.

Right then. I'd like now to offer for your perusal three quick newspapers (one silly), three live TVs, and a cinematographer.

The quick newspapers. I'll start with the silly one. Manchester is of course the home of The Daily and The Sunday 'Sport'. When I had that great return visit to the Fab Café, they – Debbie Manley and her cameraman – were also there. Please, don't again misunderstand me, chums, I do not want to suffer more at your hands! Debbie's another lovely lass, really she is. The fact that in her exclusive she had to resort to quoting passages from *Yes, Mr Bronson*, wherein I talk of the great times I had dubbing Swedish girlie films into English, has naught to do with it. Simple fact is she couldn't find anything else naughty to say about me.

But Debbie, those passages you quoted from my book were written with affection and laughter. You didn't have to head your piece in 'The Sunday Sport': 'Red-Hot Porn Secret of TV's Mr Bronson'. Surely not. Was it because you'd sent a fax of questions to my agent and asked me to fill them in? What would you expect me to answer to: 'What is your favourite position. Bulldog or Poodle?' Except: Parrot?!

Isle of Wight County Press. Great newspaper, great editorial staff, great reporters. Is that enough Chris? Chris Gardner is a very good egg. And I'm sure I've said before, he's a Sci-Fi – oh dear, I nearly said nut. No way, Chris is a devotee and he did an excellent article on me for the *Star Wars* magazine. And, whenever there's a local issue concerning me – for instance, I've recently been asked to direct Willy Russell's *Shirley Valentine* which is due at the Brighton Festival, Chichester and all points north to Edinburgh – Mr C. Gardner gives it as much coverage as he can. Thanks mate.

I should just add that *Shirley Valentine* is produced by Wihtgar Productions. And I'm able to direct it for them because of course there's only one thesp involved, Gwen Glover, and we can rehearse whenever I've got free a few hours or four.

'The Aberdeen Evening Express'. I've talked before about the Capitol Cinema in my home city, where I first saw *The Wooden Horse* – the movie which really got me going – and how it was going to be turned into a pub. Well, the Evening Express also helped magnificently well. I sent them a fax stating how terrible I thought the closing of the Capitol was, and that its change to a public house was horrendous, and the Express printed the fax verbatim. The fact that all our efforts have come to naught and the Capitol is now just another bloody pub makes no bloody difference. Many thanks Evening Express for your support.

OK. Live TVs. You'll certainly know by now that there's a *Grange Hill* twenty-first birthday party/convention in the offing, indeed it's very much planned by that super chartered accountant, Ms Pam Clarke and her cronies. If you've bought this book late, shame on you. It may already have happened.

But at the start of last year we – Mrs McClusky and Mr Bronson – were asked, along with an assorted compilation of children chums from the series, to take part in various live TV mornings. Because it was the twentieth anniversary. And a great time was had by all, wasn't it Jonathan (Lambeth, aka Danny Kendall)? The only adults always invited to these 'do's were Gwyneth and me. They were great fun and we loved them.

Light Lunch, I got Miss Perkins to make the sweet – Mr Bronson would never do that!

This Morning, Richard Madeley (without his missis then as she was recovering from an operation which had been much publicised) was terribly nice and sincere. He's presented so much, week in and out, that I'd have thought he must surely get bored, flummoxed even, by the influx of school kids. But not a bit of it. He's a nice professional man, too.

GMTV was my personal favourite. I walked on, Danny Kendall in tow, and said to the presenter, 'You, girl. Will you behave?'

'Yes, Mr Bronson,' she answered contritely. At which response I came straight out of character:

'Thanks very much, love,' said I, 'for plugging my memoirs!' And I proceeded to ask if she'd like to feel the hair – I'd been presented with, and asked to sport this most awful wig you see. She tentatively did, I stepped back, and the hair-piece was left in her hand. It was not rehearsed and she all but screamed. The original toupees by the way have long since gone to charity auctions.

The *Star Wars* cinematographer. I've written stacks about Gil Taylor already, both here and certainly elsewhere in another book, and I don't want to make him too big headed! So, having said, again, that he's a super chap and friend, and that he and his smashing wife Dionne are the most wonderful hosts – Dearly B. and I had dinner with them recently and it was quite magnificent – let me add here just a few lines about *Millennium Blue*.

Millennium Blue is not a blue movie. It's a great Sci-Fi film centred around the fact that we are about to enter the year 2000. Of course it is. But once again, as with dear Norman Wisdom, Gil has that same insurance trouble. He's getting on a bit. And it's bloody stupid. Gilbert Taylor is more with it than I am, for F's sake. But no, the insurers don't like it. But Gil has an ace up his sleeve. His son, Peter, is also now a respected lighting cameraman and the idea is that Peter will be the official photographer on *Millennium Blue* and that Gil will act as consultant. Nice one. See you soon chaps. What? Of course there's a part ear-marked for me. You watch this space!

I've mentioned elsewhere that cons are divided more or less thus: The Professional Convention, the Semi-Professional, and the totally Fan (App) run Convention.

The Professional are normally staged by limited companies, which are V.A.T. (for those of you across the water, that's Value Added Tax) registered, and are professionally run right the way down the line. One organiser of such a show – it would be more than my future guesting's worth to name names – actually told me that he didn't know his *Who* from his *Trek*, but that they could be very good earners and that's why he did them. Absolutely nothing wrong with that, mind.

The best example I can suggest of the professional con is, let's see, yes, super GenCon. There will still always be a charity auction at these gatherings – as I've said, GenCon's is world famous – but after the venue has been paid for, and the chairs, the electricity, insurance, hire of bands, cars, computers, guest accommodation, etc, *et al*, any profits will of course go to those who have taken the huge monetary risk and staged the piece in the first place.

The Semi-Pro Cons are usually smaller affairs. Such as the Wizard satellites. I use the word 'professional' here in its very widest sense. They are very professionally run, but the professionals are amateurs, if you see what I mean. There will usually be a sponsor – Wizards themselves for example – but any profits (I'm not too sure if there are any, actually, they're usually just happy to cover their costs and promote the card games on offer), either go to charity, or are ploughed back into the next endeavour.

Fan run Conventions. I know, I should really say App run, but in this context it might just be a tiny bit confusing. Fan run cons then, are simply that. A group of apps get together and decide to have a gathering of like-minded enthusiasts, usually Sci-Fi. And every penny of profit goes to their chosen charity. I've said earlier that one of the happiest weekends I've ever spent on the convention circuit, was at the Stakis Hotel in Aberdeen, with the Aberdeen *Star Trek* gang. They are amateurs. But you'll never meet a more professional group than Scott McMillan and his lot.

There's another I should mention. A Steve Parsons type convention is something else again. He and his gang are very personally involved with their charity.

I suppose that's it really. Regardless of whether your con is fan based or professional, if you want a good convention, and most of them are excellent, you have got to run it in a professional manner. (More of course later, but I've just returned from a fan run convention in Aalst in Belgium. Eddy Wauters and his team of helpers had never done anything like it before, but it was excellently run. Smooth and efficient. A joy.)

Right, Dave Prowse Promotions presents 'Multicon' at the Norbreck Castle Hotel in Blackpool. Where the heck do I start?

I would beg the question, why Blackpool, Dave? And why at the start of the Labour Party conference? It could be argued that there was a mass of people there, but that they'd mostly come to hear a lot of boring politicians pontificate. Don't misunderstand me, holidaymakers were there as well, and a goodly number came to the convention, but I'm sure we'd have liked it more, and I got the feeling that the hotels in Blackpool, bulging as they were with Labour Partyites, would have been happier, if we'd been in attendance on another weekend. The hotels didn't need us, and the apps had great difficulty in finding even a park bench whereon to rest their heads.

Security was everywhere of course, which made it even more claustrophobic and . . . hey, wait a mo! I'm giving a down side, it's true, but nobody really knew that it would be like that. If you remember, I'd popped over to Blackpool with never-on-time Miley, after my first visit to the Fab Café in Manchester. I did wonder how we were all going to fit into the city, but I don't think any of us realised then that there'd be a conference as well.

Let's talk about what happened inside the Norbreck.

Those several and some pages ago, when I was recounting my very successful trips to the Fab Café, I told you that thirty-six guests had been invited to Multicon. Well, in the end there were something like twenty-one in attendance. We were there, almost all of us, Kenny, Peter, Jeremy, Johnny Hollis, Mike Carter, Mike Edmonds, Declan, Warwick, Dave of course, and me. And there were a couple or six notable Americans, including Mark Goddard (*Lost in Space*) and a nice guy I got to know quite well at a later, American, convention, The Incredible Hulk, Lou Ferrigno.

The Norbreck Castle is gigantic. The upstairs single rooms are a wee bit wee, it's true, but sufficient enough for sleep. But downstairs is most certainly enormous. When I first saw the main hall, where the Q&As and discos etc were to be held, I remember likening it to two football pitches, and suggesting that three hundred people would be lost.

Fortunately, in spite of the outside reasons already stated, there were a few more attendees than that. I understand it was something like eight hundred on the first day and about five hundred on the second. Mind you, I'm sure Dave would have been delighted with three thousand. And the hotel could have accommodated them, the fire regulations would have allowed it. It really is that large. The fire people, or whoever it is, quite rightly set an upper limit as to how many people are allowed in a hotel, or any other public place come to that, at any given time. At the little Honiton convention, for example, the Dolphin hotel's limit was only 200. (I'm back at Honiton, by the way, for Steve Parson's next.)

The signing sessions at Multicon were a success, sort of. On the first day, the Saturday, we were all seated upstairs, on one side of a balcony which ran all the way round the football pitches. Although only on one side, the line of tables still seemed to stretch forever.

Pete and I parked ourselves about halfway down this line, between two of the Americans. And we chose well, there was plenty of space between the tables. But at the far left of us, at the start of the line, the tables were all but touching. This meant that when the apps came up the stairs and began to wander down the line, things became very congested at that end. So much so, in fact, that one of the ladies from over the water became extremely cross and decided to move her table to the far end and suggested that we should move up too. Pete and I looked at each other. 'Uncle,' said I, 'I don't think I want to move. Do you?'

'No, Grandfather,' Pete replied, 'we're quite happy as we are, thank you.'

The American lady all but spat fire, and announced to the assembled company that it was her time of the month and moved tetchily on.

I don't know if it was her doing, but on the next day we were split up – Brits and Americans – and we were moved downstairs. We were ranged along a sort of open corridor at one side of the football pitches, underneath yesterday's balcony, and they were seated at the top end of the hall.

Pete was a smidge late on this second morning. He kindly said, when he arrived, that he knew he could rely on me to find a good pitch. This time I'd bagged a table near the top of the line, number two in fact. Declan was first, on his own. Whereas Pete and I like to sit together and spark, Dec is a loner, he sparks himself! So we followed Declan, and then there was enough room for Mike Edmonds' table before a gap had to be left for the gents' loo. This meant of course that there was a virtual chasm of space before the next table down the line.

We had masses of room, and the apps had masses of space in which to come and see us and have a chat, before they passed the gents and wended their way down the line, where it once again became congested, in spite of the fact that the Americans were absent. I chose particularly well that day.

And there was even a bonus. I was able to get my own back on a certain Mr Michael Edmonds! It went like this. For as long as I've been doing card playing/role-playing conventions, a great guy and games master (as they call him, or her, who runs and referees a game), named Sean Connor, has very sweetly been insisting that he off-load on me some of the many role-playing lapel badges which smother his hat. Every time we meet Sean insists that I accept another. I wear these gifts with pride, all the way down the left lapel of my suit and all the way up the right. (I always wear a suit, Bronson style, and a bow tie.)

'IT'S VERY GOOD, BUT I DON'T UNDERSTAND IT' 1998.

Thing is that the guys, led by Father Bulloch and hotly assisted by Edmonds, have been regaling me with railway station calls, 'Mind the doors' and 'Pass right down the car'. Heavens, I even had a chap come up to me at a convention in Texas recently who'd had an e-mail from the UK asking him to say 'Mind the doors' when he met me. I wonder who sent it!

Now was my chance for revenge. I've already written where Mike was parked on this second day in Blackpool. Well, every time a gent wanted the gents, I drew his attention to the fact that there was a charge and would he please pay the nice attendant who was seated at the table next to the loo!

Silly but fun. I'd better move quickly on to . . . to what? I know: chums – appreciators – attendees. There were lots and lots of old friends at Blackpool, a goodly number of whom would not have been there if I'd not been in attendance. They came just to see me. OK, I know, it sounds big headed, but I do appreciate them very much. All of them. Dealers, such as Dave Phillips and George, Mike Parker and Tara, Fred McClure – Dukath the Klingon – and his followers. I'd first met this bunch at the aforementioned wonderfully great *Star Trek* convention in Aberdeen and this time I was asked if I'd become their Honorary Admiral – another one. So now I've got two *Trek* ships, and I've not yet even set foot on the Enterprise's bridge!

Fred McClure does much great work with the disabled supporters of Manchester United Football Club. It's one of his permanent jobs and he's great at it. Wonderfully caring. In the evenings, particularly at weekends, he becomes Friar Tuck, Professional Dee-Jay. In Blackpool he, his lads and I made a little documentary – of course the club has its own TV station! – in which we discussed Man United and Fred's hopes for the future. Fred's a very lucky guy, for as well as his job, which he obviously loves, he's a huge United fan and can name every player and team both from the present and way back into yesteryear.

We finished the documentary with the Klingon hug. Now, no one would deny that Fred is large, least of all Fred, and when you're surrounded by him and his mates and they lock arms and squeeze, you feel as though you're about to be shot into orbit!

I don't think even I can top Fred. So let's pop on to Cult TV. No, hang on. I think I can. Sorry Fred, mate.

Those of you who do not like down to earth words and good, no-offence-meant humour, should skip this next bit.

As often as not – as often as possible – there are discos at conventions. Multicon was no exception. On the Saturday there was a whale of a dance. The highlights were of course 'School's Out', plus the Conga, and a new one, 'My, My Miss American Pie'. During this latter I bumped into Mr Neil Green. And we danced, cheek-to-cheek! Read naught into this, OK? Except that we were hamming it up. I'd first met Neil earlier that day at the aforementioned signing session, and he'd given me almost the exact same excellent dedication for my book as had been suggested that long ago day in Aberdeen, at the book signing in Bruce Miller's.

'Would you be kind enough to personalise your book?' Neil asked.

'Of course,' I replied. 'What would you like?'

'Well, I was watching the movie, and when you came on, a guy jumped up and yelled . . . '

'It's the second time I've heard that one,' said I, 'it's a great slogan.'

That is why we danced cheek-to-cheek that night – in fun. Mind you Neil is an excellent dancer.

Now a second no-offence-meant joke. After Multicon had concluded, after John Hollis, Declan and I had braved the police at Blackpool North station, who were on the look out for anyone attempting to invade the Labour Conference, we boarded the train which would take us – change at Preston – back to London. After the change I think it was, Declan started on his famous 'Nun Stories'. There was a time when Dec really should have dressed as a Mother Superior and developed a solo act. He'd have been wonderful. As it is, he can now keep a couple of his chums laughing all the way to Euston.

Here follows a small sample, delivered by dear Declan in his very thick Irish brogue, as we trundled along that day:

'Now then, there was this novice nun working in the convent's vegetable garden. She was sowing seeds for the next year's crops, and the lovely birds kept swooping down and stealing the seeds just as soon as she'd put them in the ground. "Fuck off, fuck off birds," said the little nun. "Fuck off. Leave the seeds alone."

'At that moment the Mother Superior happened to be passing. "Oh no, my child," she said. "You mustn't talk to the birds like that. Shoo, shoo little birds, go away, is what you should say. You'll see. They'll soon fuck off!"'

OK, now we'll go to Telford.

It is strange you know. Something you're not particularly looking forward to can quite often turn out to be really smashing. I'd had to leave GenCon number two halfway through the final day. That wasn't too good for a start, I hate leaving before the end of anything. Then on top there followed a dash across country so that I could get to Cult TV in time to put in an appearance and make the dash worthwhile.

The dash was in fact quite exhilarating. I'm afraid I can't recall my driver's name – sorry mate – but let's call him Sid. Sid and I travelled in one of those posh new eight-seaters (modelled I dare say on the ones we'd met in Philadelphia), the ones that look as if they've been punched in the nose, and we topped 90 m.p.h. at one point. I've said before many times that I don't like flying, but on *terra firma* I'm in my element, when there's a good driver at the wheel. While I think I'm quite a good driver, Sid was superb.

I loved every minute of the trip from Loughborough to Telford, and when we arrived, far earlier than anyone expected, I even had time to check into the hotel and have a spot of lateish lunch, before I started my signing session. I sold out of books, again. Then I had, not so much a Q&A, more of a meet. I had a cuppa (or was it a dram?) and spent the next couple of hours just talking to the appreciators. And you know what? The majority of these apps were completely unknown to me, this being the only convention they attend. I hardly recognised a soul. Well, Richard 'pull a bird' Allen was present, but he's always in attendance of course.

Cult TV is a law unto itself. Cult is the operative word of course and let's face it, there's almost no one more cult than me. Not because I'm old you understand, it's just that I've happily done very nearly every TV series there's been in the last thirty years and a great many of the movies. I think it's true, I hope so anyway, that I've always been appreciated at conventions, not only because of my full bloodied commitment, but because even the most ardent Sci-Fi app can sometimes want to talk about other programmes.

And at this convention I was in my element. Everyone wanted to talk about everything I'd done – *Maggie*; *Dixon of Dock Green*; *Softly, Softly*; *Van der Valk*; *The Invisible Man*; *Dr Finlay's Casebook*; *Z Cars*; *Hannay*; *Colditz*; *Danger UXB*; *Caught on a Train*; *Inspector Alleyn*; *Minder*; *Bulman*; *The Outsider*; *Auf Wiedersehen Pet*; *Enemy at the Door*; *Airline*; *All Creatures Great and Small*; *Grandad*; *Space 1999*; *Dr Who* (Oh yes, the Sci-Fis as well); *Blake's 7*; *The Tomorrow People* . . . oh my goodness, old Uncle Ratty an' all!

Nearly every one of my eight hundred-odd TVs and thirty-eight movies were mentioned that weekend, or rather that Sunday afternoon, evening, night and the following Monday morning – unlike most cons, Cult TV doesn't finish until midday Monday.

And on that Monday morning we had School Assembly. I had all the Cult staff lined up in front of the audience and I, as that cult figure, Mr Maurice Bronson from *Grange Hill*, with an even dafter syrup than I'd worn in the series on my head, took them to task and commanded those who did not come up to my standard – which was all of them – to do their party piece. (By the way, a syrup of figs is a wig. Just thought I'd pop in an explanation of traditional cockney rhyming slang for American readers!)

It was the best Monday morning, so I'm told, that they've ever had at Cult TV and when I went back into the hall, after I'd done my Q&A, Alex (the organiser) was sitting on the stage chatting to the audience. He suddenly asked me if I'd like to return next year.

'You try and stop me,' I replied in jocular vain.

'Well, the thing is,' Alex continued, 'I've just asked these lovely people who they'd like as guests next time and their unanimous first choice is you.'

Thank you one and all. I'm looking forward to next year tremendously.

Now, I'm going to tantalise: 'The Goose Steps Out'; 'When We Are Married'; 'Daughter of Darkness'; 'Power Play' (not 'Powerplay' as in *Blake's 7*); 'The Shape of Things to Come'; 'The Winds of War' (that's the one I turned down); and 'Sadat'.

Any idea yet? He's very much identified with Sci-Fi. No? OK, I'll give you a big clue then – Lieutenant Gerard.

If you've still not got him, all that remains for me to say is: 'Dragon's Domain', in which I played Dr Darwin King. Yes, that's right, *Space 1999*. And I'm talking of a very nice man who was third on the cast list, and a regular in the series, namely, Mr – actually, because of his noble bearing, I always think of him as Sir – Barry Morse. Barry played Gerard of course in *The Fugitive*, in which programme he chased David Janssen all over the place from 1963 to '66.

I'd not seen Barry for many years, well, he'd been in Canada chasing David, hadn't he, but he's back in the UK and we met at Cult TV last year. And he doesn't look a day older. He's now into his eighties (sorry chum, but that's what my Halliwell says), and he really doesn't look any older than the day he welcomed a young thesp onto the set of *Space 1999* all those years ago. I know I look no different, but two of us, still looking the same? Incredible!

I kept quiet when I was talking of Multicon and Cult, so I could hold the coincidence, but it's strange, even weird, how things happen. You don't see someone for, let's see now, something like twenty-five years, and then you keep bumping into them all over the place. That's how it's been with Barry and me. Cult TV was first in fact, at which event he gave a very moving talk on the misery of Parkinson's disease that has afflicted his wife, Sydney, for many years. He was so gentle but, at the same time, so passionate. We were all profoundly moved.

The next time I met him – only a few weeks later – we all but stumbled over each other. It was of course at Mr Prowse's Multicon, I was coming down from the balcony, Barry was coming up. 'Hello, Michael, how are you? How delightful. I didn't expect to see you again so soon.'

Barry Morse is a delightful – I say this with a mountain of respect – gent of the old school. It's a pleasure to know him.

Chapter 14

I had a call not so very long ago from a most excellently spoken gentle-man.

'Hello, Michael, do you remember me?'

Do I remember! No one could possibly forget the dulcet tones of *Star Wars* co-producer, Mr Robert Watts.

Robert is very nice, very true blue. Not unlike my adopted-in-fun father, Mr Jeremy Bulloch. Robert has red hair, too, same as Jeremy used to have (before he went grey). They could almost be brothers. Well, indeed they are, half brothers to be exact.

If you know the Isle of Wight you're sure to have come across the various forts that are dotted about the place, several of them are even in the middle of the Solent. Well, over the far side of the island, not far from Freshwater, is Golden Hill fort, which, since the army abandoned it, has been everything from a prison to a museum. It's huge, with massively thick walls, a circular courtyard surrounded by a myriad of rooms – large and small – and balconies and things.

I can almost hear you saying: 'That would make a great nightclub, or recording studio, or film studio, or video, or . . .' You're too late, Robert and his consortium have already thought of it!

For the past number of years they've been turning it into what will eventually be the most up-to-date media complex in the south and there's a nightclub already in full swing.

It was to invite me to visit this enterprise that Robert had phoned. Wow, what a marvellous project. I've been invited back as often as I wish and I'm looking forward to working there when everything's complete. I suggested to Robert that I bring Father with me.

I've just had a silly thought. If Jeremy is my father, that must make Robert my uncle!

Now, I can't resist it! Have you noticed anything? Actually, probably not, the typeface will surely have changed during publication. But as I write, now, I can see for example that the 'dicky birds', as I have always called inverted commas, are no longer vertical, they're sloped. Yep, I've changed computers. I mentioned it yonks ago and I'm really quite proud. Let me tell you why.

Andrew (Dymond – producer of *First Frontier*) came round to see us some weeks ago and was appalled to see my dear little Amstrad 9512 sitting in the office.

'What on earth is that doing here?' he wailed. 'You're not still using one of those, surely.'

'Well, yes,' said I, 'and I love it. We've already done *Yes, Mr B.* together and we're halfway through the next one.'

'I'm not going to let you do it,' Andrew continued, 'I'm going to build you both a new one. You don't have to thank me, I enjoy it, it's my hobby, my relaxation.'

Well, what could I say? We all need something to help us wind down. My relaxation is writing. I let Andrew build us a state-of-the-art machine, which he delivered and installed four weeks ago. ('Build you both', by the way, doesn't mean one each! It's because, as the *First Frontier* producer pointed out: 'It'll be great for Ros, too, she can scan in all her pictures.')

Thus it came about. Dear 9512 is sitting unhappily behind me, wondering what he's done wrong. I'm sitting (and I say this with a deal of hesitation), slightly less worriedly than I was at his successor, tapping away. It's taken a month to even get my head around the basics, but I dare not say any more in case I lose a whole document, as I did yesterday, or the font suddenly changes, or the line spacing . . . Oh dear! Wish me luck. If all goes well, I'll see you on the Internet.

So OK, let us proceed. Can anybody tell me why the Americans are totally unable to make a good cuppa? It's always a pot of what I concede was probably once boiling water, but by the time it reaches your table it's, well, let's just say that it is very rapidly cooling down. And the bloody tea bag has yet to reach said pot, it's lying in the saucer for heaven's sake. Why is that? They had the Boston Tea Party after all (in 1773 the tea fell in the sea). Maybe that's it. Maybe the Americans are still trying to show us that they don't like tea!

Anyway, it was thus at the Harvey Hotel in Dallas when a brace of Admirals went across the water to do Ben Stevens' convention. (Yes, *The* Harvey Hotel, the original one as immortalised in the Judy Garland movie.)

Ken Colley – the other Admiral – is of course a great guy and we had a super time, but my, is he accident prone. I arrive at Gatwick, check in, and pass smoothly through immigration with no problems. I haven't met up with Ken yet and indeed I'm beginning to wonder if he's missed his train. But no, here he comes, a wee bit harassed perhaps.

'Michael,' he gasps, 'sorry I'm late, but I'm having a bit of bother. Do you know where we're staying in America?'

'Haven't a clue, mate, why? By the way, how are you?'

'What? Oh fine. Except that that man at immigration wouldn't let me through because I didn't have an address in America.'

'Well, you're here now,' I pointed out.

'Yes, but only after I insisted that we had a definite booking. And the man still said that they'd never let me into America without an address. Do you think we should ring Doug (Murray) and ask him where we're staying?'

I confess that I was now beginning to get a smidgen concerned myself, but I couldn't see any alternative but to go on and hope. 'It'll be OK,' I said with rather more confidence than I felt. 'Come on. Let's have one for the air. At the moment I'm more concerned with leaping off the ground in a tin can!'

I'll tell what befell Ken on the return journey in a moment. Suffice it to say for now that there were no incidents on our arrival in Dallas, after a very pleasantly passed six hour flight. Very nice chats with Ken about everything from the state of the business (as always with thesps) to – oh, Julian Glover. Julian had been due to join us, a triad of officers – or is it triangle? – but he was working in the theatre, again. Lucky man. There was also nice food, nice movies, nice couple of drams, nice (small) kip. If you remember, have more than a wee sleep on the way out and you'll never be at your best.

So, we've arrived – tarra! Now what? In fact we had a superbly great time. Lots of appreciators, wonderful hosts – apart from Ben, of course, those that particularly spring to mind are 'Scoop' (Kathy Edgar) and 'Perqui' (Denise Clarkston). These two ladies were our liaison/drivers and were totally on the ball and always affable. At one of the excellent complimentary dinners we were invited to, they gave me the following key to the speaking of Texan. I understand that if you say it with a drawl, it comes out just right:

M R DUCKS
M R NOT
M R 2
C M WANGS
LI LL B
M R DUCKS

And if you can work that one out, you're a better man than I! Don't please ask me to explain it, ask them.

We did have a happy convention in Dallas. I've said before, somewhere else, that although I'd not like to live in the States permanently, I very much enjoy my visits.

Now, this is not a political volume of course, but before I tell of the second clutch of Colley mishaps, I'd like, for a moment, to take you to the scene of the President Kennedy assassination. On our last night in Dallas, after another scrumptious evening out, we were asked if we'd be interested in seeing the location of that horrific day.

Doug Murray is a crack shot, a marksman, and I've asked him if I can tell it as he told it to us that night:

'OK. If you stand at the junction, as we are doing now, looking down the road in the direction the car was travelling, the book depository, from which Oswald fired, is on our right – that oak tree, which would obscure the line of fire today, was much smaller then of course – the grassy knoll, which is exactly as it was on November 22nd 1963, except for those road signs, is in front of us and the Dal Tex building is on our left.

'Now, I'm still a pretty darn good shot, but during the Vietnam war I was an above average marksman. Even at my best I could never have dispatched three bullets in the six seconds that Lee Harvey Oswald had at his disposal. It's quite impossible. Oswald's army records show that he was only average, certainly no marksman. And it was a bolt action rifle, remember, which meant that it had to be lowered between each shot and then re-aimed.

'There had to be another rifle, probably two. One behind the knoll, there's a railway track down there which would have made escape easy, and one on the second floor of the Dal Tex building.

'The FBI and the KGB also say that there must have been other shooters. And experts, using laser technology to determine the line of trajectory, are convinced that others were involved. So am I. Oswald was simply an incompetent patsy.'

Standing there on that late summer evening, with the shadows beginning to fall and the dark shapes of the tall buildings – book depository and Dal Tex included – looming eerily above me, I forgot for a moment that the assassination took place in broad daylight. But when I imagined sunlight I still readily agreed with what Doug was saying. Of course I'm no expert but, heavens knows how, I too was a marksman, very many years ago when I was one of the last to do National Service.

There is absolutely no way, I'm convinced, that anyone could have done that deed, on his own, from the book depository.

Let's leave it there. I should add, though, that it is not morbidness that brings the American people – and indeed those of us from around the world – to that road junction in Dallas, it is our disbelief, our incomprehension, our amazement, that such an atrocity could ever have happened. And yes, our determinedness to get to the truth, which of course we never will.

I'm off to a convention in Rhyl now. I'll finish this episode on my return.

OK, it's been a very long but as always a most enjoyable weekend. Now then, Ken Colley and I arrived at the airport the next day for the start of our homeward journey and said goodbye to Lou Ferrigno. It had been good to see Lou again at this con. He's a nice man. I'm sure his hands are even bigger than Pete's, I must remember to check next time we're all three together. We'll have a hand contest.

Lou disappeared to catch his internal flight to LA and as we had a wee bit of time before ours would be called, we made our way to International Departures and wandered into the concourse shops. We each bought a little something for our Dearly B.s, before it was time for our flight, and we approached security.

I've talked about airport security and immigration and I've also said that of course it's extremely necessary. I've written, too, that the Americans are particularly vigilant, and after what

I'd seen at that crossroads in Dallas, by the book depository, this is, alas, very understandable.

But that evening I went through the X-ray machine with no problem. I put my loose change, my keys and the metal present I'd just bought in the plastic container – I still think this part of the procedure is archaic, but never mind – and walked through the X-ray arch without let or any hindrance. Then it was Ken's turn, and all hell broke loose. There were high pitched wails, screeching sirens, and the garrison of guards which descended on poor old Kenneth from all parts of the airport all but smothered him.

Guess what it was? Mr Colley has a very favourite belt with which to keep up his breeks (trousers to the sassenachs among you). This belt is covered with very large metal studs. He'd worn another, innocuous one on the way out, but here, in Dallas for goodness sake, he'd decided to wear his pride and joy.

Poor old accident prone Ken. He was somewhat shattered by the experience and when we finally boarded our flight – after I had gallantly gone to the aid of my friend and told them that he really was just a very nice thespian from England – the stewardess gave him an extra large dram.

Hey ho. Since I wrote the above I've not placed a finger on the keyboard for over a fortnight. If I tell you that it's now almost Christmas I'm sure you'll understand why. Yuletide is of course very convention orientated. But this year there is an extra reason for hecticness. Let me tell you about that first.

Quite a number of pages ago I tantalised you by briefly mentioning a chap named Danny Flynn and the fact that he could be responsible for a change in the direction of my career. Well, not a complete change, perhaps, but most certainly a fascinating diversion.

I've done masses of voice-overs, narrations, and re-voicing over the years but I've never been the voice of a cartoon character. Now, however, we've just laid down the soundtrack for the pilot of a beautiful new animated series called *Manic Moonsters*. Based on characters created and painted by Danny, it is completely delightful. I'm going a wee bit out on a limb here, but I'm sure I'm OK in telling you that these creatures (the Moonsters) live inside the moon and I play their leader, one Professor Nubrubble Smith. He pronounces his name New-brubble and all the others say Nub-rubble. This happened almost by accident at rehearsal – I just naturally said 'New' – but it works beautifully, making Smith just a teensy bit pompous.

I'll say no more here – mustn't let the manic out of the bag! Except to add that, as I say, we've just completed the voice track, which, coupled with what I'm about to mention, makes for an extremely busy couple of weeks.

On the Sunday I was in Sheringham, at the invitation of Jenny and Terry (MidCon, still to be recorded) Elson, to turn on the Christmas lights. Preceded by the Town Cryer, I, seated in a gigantic Mercedes and feeling like Lord Muck, was slowly and majestically escorted to the centre of the town. It was lovely. And I sold a goodly number of books, too.

On Monday I travelled to Banbury in Oxfordshire where the *Manic Moonsters* studios – AudioMotion – are located. I'd been there the week before in fact. That's when we rehearsed and I came up with 'New'. This time we were going to actually record the voices and lay down that track, which would then be matched by the animators. Oh yes, gone are the days when the actor has to synch his voice to what is on the screen, now we do the track first and the animators animate the computerised characters so that their mouths match our words exactly. And I assure you it's bloody wonderful. Particularly this one, as produced by Mike Cox and directed by a super guy named Chris Taylor. Chris has done masses of animation and has recently been working on *Lavender Castle* with Gerry – *Thunderbirds, Stingray, Space 1999* – Anderson.

There, I told you Chris didn't I, that you'd get a mention? You'll get more than that in the second half of my memoirs, (due in thirty years!), particularly if *Manic Ms* goes to a series. Chris very kindly gave me lifts from the hotel to the studios on the very early mornings we were due in super Des Tong's sound studio.

Now, who was it who said 'And there's more'? 'Course it was – Jimmy Cricket. Well, there is more! I may have already delivered this manuscript – sorry, floppy disc – to my publishers, but they've given me permission to pop in the odd little extra. So here goes.

First, and shame on me, I haven't yet mentioned a lovely man, Mr Bruno Brookes. Bruno, heavens, has done everything in our business, everything from DJ to what he is here, entrepreneur extraordinaire.

He really did pull *Manic Moonsters* together. In his own words, and I quote from his speech at the private première:

'I was watching the World Cup – Scotland v. Brazil – and this chap Danny Flynn came to see me with his art work. And, do you know, I found my attention shifting from the TV screen to Danny's wonderful paintings. Unheard of, I've never turned off a football match in my life! But I did, and I phoned my chum Rieny right then and told him that we must talk, because here were the ingredients for a wonderful animated series.'

I saw the pilot to said series last week and it and I are . . . wonderfully marvellous!

OK. We did the voices on Tuesday and on Wednesday I trained it all the way to Manchester. Of course you remember the Fab Café, well, I'd been invited back again for their Christmas party. And oh, what a night, what a night, what a Wed-nes-day night! I sang 'Danny Boy', 'Underneath the Arches' and 'Strolling' with a guy I pulled from the audience who was wearing a splendid red velvet jacket. I'm afraid that Mark Slater from Stockport will, forever more, be known as Mark 'Danny Boy' Slater.

We finally left the café at four in the morning. I was staying with Paul, co-owner of course with his brother Steve and Mike, of the Fab, because there was a Chelsea/Man United football match that night and there wasn't a hotel room to be had. No room at the inn? I was much better off in the stable. Treated right royally I was, cooked breakfast an' all, and delivered to the railway station by Paul in time to catch the ten-thirty a.m. for Cardiff. And I slept all the way.

And what a night that was, too – the Thursday. I can't remember much about the journey to the hotel. Except that, as I walked all the long way down the long road to Cardiff Bay (no taxis), I kept thinking that this is where Shirley Bassey came from – Tiger Bay. If it looked rough now, what must it have been like then? But when I finally arrived, I saw that whoever it is that decides what should be done with the run down edges of cities had really gone to town. Or was certainly beginning to. A whole new development of houses and hotels – I was booked into one of these – and a gigantic sports and leisure complex (which included about ten cinemas) came into view.

After the première of the new *Star Trek* movie, *Insurrection* (at which I was honoured to be the honoured guest) had been held in the largest of these, and a huge sum had been raised and donated to the Christian Lewis Trust, a charity caring for

children with cancer, there was a charity auction, also in aid
of the Trust, at which I was the auctioneer.

It's fantastic that the auction raised another £4,000 and at
the end I was presented with the most exquisite replica of
Vader's star ship – my ship. It lights up when you turn on a
special battery, and it now stands very proudly on top of our
corner cabinet. Thank you, Cardiff.

Right. I rushed home from Cardiff on Friday so that Dearly
B. could get me organised (pop my dirty shirts and things in
the washing machine, bless her) and I then was off to Derby.

Dear Derby, oh dear. I'd met Neil Green at Dave's Multicon
of course, we'd actually danced cheek-to-cheek (at the disco,
very late at night) and I'd agreed to pop down to Derby for a
small, a very small as it turned out, get together at the Alfreton
Leisure Centre. Don't misunderstand me, Neil and his gang
did a super job, they pre-sold all the tickets, arranged great
digs for me with the parents of one of their mob, Bob and
Gill Ravenhall, and introduced me to Peter and Brenda
Hemstock who run film fairs. I'm doing one in Nottingham
for them shortly. There were only two problems. One party
of fifteen didn't turn up for whatever reason, and another
fifteen teachers, who were coming especially to meet Mr
Bronson and see how the job really should be done, had an
emergency school meeting called at the last minute and so
they didn't arrive either.

They'd all paid mind, as I've mentioned, so Neil didn't lose
out financially, but the Derby gathering was somewhat
depleted from it's capacity of fifty! But we had a selectively
happy time and a great trip to the pub afterwards where the
constantly paralytic local, Nobby, bought the last remaining
copy of The Book I had with me, indeed he vehemently
insisted.

'I want a copy of that fucking book, er – what's your name? – Yeah, Michael. Really, I must have it. Come on, give me the fucking book.'

'OK, Nobby, it's yours, but it'll cost you a fucking fiver.'

'I'm not bothered with a fiver, here, take twenty.'

I settled for a fiver and a dram, upon which he also very strongly insisted. Nobby was a very nice gentle-man. But I'd love to know what he thought when he woke up the following morning . . . 'What the fucking hell is this book I've got?' I feel sure, though, that after he'd read it, he was glad that he'd not take no for an answer when I asked him if he was quite sure he wanted to buy!

And yes – I'm adding this bit during my final edit – Neil rang last Sunday and said that they'd re-visited the pub. And as they walked in, the first person they saw was Nobby. He bounded up:

'Hey, you. That fucking book I bought. I've read it, and . . . it's fucking good!'

Right then, I scampered back from Derby, spent the night in London, Simon – son number one, the accountant – took me out for dinner, and at seven blooming thirty the following morning I was having breakfast in the Wimpy opposite the Vicarage Fields shopping centre in Barking. I was waiting for it to open, because I had a date at the 10th Planet Sci-Fi shop to do a book signing. And Derek was late. There was no one there.

Yes, OK. He's asked me to say that he'd been delayed (no fault of his) and he did turn up fairly soon, full of apologies.

Bearing in mind that it was a Monday and at the start – eight-thirty to nineish – it was, well, pretty quiet, it got Christmassy by midday. All went well and I'm looking forward to a return visit to Barking with my new book – this one. Thank you all.

Phew. There's so much I want to say. And there's bundles more. I've more friends I want you to meet, and there's MidCon, Plymouth and the enigma, and Rebellion, to tell you about, and heavens, Manopticon, I've not done that, and . . . and Panopticon!

But now I want to talk about ConeXion and Twisted Toys 2, which I've already tapped on, but not elaborated.

I returned in triumph not too long ago to do another of Mike Parker's Twisted Toys, this time with Jeremy Bulloch. On the eve, we had a jolly evening, Father, Maureen (Mrs B.) and I. On the day of the fair – for indeed, again, that's what it was, we were all in an annexe of the hotel and Jeremy and I sat at one end of what would normally, I guess, have been the ballroom. Last time, if you remember, Warwick and I had been in the centre of a sports arena.

I sold a goodly number of books. Then I had to rush off. That same evening I was due in Northampton for Neil Meadows' first Rebellion. Almost all the way across the land I went, and arrived on time. It was a Saturday and I trained it. Wonders will never cease.

I'm very much looking forward to returning to Twisted Ts shortly with Ken Colley – a brace of Admirals again. Mike and I discussed this possibility at Basildon so see you soon.

ConeXion. Dear weenie, teeny little convention, held just outside Glasgow, in Paisley (never call it a suburb), which is best known, I think, indeed I'm sure all would agree, for being near to, and thereby serving, Glasgow airport. Mind, it has a University all of it's own and it was there that ConeXion was held.

Rather, is held, every year. Again, I was a sort of guinea pig, a first. And as of old I worked my guinea socks off, but only because it was such terrific fun. My special memories are: The Fancy Dress, what a job that was, choosing the winner;

the swearing in of the new *Star Trek* recruits, including my pal, Allan Green; the fact that the Wallace came over frae Aberdeen to see me and got pissed, as usual! We all had a great time and I'm going back to Paisley again next year, work always permitting. Funny, this time I remember my hotel bedroom, too. No, not really funny actually, because this one was different, that's why. Under the eaves it was, huge, with a very small door leading to the bathroom. I was very fond of that room. I've asked for it again.

There's one other recall from that weekend which I ought to mention, even though it does not redound to my credit. I am of course an honorary *Star Trek* Admiral, twice over, but I don't wear my Admiral's pips etc, unless I'm attending a *Star Trek* convention. ConeXion is a *Star Trek* convention.

On the first morning I came from the dining room and my super cooked breakfast (I only allow myself cooked breakfasts when I'm away from home), to await the transport which would take me to the convention venue. I was all dolled up in my Trek finery (by that I mean all my badges were in place, not that I was in costume), and I was raring to go. Happily for me it was dear Janet (Stewart) who arrived. Once we were in the car and under way, she glanced at me and said very sweetly, 'Michael, I think I should tell you before we get there that you've got your communicator on upside down.'

Shame on me!

Is it possible to talk of doing something at the eleventh and three-quarters hour? Maybe it's almost the twelfth hour. Anyway, I said up above that I'd been invited back to ConeXion next year. Well, now it *is* next year and I'm proof-reading these pages having been given permission to add a few more lines, because I've just returned from my second, of course, ConeXion.

Once more we had a really lovely time, with one rather large fly. Before I recount that, however, I'd like to tell you of a question that was asked during my Q&A on the second day. One of the group is a super bubbly lass (no, I'm not going to name you – yet), who co-organised last year's bash and is doing next year's. She fell asleep after the convention was over when we all went to the cinema to see a special screening of *Insurrection*. (She had, it's true, seen it many times before and had worked very hard over the weekend, even though she wasn't officially involved this year.)

The young lady knows that there's a reason why I'm prattling on like this. At the Q&A, said young lady asked the following, 'Michael, are we in the new book?' and do you know, I couldn't remember. I knew I'd written of Janet (Stewart) and my upside down communicator, but for the life of me I couldn't recall what else I'd tapped about last year's event. (Aren't these new machines great, by the way? I was able to do a very quick name check before I started this wee bit. I still love my old Amstrad, but, with the help of invaluable lessons and tips from the likes of Arthur James Forbes last weekend, I'm becoming increasingly fond of this new computer.)

I didn't let on though, did I chums, that I couldn't remember? I said that, although I loved everyone, I couldn't possibly write a book of names, and that just because your name didn't appear, it most certainly didn't mean that you weren't special. I also added, 'Wait and see. If I tell you you're not there, you might not buy the book!'

OK. You've read what I wrote about ConeXion last year and there ain't no mention of nobody, because of the slant it took. That's no excuse, mind, and I'd like to put the record straight by proudly presenting: Miss Claire (. . .) Anderson. The (. . .) is an indication that there is a middle name, but it's not enjoyed by Claire and as I'm a gent, I would never divulge a lady's name. Unless I'm not invited back to ConeXion next year, in which case I will! It was plain Claire Anderson, then, who asked the question in the first place and loves a good snooze at the flicks. Miss Rosaleen (Rosie) Hendry is another super lady. She co-organised this year's event and looked after me delightfully. I've been humming that old Al Jolson song ever since, 'Rosie, you are my posy . . .' And there's another. Co-organiser with Rosie this year. Big man, glasses, almost as much gift of the gab as I. Took me to visit the children's ward at Paisley hospital on my way to the airport and home. (The children's ward is ConeXion's charity auction beneficiary this year.) What *is* his name? Of course! Big Peter Bradley is a great guy and if I'm invited back next year, I've promised to get him a date with Claudia Christian. (If I can Peter, if I can!)

I mentioned a fly. Please Paisley University, if this wonderful bunch of people hold their future conventions on the campus, don't make the attendees walk down one street, across another, down to the bottom of a third and get lost. Open the bloody main gates. PLEASE!

Chapter 15

I'm delighted to have this opportunity to raise a huge glass of thanks to two very nice, very clever men. George Lucas and Irvin Kershner. I'm just glad that I had the chance to work with them. Irvin once, and George twice – the second time being *Indiana Jones* of course. (Actually I have, technically, worked with George three times. Those of you who've not read *Yes, Mr Bronson* and will be unaware of this fact, better hurry up and find out!)

Here's a man I like tremendously and he's always been exceedingly nice to me, too. Although there was a time, wasn't there . . .

Julian Glover (General Veers). It went like this: Eric Sykes was making one of his specials. This one was about an inept Scoutmaster (Eric) and he wanted some cubs – don't ask me why as a Scoutmaster he needed cubs and not scouts, as I haven't the foggiest. But my then agent, June Epstein, rang and asked Dearly B. and me if we'd like Rupert – son number two, now the teacher, and then a little lad who had his ninth birthday on the set – to attend Eric's auditions at Thames TV in Euston Road.

It was holiday time, or it would be when the piece was shot, so we asked Ru, he seemed keen, and I took him up to London. And the first people we bumped into were Julian and his lad.

The rest was, well, a triumph for me and Rupert and a failure I'm afraid for Julian. They, Eric and his producer, were seeing the lads, of which there were many others waiting, in fours, and it just happened that Rupert and Master Glover were in the same quartet. Up they went to the office, we all waited, then down they came. Well, you know little lads. Rupert had a huge grin on his face.

'Dad, they've asked me to wait.'

This all but meant that he'd got the part and they just wanted my consent in writing.

Master Glover just burst out crying, 'Can we go ho-ho-me Daddy?'

Before I continue, I'd like to state for the record that Julian's lad has gone on to become a very excellent thespian and I'm sure he will go far in our profession. Rupert? Well, he's recently started his own A-level politics department at Guildford High School for Girls. But he did enjoy being a cub. Particularly as his ninth birthday came during filming. The caterers made two lovely chocolate birthday cakes. One of which Eric all but fell into – he produced it as if by magic, did a pratfall, just for Ru, and only managed to avoid crushing the delicacy by a whisker. Then they all sat at the roadside in Wisley in Surrey for a tea break and completely devoured the scrumptious treats.

There's another Glover I'd like to pop down, the Paladon *Dr Who* convention in Basildon – yep Basildon, again!

It went this way. I was the MC at the Paladon *Dr Who* convention. It was my job to introduce the guests, to scurry around the auditorium with a radio mike and gather the questions. Right, I introduced Julian and his lovely wife, Isla Blair, and a question was asked. 'Julian, how many *Dr Who*s have you appeared in?'

'Ah, well now,' came the reply, 'I've been very fortunate. You see, they, the BBC of course, didn't like you to do more than one story, but I was fortunate, I was offered one with William Harnell, right at the start of my career and then I did another, almost at the end. Of *Dr Who* that is, not my career! So I did two.'

I was with the audience as I've said, with my radio mike, and I promise I only made a very small 'Ah hum'. It was the audience who did most of it, and one very nice lady stood up and shouted very loudly (I was at the other side of the hall, so couldn't reach her with the mike):

'Michael has worked with all the Doctors except Patrick Troughton, and he did two stories with Tom Baker!'

I need not report, I'm sure, the dignified way in which Julian Glover accepted that outburst.

Very nice gentleman, Julian. I recommended him, and I'm delighted he's coming, to Neil Meadows' next Rebellion in Northampton.

OK, Barry, here we go. Barry, the enigma. I feel I have to mention this story because, apart from owt else, it has a bearing on the paragraphs I wrote earlier about the differing types of convention guest – the amateur versus the professional. And I've just, this minute, got off the phone to Jeremy who's given me another example which I may drop in later.

Barry Poland first, though. I first met Barry at Steve Parson's Honiton convention.

'Michael, noice to meet you. A great honour, I mus' saye.' (This in a splendid Devon accent.) 'Oi'm doin' moy own convention in Plymouth next month, I'd be 'onoured if you would be moy guest. I 'ad Jeremy laast toime, but 'e can't come.' (I'm still trying to give you a feeling of the Devon accent you understand.)

'Great,' I replied. 'I'd love to.'

'Thas alroit then. I'm 'oping to get sum othurs along tu. Got any idears?'

There must be an alternative phrase to describe working one's socks off, but I can't think of it. So, I worked my socks off that day in Plymouth. I circulated, I did the rounds of the dealers, and I bounded up on the stage. I called everyone in, and chaired an impromptu Q&A session, when Barry came and begged me to find the others and get something going because the apps had been promised talks and nothing had happened (as well as Uncle Peter, Kenny and Mike Carter were also at this one).

Yes, I had a good time, yes, Peter and I did well sitting next to each other as usual at the signing sessions, yes (he says with modesty), I was certainly one of the stars of the convention. And yes, after it was all over, it was I who sat with Barry and his wife for a debrief, this having been Barry's first big one.

'Hello, Michael (we're now at Multicon) ''ow ar' you? You ar' comin' to moy next, aren't you? I do 'ope so. Everyone is sayin' that it will not be the same if you're not there. Every day oi 'ave folk comin' up to me and askin' if you're comin'.'

'Thanks, Barry, yes, I'll be there. And if I say yes, it means yes, except for thesping duties of course.'

'Thaas always understood, Michael. And thank you.'

'See you on the green then, Barry. I'm looking forward to it.'

Now, you'd think that was a positive invitation wouldn't you? But after that exchange there was no word from Plymouth – not a fucking phone call, no letter, nothing. I tried to get hold of Barry but it was completely in vain. In the end I telephoned Steve Parsons in Honiton, because he's sort of in Barry's neck of the woods and Barry is sort of on Steve's committee, and asked if he knew what was going on. Steve very kindly said he'd try and find out and indeed he called me a couple of hours later. 'Hello, Michael. I've managed to track Barry down and he says he's decided not to have any guests that he had last time. Tell you what though, I've told him that we, our group here in Honiton, will be honoured to pay for you to go to Plymouth.'

Dear Steve, you daft halfpenny, I couldn't have accepted your generosity in a month of fifteen blue Sundays. So I e-mailed Barry, on my posh new computer, which I'm still trying to get my head to go around, and told him that I was sorry, but I wouldn't be joining him and old chum Declan.

I was very sorry not to have met Michael Culver again. He was another guest that Barry had lined up, and he's yet to be individualised in these pages.

So, sour grapes on my part? No, I'll always go where I'm wanted, Barry. But, please . . . life's too short to piss about.

(Dear Dec Mulholland, by the way, sent Pam Clarke – the accountant/convention nice lady from up north – a Christmas card this year which read, 'I met up with Michael the other week and he led me to the drink.' Not true Dec, twas t'other way around!)

And, to quote Jimmy Cricket again, 'there's more'. Well, there is. Kenny, Peter, Dave and I were in Belgium. Kenny asked Dave, 'Who's going to Germany, then?' (After Multicon, Mr Prowse had organised a week long tour of Germany for December.)

'All of us,' Dave replied, 'except Michael.'

Perhaps my face dropped, I don't know, I really don't think it did, because I had masses of offers for the weeks coming up to the festive season, but Dave added very hastily, 'Only joking, Michael, I just wanted to see the expression on your face. Here, I haven't got your info. I need your address, phone and fax numbers so I can get back to you with details.'

Sorry chum, but I think it has to be said, you shouldn't say something unless you mean it. How the hell was I to know that all the Germany berths were already taken?

Perhaps it's just that I'm a professional actor who enjoys conventions.

Now then, MidCon – at last! Father Jeremy was in attendance here as well. Virtually just the two of us again. Oh there was a stunt man chappie of long acquaintance –Terry Walsh – and the odd American from *Star Trek* or somewhere, but it was we who were the stars. Hang on, I might just be carrying myself away with the ether of it – only kidding, folks!

My, but this was a good 'un. And I must have been good, 'cos I was invited to no less than four other conventions over the weekend and Jeremy only got two!

The most important report I have to make about MidCon is that it lives on. Jenny and Terry Elson had decreed that this one was to be their last. Heavens, they'd retired from Leicester, where they used to live and work and mount MidCon, to Sheringham (Norfolk) several years previously, but they'd still returned – to Leicester – every year, to organise MidCon.

But this one, their seventeenth, was to be their last. Until that is two other guests – Steve Gillis and Dave, both writers – sat down on one of the MidCon evenings at the Holiday Inn, Leicester, and chatted. I think I might have been there too, egging them on. The result was that, after hasty discussions with Jenny and Terry, which have since been amicably prolonged, it was announced at the closing ceremony that Steve and Dave would take over MidCon. And thus it certainly does live on. And guess who they asked to be their first guest?

I'll see you. And as my dear old chum Maurice Bronson would say, 'You *will* be there!'

Lucinda Curtis played a teacher in *Grange Hill*. At that time she was married to Michael Culver (Captain Needa). When Lucinda joined the *G.H.* cast, it was a connection Michael and I had in common.

Michael is another very nice man. I first met him on the set of *To Encourage the Others*, the first, I think I'm right in saying, movie of the Craig/Bentley murder case. It was written by David Yallop and no, Michael wasn't in it, but his father, Roland Culver, was. Roland played the judge, Lord Goddard, who many historians say cajoled and bullied the jury into finding Bentley – who had not fired the fatal shot which killed PC Miles, but who was over sixteen and therefore legally responsible – guilty of murder. The sad result of course being that Derek Bentley was hanged. It must be added here that I'm very delighted that, after so many years of campaigning by his family, Bentley has at last been posthumously pardoned.

Mike, then, popped into the studios to see his Dad, and as I say, that's where we first said hello. Apart from *Empire*, another meeting I particularly remember was at the then *Grange Hill* producer Ronald Smedley's house in Ham, near Richmond. I'm sure it still is a tradition that the current producer holds a summer party for the crew and cast. (My first producer and chum, Ben Rea's, was astronomical.)

I still think it's funny that there are some days you can remember like there really are no tomorrows. Ron Smedley's party was one of these. The Sheards lived in Send at the time, a tiny Surrey village twixt Guildford and Woking, no distance, car-wise, from Ham. Ha! Up and down the A3 I went and could I find the exit for Ham? No I bloody couldn't. I went halfway to London, came back through Richmond park and was about to stop and phone, when suddenly a policeman appeared, striding up the road towards me. I stopped and he laughed when I asked for the road in which Ron lived. 'It's just over there, Sir,' he said and pointed to literally the next turning.

Heavens, I'm supposed to be telling you about Michael C., not giving you a history of South London roads! OK, I got to the house and I gave Ron a vine seedling, which I'd brought on myself from a grape. He planted it in his garden and as far as I know, it flourishes now as it did then. Then I entered the house, and I found Michael sitting next to Lucinda, on the best sofa – well, he would, wouldn't he?!

I'd no idea he'd be there. We had a good chat. I have to say that I did feel he was a wee bit uneasy with the *G.H.* lot, and sadly, in less than no time later he and Lucida had parted company and divorced. Very sad, very common, and nothing to do with *Grange Hill* of course. Thank whatever there may be that Dearly B. still puts up with me after all these years.

I'm looking forward to seeing Mike, by the way, at a convention in Basildon shortly.

I've just had a call from a guy called Amego Schpiel asking if I'll do a convention in Rottenberg, in Germany. I've said yes. Well, Chicago have not confirmed their dates and these are firm. Mind you, I hope they don't clash. I'm greedy and I'd love to do both!

Eddy Wauters came to Pam Clarke's Regeneration convention – the Heathrow Airport one – and before he returned home to Belgium he asked me, Kenny, Peter and Dave if we'd be guests at a convention he was going to set up in his home town of Aalst, which is not that far from Brussels. We all said that we'd be delighted, then thought no more about it. Well, it does happen fairly frequently, an appreciator has a great time at a convention, thinks, 'I could do this', and then, in the cool light of the morning after, decides that perhaps it wasn't quite such a good idea after all. There's a hell of a lot of work involved.

The above said, there are, happily, a good number of these ventures which do go ahead.

Some only last the once – for varied numbers of reasons. The Matson twins in Peterhead for example are taking their end of school exams (highers, they're called in Scotland); Capsicon in Edinburgh didn't go to a second this year, mainly due to the happy event of Karen (you remember Mrs McClusky the Second of course) and Colin's wedding. Let's hope that these and all the other one-offs make triumphant returns.

Then there are long established events which come to an end. This is particularly sad. Polycon has, I think, really flown now, because the organisers, Meachelle and Gordon Hudson, have parted I'm afraid, and in spite of Jonjo's efforts, I can't see Infinity going again, certainly not in Cardiff. I hope I'm wrong, mind, I'd love to see them make a comeback.

Then there are fledgling convention entrepreneurs who simply get it wrong the first time, lose money and thus heart.

Oh, dear, this is all a bit downbeat. Let's have a peek at t'other side of the coin: at those conventions which, kindled with the enthusiasm gained at someone else's con, have made it at the first attempt and are about to establish themselves on the circuit, good and proper. There's Mark O'Grady's Battlefield in Exeter; Neil Meadows' Rebellion in Northampton; and the Eldridge's UK Games Fest. I'm flattered to report that Jan and Karl Eldridge have even changed the date of their 'do' so that I'm free to attend, and I'm delighted to remind you that I had some small input into the mounting of both Mark and Neil's first. Both have very kindly invited me to return as a guest. Once again, very sadly, I've had to say sorry to Mark because of other commitments, but I'll see you in Northampton.

I've barely tickled the surface of the convention calendar, there are so many around the world that I'm sure nobody knows the number. I was endeavouring to come to terms with the Internet on this new machine of mine the other day and I came across an American convention list, or rather a listing for the district around New York only, and there were something like three hundred of them. I think it's amazing, and I'm delighted, long may it continue!

These here mentioned are of course just a few of those which have touched me, and I must offer you another, mustn't I? Because I started this section with Eddy.

In no time at all, Eddy had got back to us with dates, venue, an offer, the hotel, even flight times, and there were nearly five months still to go. You'd never, in a month of conventions, have thought that this was his first.

The hotel was smallish but excellent, with an internal circular reception area on the ground floor that had its glass-covered roof eight floors up. You could look down into the belly of reception from outside the lifts on any of the floors, and Peter and I took great delight in playing the balcony scene from *Romeo and Juliet*. He was on the ground floor, I on the fourth. Even though you would expect Pete to be him and me to be her, for some reason we both took it in turns to be Romeo.

Peter: But soft, what light through yonder window breaks.

Me: It is the East and Juliet is the Sun.

And I did get that old chestnut in. I got Peter to say Juliet's line, 'Romeo, Romeo, wherefore art thou Romeo?' and I replied in time-honoured music hall fashion, 'Up here in the balcony dear, it's cheaper!'

The venue itself had been excellently thought out. A large recreation centre was arranged thus: dealers' tables, including our signing tables, were set around the perimeter, with two large tents – yes tents – in the middle. At first, I confess, I wondered what on earth was going on. But it worked splendidly. Pete and I were teamed together and Kenny and Dave formed another twosome, and every so often throughout the two days we would do musical chairs. When Pete and I were doing a Q&A in one of the tents, Kenny and Dave would be either signing, or taking coffee with just a few apps in the more informal atmosphere of the other tent. Then we'd musical chair/change about. And you know something? When you were in one of those tents, you may have been having a bloody good loud laugh, but although those outside were not more than a basket ball pitch away, they hardly heard a thing. Something to do with the way they make tents in Belgium I guess!

One other morsel I'd like to mention about that trip to Aalst, is Eddy's restaurant. We ate superb food there every night and I had frogs' legs!

Chapter 16

In another book, I told the story of a lovely cockney character actress named Rita Webb and how she dealt with being given a dressing room down in the depths of the BBC. Rita was a marvellous redheaded lady, who always spoke her mind. She was small and dumpy and never seemed to be out of the BBC TV centre and its studios, in the good old days of yore.

Claire Davenport (Yarna d al Gargan) was, I'm sure she'll allow me to say, not a redhead, small and dumpy, but a nicely rounded large blonde lady, who, when I knew her in those same seemingly far off days, also spoke her mind, and she also was never far from Auntie Beeb.

Except when she was in Germany on a photo shoot. The German men clamour for large blondes with big 'assets' of course, but if Claire wants to tell you about those trips across the North Sea, it's up to her. I must just add, however, that even though it's something like twenty-odd years ago, she didn't 'alf keep us in stitches in the BBC Acton Hilton rehearsal rooms telling us about her 'little German jaunts'!

Claire, when she wasn't on the continent, seemed to be the mainstay of the BBC supporting roles. There were dozens. I did so many with her that I can't be absolutely precise, but I certainly remember our appearing together in *Dixon of Dock Green*, *Softly, Softly*, *Dr Finlay*, *Task Force*, *Dr Who*, *Z Cars*, *The Dick Emery Show* and on to another Old Uncle Ratty an' all – there have been so many. Suffice it to reiterate that Claire did a hell of a lot of tellies.

Ken Colley, who knows her well, tells me that Claire has not been too well recently. Please get well soon luv, so you can keep us laughing. And listen, do some conventions.

Well now, what can I say? I've hinted at Rebellion. I've stated how I raced across the country late one Saturday afternoon, after I'd done a day with Mike Parker, Tara and Jeremy at a Twisted Toys 'do' in Bristol, to reach Northampton in time for the celebrity dinner. I've told you that Neil has invited me back again this year, but I've not reported on it. Not yet that is.

OK. I'm going to put that right, now, by putting it into two or three or perhaps five nutshells.

Nut one. The first person I met on my latish arrival was Neil himself. No, I tell a lie. Neil's dad, Mick, had picked me up at the station, and on the short journey to the hotel, told me how excellently things were progressing. Indeed, perhaps one of the reasons why everything seemed so relaxed was because – again this was whispered to me in the car – Rebellion had already broken even. Before it opened and the 'ticket at the door' punters arrived. You know, that's bloody marvellous. Your first convention and you square the books before you start. No wonder Neil's doing more. Let me make it very clear, though, his conventions are fan run. In fact he told me in all seriousness that he wouldn't mind if he didn't make a profit, 'Just as long as everyone enjoys themselves, Michael.'

Nut two. We most certainly did. There was no Father Jeremy at this one, he'd stayed on in Bristol for a 'Robin of Sherwood', and no Mr Prowse, but the rest of us were there. Pete and I were once again a formidable double act. And there was an additional bonus for Pete. He bought a superb original painting of Alec Guinness as Ben (Obi Wan) Kenobi, at the charity auction, signed by Alec. I know Pete got on particularly well with Alec and was therefore delighted with his purchase. Signed pictures of Sir Alec are now almost non-existent.

Nut three. Guess who was the auctioneer at that charity do? Moi, with a smidgen of help from my friends – Declan, Pam Clarke, and Peter. We had a great time.

Nut four. I've only one complaint about that very super day. It was just that, one day. I'm delighted that Neil's next is to be a two dayer. A weekend is so very much better. More time. More time to chat, more time to party.

Nut five. We did have the celebrity dinner on the Saturday evening of course, so perhaps it's unfair to call Rebellion simply a one day affair, let's say one and a tiny bit! The dinner was delightful. We, the guests, had a table each, full with about a dozen apps. At the course change overs I did my usual walkabout and greeted the people at the other tables and I got my fellow guest chums to do the same. That way we all met everyone.

Final nut. Because our diaries don't always combine, Pete Mayhew and I have not done a show together for a couple of months. We're glad to be teaming up again in Barcelona in a few weeks. You can't keep a good act down.

Epilogue nut. I'm terribly looking forward to the next Northampton one, Neil. See you there. And you, and you and you!

Tell you what I'm going to do now. I'm going to put the three leading *Star Wars* actors into one packet. It seems daft, I know, but there's a valid reason for it.

Let me explain. Harrison is a great guy, a good friend, with whom I've worked four, or is it five, times. But I've told you so much about him already. His kindness, his excellence on the screen, his relaxed, cool acceptance of that which is happening around him. No. Perhaps I should say his 'seeming' acceptance, don't misunderstand me, Harrison is certainly his own man. I'm very sorry he was unable to join Roger (Moore) in doing a foreword to *Yes, Mr Bronson*. He was uncontactable, filming in the Tibetan jungle. I look forward to working with him again. He's a great guy and actor.

Carrie and Mark do qualify for a mention in my book because I did bump into them on the stairs. Almost literally. We all but collided.

Having said that we said 'Hi', there's not much more that I can add. Except that I'm not, I'm afraid, familiar with Mark's other work, and I think Carrie was simply great in *When Harry Met Sally* with Billy Crystal and Meg Ryan. She's still very active in the business, and I love her mum the best. In fact it's about time the Sheards saw *Singing in the Rain* again, I think I'll suggest it to Dearly B. for this evening . . .

Manopticon – Panopticon. 'Man' stands for Manchester of course where it used to be held. 'Pan' means across the continents I imagine, certainly not Coventry, where this Andrew Beech extravaganza is staged every year.

I've been thinking about these two *Dr Who* conventions off and on since I started these pages and have been wondering how to present them. How about snippets? Don't ask me why, but I do tend to recall these events in snippets – isolated incidents. Perhaps it's because of the sadness pervading both. The last time I saw Don Henderson was at Manopticon, and Jon Pertwee was in great form at Panopticon just before he died.

Anyway, snippets it is. Let's take Manopticon first:

I could only do one day, the Sunday . . . a gold paint-filled signing pen exploded and splattered all over my suit . . . the cheer which greeted the announcement that I had arrived . . . a bomb scare at Manchester's Piccadilly station on my return . . . signing on my own after the others had finished, because I'd arrived late . . . the warmth . . . the laughter . . . losing my room key, then finding it again, on the bar . . . losing my way to the station of course and being directed there by Chris (see my second Fab Café visit) . . . walking into the dining area and being greeted by a sea of happy, smiling faces cheering me . . . Andrew Beech (Panopticon) saying, 'What on earth are you doing here? I was going to invite you to mine' . . . me replying that couldn't he make an exception because I'd just had a book published . . . joining the closing ceremony after it had started, again because of my signing duties, just as Nick Courtney was being asked what was his greatest nightmare – we got the loudest ovation of the whole blinking weekend when I shouted, 'Me Nick', and he replied, 'Yes, I rather think it's Sheard!'

I've done more than one Panopticon. I certainly did one before Manopticon because Andrew Beech made that exception and invited me back 'cos I'd been such a hit at my first Panopticon. Anyway, Panopticon snippets . . . having dinner with Sophie Aldred, talking over the old times when we used to share an agent . . . Sophie kindly suggesting that if ever I wanted to change, she'd be more than happy to recommend me to her new agent . . . the gigantic signing queues which spiralled all the way up to the very top of the hotel stairs . . . having breakfast and chewing the fat with Barry Letts, one time *Dr Who* producer . . . the celebrity dinner, where I first introduced the guest table-change between courses . . . early on the second morning, popping out and walking miles to find a phone that worked to call home (never from the hotel remember) . . . the excellent repast offered in the guest's green room . . . seemingly huge numbers of radio interviews, actually staged in the hotel, for broadcasting later . . . the problems of finding a quiet place to do them, usually out on a landing . . . once again the warmth, the laughter and the happy smiling faces . . . the books, I sold a heck of a lot and took those masses of mail orders . . . and Nick again, doing a Q&A together and finishing with that most enchanting rendition of 'Me and My Shadow' (that great Flanagan and Allen number composed, of course, by Billy Rose, husband of Fanny Brice of *Funny Girl* fame).

Happy conventions, very happy. The sadness came later. But I feel definitely certain that Jon and Don would want us to remember the happiness.

I'd like now to give another Dr Who a sentence or two to himself, but you know, I can't think of anything more newsworthy to say about Colin Baker, I've used up all the Baker news!

The same's true indeed of Sylvester McCoy, and Louise Jameson. And I've written so much about my chum Sophie Aldred that there can't be more. Or can there? Let's see.

Colin Baker. Colin had played the game we played at the Regeneration Easter convention before, on TV, that's why he was so good. The 'game' is a sort of crossword, with two teams. The clues were read out in this instance by the convention organiser Ms Pamela Clarke, and the correct answers appeared on a screen behind us. Throughout we could have a go at guessing the answer to the whole thing.

I was much better when I was sitting in the body of the hall as an observer, but Colin was masterly. Mind you, as I say, he'd played it before. Maybe he already knew the answers – no, I don't think so!

Syl. I had the opportunity of doing a Joe Orton play, *Funeral Games*, with Sylvester McCoy. It was to be staged in London and I'd have liked to do it. No, that's not quite right, I know I'd have enjoyed working with Syl, but the concept, as outlined by the director, did not, I confess, appeal to me. Make no mistake, I'm all for exploring new ways of presentation. I think the American *Pirates of Penzance*, and Jonathan Miller's wonderful reworking of *The Mikado*, with Eric Idle as Ko-Ko, are brilliant, but one should never do something just for the sake of sensationalism. I'll say no more, except that I never saw the production, but I'm told that Sylvester was smashing.

Louise. What a trouper. And what a lass! Louise works tirelessly for charity, perhaps not everyone knows that. She's compiled a tape of readings by as many of her chums as have been available. It's great and the proceeds all go to charity.

Sophie, dear Sophie. I've searched through these pages, with the amazingly quick help of this wonderful new machine of mine, and I've not spoken of the time Sophie kneed me in the goolies!

I don't think even I can top that. All I should perhaps add, in case anyone gets the wrong idea, is that it was done in *thespian* anger, not the real thing. Do you remember the scene in *Dr Who*, 'Remembrance of the Daleks', where said exchange occurred?

By the way Sophe, what's happened to your book?

Now do you know what, I've not given Pat Troughton full rein, have I? No, I didn't work with him in *Dr Who*, but we did masses of other tellies together. *The Sweeney* – hey, I was a headmaster again, I'd forgotten that, and Pat was the baddy – and in numerous numbers of filmed TV series, which were made in the late sixties and early seventies.

When I did *Maggie* for BBC Scotland, the only other sassenach Scot was a very nice lady actor called Alison Groves, who is married to David Troughton, one of Pat's sons.

The descendants continue. The David Troughton's now have budding thespians of their own.

Now then, what follows was a first, even for me.

A short few Fridays ago, I was having lunch in Matchams Restaurant, which is situated within the Theatre Royal complex, Newcastle-on-Tyne. But this was no ordinary lunch, this was my very own first Literary Lunch!

I've been invited to the London Book Fair, ever since *Yes, Mr Bronson* was first published, and I think that's great. But as I said to Dearly B., to have one's very own Literary Lunch, well, it must mean that I'm a proper author, mustn't it?

There were over forty dear people, who'd paid lots to come and dine with me, the author. Yes OK, the two do mingle – author/thesp – they must do, but this lunch, my Literary Lunch, was primarily because of my book, *Yes, Mr Bronson*. And because *Yes, Admiral* was following, and because (I have let it slip a couple of times and the Internet grapevine flourishes), there's the possibility of a follow-follow-up coming along in the fullness of time.

But I'm getting carried away with the headiness of it. Let's dwell for a moment in that great theatre in Newcastle, which I liken a smidge to that lovely theatre in Perth where I started my professional career and where I met Dearly B. Peter Sarah, the manager of the Theatre Royal, Newcastle, gave me a tour before we started My Lunch, and it is truly magnificent. Matchams Restaurant, by the way, is named after Frank Matcham, the architect of the Theatre Royal, who also designed the Haymarket Theatre in London, and on the walls of the restaurant are some of his fascinating original drawings.

The auditorium, though large – no blow it, it's vast and can seat something over twelve hundred – is so designed that it still gives a feeling of intimacy. We were standing on the stage where *Martin Guerre* would be staged that evening and to which, thanks to Peter, I'd been complimentarily invited. And I turned to Peter and said, 'My production of the one-woman play *Shirley Valentine* could be staged here, no problem.'

It's not happened yet, but as always, watch this space!

Right, now. Credit where credit is due. My wonderful Lunch and the great Q&A we had after – mind you we'd blethered all through My Lunch and even before it started – was the brainchild of that lovely accountant Ms Pamela Clarke, and

I'm truly, madly and deeply honoured. I try to come clean, always do. When it was first suggested, I trembled a wee bit. I thought that nobody would come. It's one thing to have a book published, which has been well received, but a whole darn lunch dedicated to that fact?

I had melon, orange and kiwi cocktail for starters, supreme of chicken with a green peppercorn sauce for the main course, and home-made apple and cinnamon pie served warm, with vanilla ice cream. De – licious!

My Literary Lunch was a gigantic success. I've been asked to do more lunches, and I'm terribly grateful to Pam and her Friends of the Theatre Royal.

My trip up north is not yet done. I'd like to take you back to supper the previous evening. No, this wasn't my supper, as in My Lunch. It was Pam's. And I was delighted that the two 'do's coincided.

It's been suggested that I give mention to the Tyne and Wear Society of Chartered Accountants' Chairman's Supper – supper, not dinner for some reason, they're very strict on that – because then I'll sell masses of copies of my books to all those who were present.

No, I want to talk of this supper because Pam is the chairman this year. Chairman – not woman – or person even. They're strict about that, too!

The Tyne and Wear Society of Chartered Accountants' Chairman's Supper was held in the Tyne Suite, on the ground floor of the Forte Post House in Newcastle. Small world: I'm due to do a 'Neutral Zone' convention there next year – in the next millennium!

At the top table sat all the top people, including of course Pam, wearing her chain of office – well, almost wearing it. The original had been lost or something and its replacement was so heavy that Pam had abandoned it. Next to Pam sat Dennis Taylor, former world snooker champion, who gave the most superbly great after-dinner speech. Dennis and I got on like houses on fire and he's invited Rupert, son number two, who is also into sport, and me to the next Masters.

Lots of other tables, at which sat at least three hundred Tyne and Wear accounting types and their guests, were ranged around the Tyne Suite. I'm sorry I couldn't name you all, maybe, if I had, I'd have made even more sales!

I, together with the others from Pam's own company, were seated just below the top table, on, I guess you'd call it table one, if top table has no number. There were a dozen of us, including Peter, Pam's partner, Tina Pole, Pam's secretary and friend, who'd come up with Pam to Glasgow to visit me at Continuum, and Mr David Scott of whom I wrote earlier. He was the guy who spoke so disparagingly about actors. (My, but I had to keep sober this evening, otherwise I'd have proved him right!)

A great evening, made even greater by melon and pineapple cocktail, rack of lamb Dijonnaise and strawberry shortcake, all washed down with a great Rioja.

Thanks all for two wonderful days.

It is now perfectly proper and fitting that my final thumbnail should be reserved for the super lady who started it all for me – and for many others, bless her – *Star Wars*-wise. The director and producer may actually do the hiring, but it is the casting director who puts your name forward in the first place and pushes and convinces, if need be, until the hirers hire.

I'm feeling modest today – probably as I've just been recalling some glorious *Dr Who* times and my Literary Lunch – but I must just mention *Yes, Mr Bronson* once more. Because in that companion biography I've explained in much grateful detail the many times Irene Lamb has been responsible for putting my name forward. If the movie's director and producer are American, which they mostly seem to be, they haven't a clue about the British working, character thespian, and that's where, to have a chum like Irene is an absolute must. I know you won't misunderstand me, no casting director would suggest you out of friendship alone, they also have to respect your abilities, your talent and, indeed, the way you conduct yourself on the set. In fact of course, friendship comes later, after the above requirements.

Apart from *Star Wars – Escape to Athena* (Roger Moore, David Niven, Telly Savalas, Stephanie Powers); *Force 10 from Navarone* (Harrison Ford, Robert Shaw); *Les Miserables* (Anthony Perkins, Richard Jordon); *Green Ice* (Ryan O'Neil, Anne Archer, Omar Sharif); and *All Quiet on the Western Front* (Patricia Neil, Richard Thomas, Ernest Borgnine) are just some of the super engagements which Irene has introduced me to. Thank you, luv, very, very much.

Now, I'd never *report* anything that's not yet happened, of course I wouldn't. But on this occasion I have to work very fast. The floppy disc/manuscript is already with the publishers and although I've not yet set foot in America this year, my dear publishers have said that they'd like another American nosegay.

So, if I let slip that I'm dropping the next couple of paragraphs in before I depart for Roanoke, Virginia, USA, I'm sure you'll understand. Actually I've even promised to write the report on the aeroplane, as I return, so that it can get to Summersdale in time.

But there have been preliminaries, which I can already chronicle. Things like: 'Where would you like to fly from?' Me, *like* to fly?! I don't really mind and, as always, I'll steel myself. Good grief, John Franklin and his gang are paying me to go halfway round the world to join them so I'd better grit my teeth and get on with it. I'll see you on the return journey . . .

... Right then, here we are. I love Laurel and Hardy – their rendition of 'The Blue Ridge Mountains of Virginia' is wonderful – and I've lost count of the times I've sung along with John Denver or Olivia Newton John when they've been on their way home to 'West Virginia'. Well, right now I'm sitting at a table in the restaurant at Roanoke Airport and actually looking out at those blue ridges. It's simply one of the most beautiful views I've ever seen. The sun is shining brightly and every so often an aeroplane takes off. A small one, so as not to break the spell.

But one flight does not take off. My flight to Philadelphia has been cancelled. I've got to wait for three hours before flying to Pittsburgh and changing on to their Philly flight. But that's OK, even though it means an extra take off and landing, because I can sit here and look to the hills for inspiration, as I write these lines. I'll still be in time for my Gatwick connection, and there must have been a good reason for cancelling the Roanoke/Philly flight. Oh dear . . . I don't think I want to follow that line of thought! I'll look at the hills instead.

It's been a very great weekend. I've been made superbly welcome. I know they'll appreciate that I can't name everyone, but, apart from John, Emily the guest liaison lady, looked after me wonderfully. Kym, who was in charge of the dealers' room where I did my signings, brought me great cups of coffee and wore the most exquisite pair of very short shorts, and Christy provided a running buffet, from a revamped hotel bedroom, which would have put many a hotel's catering to shame.

Hey, I haven't told you. The convention wasn't in fact held in Roanoke at all. I felt a bit of a twit actually. I'd been talking on the Internet to John for months, but when I came to fill in the immigration form, on my outward journey, and the first question was 'At what address will you be staying in the USA?', all I could put was Roanoke, Virginia, and two e-mail addresses.

I had remembrances of Ken Colley and our trip to Dallas – it's a wonder they let me in!

Technicon, the sixteenth convention for VTSFFC (Virginia Tech Science Fiction and Fantasy Club), was held in the Best Weston Red Lion Inn, in Blacksburg, and Blacksburg is a three-quarter hour drive from Roanoke. Mind you, to the Americans, who think nothing of driving 300 miles for an evening out, that's only just down the street.

As this is the last convention I'll be reporting for this trip to the publishers, I'll repeat myself: I had a wonderful time at Technicon. Being a University town, almost half the apps were students and a goodly number of the remainder were ex-students. It was like old home week for them, a reunion. The two things that impressed me most out of a lot which impressed me, was the true affection – love almost – that this crowd had for each other, and the organisation of the event.

The big cheese – at American cons he or she is called the Chair, and was in this case of course John Franklin – oversaw everything, certainly, but his team all had their various responsibilities and duties, and they carried them out to the letter with enthusiasm and very good humour. One moment that sticks in my mind was when John had to leave to pop into town. He called out to the Deputy Chair – James 'Not Matt' Roberts – 'You have the con, James.' James quietly and efficiently took over the reins.

Let me give you just three nice snatches from a weekend which had so many.

Nakani – his name is pure American Indian – is a huge man. He'd hardly slept the whole weekend, and when I came through the hotel lobby at midday on the Sunday, he'd finally succumbed. He was stretched out on a very long sofa, fast asleep, with his head on his girlfriend's lap. 'The Sleeping Beauty,' I whispered.

'Perhaps,' his lady replied. 'But I'm just glad he's not snoring. That's something you do not want to hear!'

'So how have you prevented it?' I innocently whispered again. The lady winked.

'I've turned his nose downwards into my crotch,' she replied!

Bambi – at the end of the convention, I was coming down from what had been the upstairs dealers' room, carrying a large stack of books for one of my new dealer mates,

'Trouble is,' quoth I, 'you can't see your feet and you're liable to go arse over . . .'

At that precise moment, Bambi, a wonderfully statuesque black lady, who had given us a superb exhibition of the belly dance at the previous evening's cabaret, came round the corner. I couldn't stop myself and added, '. . . tit.'

Bambi laughed like a drain.

'In that case honey,' she said, 'gimme a big tit hug!'

What a nice lady.

The App – a little later I was in the lobby again when an app approached me.

'Can I buy a copy of your book, please? And will you sign it for me?'

'Yes to both questions,' I replied. 'But which one would you like?' (Although not yet published, dear publishers had come up with a great order form which, as well as offering *Yes, Mr B.*, also included *Yes, Admiral.*)

'The one where you get killed.'

'I've been killed more times than we've all had hot dinners,' I replied, 'do you mean the best death ever?'

'Yeah, I guess. But if you've been killed all those other times, I'd better have both books.' All of us in the reception exploded with laughter, including the recipient of both books. Long Live Death!

OK. Now I'm being very brave. I'm millions of miles above Mother Earth. Oh my God, I've just looked out of the window, I can actually see the sea beneath me! They'll soon be serving supper/dinner/breakfast – I don't know, I haven't a clue what time it is – dinner, that's it. Then there's the movie. A new one of course (always is on flights) Holly Hunter and Danny De Vito in *Living Out Loud*. I've heard good reports. Anyway, it's bound to be better than the outward bound offerings, *How Stella Got Her Groove*, and particularly *The Echo of Thunder*. Oh dear, not very appetising. But here's dinner, which is, so I'll eat, then continue, and try to get this written before the film starts.

OK. Dinner – which was good, I had the steak and a half bottle of wine – and film were served at the same time. So both are now over and I can continue in peace, or should it be roar (of the jet engines)? Actually I'm feeling quite pleased with myself. I've got this far and the aeroplane seems steady. Um, maybe it's the wine, but perhaps I'm getting better. Let's continue.

Carrying on from 'Long Live Death' then – not a bad film title that. I bet it's been used already, I'll look it up when I get home. (Added from home on my return. No, my Halliwell records a movie called *Long Live Life* with Charlotte Rampling, but not 'Long Live Death'. So it's mine, and don't you dare nick it! I now return to my seat in the air above the Atlantic.)

By the way, I made it to Philadelphia via Pittsburgh. No time alas to visit that pawnshop on the corner. ('There's a Pawn Shop on the Corner in Pittsburgh, Pennsylvania.' Dearly B. doesn't think that's the title of the song. Can anyone verify it?)

I've got just one more thought regarding Technicon. Technicon was the driest convention I've ever attended, dram-wise. As Warren Lapine, editor of numerous Science-Fiction magazines and one of the American guests, observed, 'My

Australian friends say, America got the puritans, thank God we got the convicts!' Don't get me wrong, please, I'm not against abstinence. But I have to admit that it is a wee bit daunting when you've had a super day and the hotel bar is shut because it's Sunday.

But there is another reason for the dryness at Technicon. The legal age for drinking, throughout America, is now twenty-one. There were so many road deaths among teenage drivers that the government put pressure on the States to raise the legal age limit from eighteen. I didn't know that. Great decision, those continuous six lane motorways – something we don't really have here in the UK – virtually beg you to go fast. That said though, I'd have loved a little dram at the end of that hard day. I wasn't driving and I'm twenty-seven!

Thank you Blacksburg, John, *et al.* I had a very, an especially great time at Technicon. And, I've been invited back next year. The assembled company insisted. Thank you *very* much, I can't wait. Eat your heart out fellow Starwarians, this one's mine!

Before I leave this – I was going to call it a snippet, but it's grown – before I conclude this chapter, let me now introduce you to Perdue's Quality Improvement Process Director, Mr Shaun McKenzie.

I was engrossed in continuing the draft of this in one of Philly airport's many bars (I must assure you that the whole county's not dry), when Shaun and I got chatting – he's going to buy both books, and yes, he's also going to send me some of Perdue's – that's Perdue, Salisbury – choicest chickens!

Shaun – who is of both Irish and Scottish extraction, hence his name and his blarney – and I spent a great couple of hours whilst waiting for our respective flights and here is one of the great stories he told.

Shaun travels a lot in his job and as he's based in America he mostly flies. On one of his many trips the Captain came on the radio to make the customary Captain's address. Shaun was interested in the fact that the Captain was obviously a woman, as it was a female voice, and mentioned it to one of the cabin crew.

'That's right,' said the steward, 'our Captain is a lady, and what's more our co-pilot is a lady too. We're thinking of changing the name cockpit to . . . !'

Chapter 17

Right. Now I do, in fact, need to open the other book again. Very many people have been so very kind about *Yes, Mr B.* and masses have said that their favourite pages are those devoted to *Grange Hill* where I used the alphabet system. You know, A is for: Agent, Actor, Availability, etc.

Well, I've got lots of bits and bobs still to pop into this one and I thought I'd like to adopt that method again. The idea came to me whilst I was giving you the Man and Pan – opticon snippets. So, that explained, here goes with the rest of my Sci-Fi, conventions, and the odd extracurricular:

A is for:

'Aberdeen Evening Express' – again
I've talked before of the Capitol Cinema in the city of my birth, closed last year by the Donalds and how the Evening Express printed my fax. I'd like to add that I feel sure all of us, the Evening Express, the people of Aberdeen – particularly those in the Art Sutter Chat Show audience on Grampian TV, where everyone was clamouring for a stay of execution, helped a wee bit to slow the tide of stupidness. Let's keep it up, our lobbying. I understand that the stage and projection room are still as they were, they've not yet been removed.

Long live The Capitol Cinema. Come back soon.

Alex Armstrong
Is a very nice man. I met Alex at GenCon a couple of years ago and he invited me to join him at a gaming day he was organising in central London. It went very well and he was talking of doing masses more, almost all over the world, with me as the figurehead, but I've not heard from him for nearly

a year. Neither has anyone else. If you read this, mate, get back in touch, and let's go!

Always
Always be bright-eyed, bushy-tailed and approachable when you're a convention guest, even if the vino has fully flowed the night before, or those dastardly Klingons have proffered another of their dreaded brews, which at times, coloured a ghastly purple, blue or pink, can be even stronger that the Matson's (Peterhead) whiskey, a tall order considering that it was 120 per cent proof!
That, as I see it, is my job.

Audio
Frank Cronogue and Dave Willcox have asked if I'd be interested in an interesting little venture. I'm to be one of the first *Dr Who*ers to do an audio tape for Frank's company. It's to be in a sort of Tardis form – forward and back in time. A discussion of my career. I think it's a great idea and I've already done quite a hump of preliminary work.
Frank and Dave originally asked Anneke Wills and Michael Craze to be the guinea pigs for this new venture, but after poor Michael passed away they thought that Anneke would no longer be interested, so they asked me. Thing was that she was still interested – quite right, too, mind, a sort of tribute to Michael. I'm pleased to say however, that Frank and Dave didn't want to lose me. So now, instead of there being a double act for the first tape, there will be two singles.
Wish us luck. Mind you, I'm all for new ventures. Always have been.

Anchor
Dearly Beloved. I don't want to sound soppy, but I couldn't have done it without my missis. Thanks love.

Author
Me! I get an invite every year now to the Book Fair at Olympia in London. And now my very own Literary Lunch. Yes, I admit it, I'm very proud and extremely grateful. Grateful particularly, because people have read the book as I hoped they would, with enjoyment, as I wrote it.

B is for:

Bait
Sometimes, when I've got a couple or six hours free, Sophie and I take the fishing gear and trot down to the seashore. I bait the hook and cast the line, as in the days of fishing with my Dad in Aberdeenshire when I was a wee bairn and he was a Minister of the Kirk of Scotland. Sophie bounds up and down like mad and is forever meeting her many doggie chums. I never catch much but a great time is had by all.

C is for:

Cable and Wireless TV
My mate Mei Trow (M.J. Trow), as well as being a prolific author (of *Lestrade* and *Maxwell* novels) and writer of screenplays, also happens to be a history teacher at one of the local schools, so when this company (C&B) contacted me and asked to do a 'Bronson' interview to mark the twentieth anniversary of *Grange Hill,* I gave him a ring. The result of his help was that Samantha Penfold, from Communicopia Ltd., who make programmes for C&B, came up to Mei's school and we did a great interview actually in one of the classrooms.

Car
I've said before that dear Kenny B. has the most fantastic Rolls Royce ever. But it did break down when he left Plymouth.

Mind you, I'm not surprised. Lots of happenings happen at Barry Poland's Plymouth weekends!

Poor Kenny and Val had to wait ages before being towed home and they missed a holiday they'd arranged on the Isle of Wight. One of Ken's old stamping grounds. He's played every theatre and hotel in the country, has Ken.

Car again
My Honda. Bless its little cotton tyres. Because either I'm provided with transport, car-wise, when I'm over the water in England, or I let the train take the strain, my dear little Honda Civic is so underused nowadays that its battery has almost gone flat. A far cry from the *G.H.* days. Five hundred miles a week round the M25 – in a Rover. No disrespect to Honda, mind.

Canada
I'm off there quite soon to do a compilation of events.

Computer
Please wish me luck, I'm still hoping to get my head around this new blinking machine. We've had cartridge trouble today. And each time I press paragraph, it goes from the typeface I want, into . . .

this . . . which is tiny and I most definitely do not want!

Chums
Thank you all for making my visits to conventions, book signings, charity events and everything so hugely enjoyable. Let me give just two examples of your kindness. I arrived at MidCon and found that I'd left my re-chargeable razor in Rupert's flat (son number two). I couldn't leave the opening festivities to buy a replacement throwaway scraper that could

fill in for the weekend. At least a dozen apps offered to do the shopping for me.

I put a call out for photos for this book. If I tell you that it took Dearly B. and me almost two days to whittle the hundreds that I received down to the comparative few included here, you'll get an idea of everyone's kindness. If I've not thanked you before, THANK YOU ALL VERY MUCH!

D is for:

DOG. Dandy, Dapper, Daredevil, Daring, Dashing, Darling, Dazzling, Debonair, Dependable, Dignified, Devoted, Disciplined, Domesticated. Over the years we've been honoured that Lance, Bengie, Haggis, Monty, and Sophie have shared their lives with us. Sophie - our first lady - is still sharing of course.

E is for:

Edinburgh – Live TV

I remember this one because it was early. Very early in the morning, that is, not my career! It was the Capsicon weekend on the morning of the first day. The idea was that I should be driven from my hotel to the studios, do the interview, and then be taken to the convention venue. Nothing much wrong with that. Except that it's not too easy to be the bright bushy convention figurehead, when you've had a rather late night and you're due at the venue at eight a.m., which means you have to leave for the studio at six-forty-five, too early for the hotel to give you breakfast. Actually, I can be, and am, bright at any time of course!

The idea of these pre-convention interviews, be they TV or radio, is of course to publicise the event and we, the very comely Scottish interviewer lassie and I, had a great time pushing Capsicon. The numbers attending the convention were certainly improved. Although, as I've already reported, I, and others, think it was not a good plan to hold Capsicon during the Edinburgh Festival. Far, far too many other distractions.

E-mail
How do I do it? For this, the alphabet section, I typed in some of the headings first, as they occurred to me. I'm leaving for rehearsal shortly, and I thought I'd check to see if there are any e-mails. This coincided with E in the alphabet. How's that for timing? By the way, what a great boon the e-mail is. I've e-mailed all over the world, everybody. I think I can work it now. Mind you, I still can't believe that I can e-mail as many people as I choose, but Karl Eldridge (and he should know) and others tell me I can, and all for the cost of a local call. Marvellous.

I've just returned from rehearsals and it occurred to me on the way home that I must tell you about the stuck e-mails. We've all had blocked loos, well, this time I had blocked e-mails! As I've said, I'd sent a pile of the things, and I got not one solitary reply. OK, not everyone answers, but none?

As I'm very new to all this, I rang my server.

'Ah,' the very-young-man-who-knows-all-about-computers-that's-why-he's-in-the-job, said, 'you've got a blocked one.'

'But what do I do about it?' asked I.

'Oh that's very simple. Just do this, and a little bit of that . . .' yeah, then turn around the corner and stand on your head!

But I did do what he said and I was suddenly flooded with forty-eight, yes *forty-eight*, e-mails. I'm still trying to sort those forty-eight out!

F is for:

Fun

That's what it's all about and I pity anyone who attends conventions and does not enjoy themselves. I know that Kenny, Peter, Jeremy, Michael, Julian, Angus, Mike, Declan, Nicholas, Colin, Sylvester, Femi, Caroline, Sophie (Aldred not the dog!), Warwick, Ken, *et* most everyone else (and if I haven't mentioned you, please forgive me) would certainly agree with me.

Fiona

Fiona Templeton is a) a super Scottish lassie and b) one of the most dedicated of apps. She it was of course who posed with me, at Sandy's Aberdeen DrakCon, for the great cartoons which intersperse these lines.

The second, or perhaps it was the third time I met this lady I didn't recognise her. Fiona and I had chatted at Scott McMillan's Aberdeen 'do', but when the time came for the fancy dress parade, I had no idea that Pinhead, with all those ghastly needles sticking out of its head just as they were in the movie, was in fact Fiona! She won the fancy dress, as she has on several subsequent occasions. Not, I hastily add, because she is a nice lady, but because the head, the costume and all the accessories – have been made by her and are truly excellent. Woe betide anyone who enters a fancy dress with Fiona!

Future Plans

Happily there are always lots of those. Where to start? Let's see, I've talked already of *First Frontier*, *Millennium Blue*, *Manic Moonsters* and (your movie!) *Day of the Anorak*. But have I mentioned *Maxwell*, which will go, and *Chaos*, which probably will not? (Actually, probably it will, now. I'm skipping through these pages for a final time before taking them to Stewart (publisher) and last week I had a fax saying that *Chaos* is back on. Hooray! Garrick Hagon, I and all are delighted.)

I know what I've not talked of, *Connemara Days*, 'cos it only came up just now.

In the list of my very favourite movies, *The Quiet Man* rates extremely high and I've just heard, by the post this morning, that there's a script on its way to me for a film called *Connemara Days*. I'm thrilled to bits. It tells the story of the making of *The Quiet Man*, and Andrew V. McLaglan – his dad, Victor, of course, played Will Danaher, 'Squire Darlin' in that lovely 1952 John Ford classic – is to be an adviser. I gave one of my four Hitlers in *The Dirty Dozen – The Next Mission*, a movie which Andrew directed. I'm looking forward to meeting him again.

And there's lots more happening. Book signings and Literary Lunches, and my convention diary reads like a 'Who's Who' of, almost, the world – Nashville, Virginia, Chicago, St. Louis, Barcelona (Dearly B. is coming to that one), Germany, Belgium, Australia, and nearly every city and town in the UK – Manchester, Dudley, Bournemouth, Newcastle, Ruislip, Birmingham, Northampton, Cambridge, Liverpool, Edinburgh, Belfast, Chesterfield, Glasgow, and I've just had an e-mail inviting me back to The Norbreck Castle in Blackpool, scene of Mr D. Prowse's Multicon.

Oh it goes on, hopefully forever!

Famous
Nah, not me – well, just a wee bit perhaps!

G is for:

Grampian TV
Do you remember that Peterhead convention where we were snowed in on the first day, and Scott and I were invited to the Matsons' for dinner and had that 120 per cent proof? Well, in

the afternoon of that second day, Grampian TV, in the shape of a young lady (who looked, to my semi-veteran eyes at any rate, as though she was about ten) slushed her way from Aberdeen sixty-odd miles away to do a wee piece about me.

And she did the lot with no crew, she was entirely on her own. Having driven herself through the fast thawing snow, she operated the camera, asked the questions and she'd have held the mike, too, if I hadn't offered to take it from her. It was about three-thirty p.m. when we finished and she'd got back to the (former tram depot) studios in Aberdeen, had edited the film (herself) and we saw it that same evening on the six o'clock news. And it was darn good.

Eh, they don't 'alf work them hard!

Glasses

In fact another Peterhead. The bar in the Palace hotel was huge – it has to be my imagination, but there seem to be more large bars in Scotland than anywhere else – and it was always full. Great for the owner and also great for me, because we were snowed in on the first day. The only customers able to reach the hotel were the locals and a contingent from a nearby RAF base who had skied down the hill for all I know. These lovely people had come for the drink you understand, not the convention. Anyway, on the Saturday night the place was really packed, it was worse than London's rush hour on the underground. We were literally shoulder to shoulder.

I was in my element. Having thought I'd not sell one book, I just stood at the bar and people all but clawed their way to me. It was marvellous. Except that, in midst of the foray, I heard this voice, 'I want a souvenir of Mr Bronson', and a hand came round from behind me and my glasses were whipped off my nose. I turned round as smartly as I could, but the souvenir spectacles and hunter had disappeared in the crowd.

Thank God I always carry a spare.

George

I told George Merrill I was going to pop him in.

George was aged only eleven when we met but he was one hell of a pain! It was at a *Dr Who* convention, during the Q&A. Every time someone asked me a question about a part I'd played, before I had a chance to reply George would pipe up:

'I didn't like it. I hated that. I wouldn't even watch that one.'

In truth it was really quite amusing and it got to the point where I'd defer to him before I'd answer. But his Dad was obviously embarrassed and took him outside, in spite of my protestations that it wasn't necessary.

About ten minutes later they returned and George came up to the stage and handed me a scruffy piece of paper on which he'd written the following – I read it out to the assembled audience who loved it:

'Dear Mr Sheard. I don't hate you. I hate the parts you play. You play them very well but I hate them. I like you. Honest.'

Games

I love my sport and used to try my hand at most. Cricket (I was pretty good at this, remember that end of year cricket match in *Grange Hill*? I choreographed it), bowls, hockey, tennis. But nowadays I don't seem to have time to do much more than catch the football results. No, hang on. As mentioned under B for Bait, I do pop down to the beach occasionally for an auld lang syne fish with Sophie, and about twice a year I get on to a golf course.

Gwen

Gwen Glover is my discovery. I told you about my production of *Shirley Valentine*, well, we had a dress rehearsal last week to which a few special guests were invited. Dearly B. thought Gwen's performance was one of the best she'd seen. On the opening night she got a long standing ovation which made headlines in the press: 'Standing Ovation for the Great Shirley'.

H is for:

Happiness

I'm happy. Dearly B. will say that I'm being sentimental, but, yes, I am – happy. I've got a great family – two wonderful sons and Doctor Susannah is about to make us grandparents again this year – a smashing artist wife, a super career, many great mates, some lovely things coming up. I hope you are happy, too. Those of you I've met at conventions most certainly seem to be.

Hope

Here's hoping that it continues!

Hepworth

Andy Hepworth, the flippin' marvellous artist of numerous games manuals. We first met at Edinburgh's Capsicon and he shouted at me, 'Oh do stop talking, Michael. Stop trying to sell your book. I'll buy a copy from you, so long as you stop talking!' Of course I didn't, and I sold out, and he did, despite everything, buy a copy. We've become the very best of mates.

I spoke to him on the phone yesterday and when I asked him if he'd like a mention, he said, to my amazement, because he is a very quiet chap, 'Yes please.' He must like the idea of the publicity, that's it! And that also means that he thinks this one will sell well, too. I'm delighted, Andrew, to give you full recognition in these pages. Thanks for becoming a chum, mate. I'll try and be quieter next time.

Hannam

John Hannam is a show business reporter, who has his own local radio show along the lines of 'Desert Island Discs'. I've done it several times. John is a very nice guy. Even got me a job for Meridian TV. They were doing a celebration of the works of Alfred Lord Tennyson – who spent many years on the Isle of Wight – and they asked John if he knew of a resident who could read some of Tennyson's poetry. I'm a resident as often as I can be, so John asked me. The programme was great! I was filmed walking along the cliff edge on Tennyson Down, near Freshwater Bay, reading from a book of the great man's poetry. I was wearing a long full-skirted, romantic looking black coat (borrowed from John Hannam), and was almost blown over the brink in the force 8 gale!

I is for:

Icons
Icons Authentic Replicas, Inc. This is the organisation we mostly work with when we do conventions in America. Some of the very small ones operate independently – Virginia for example and my convention trip to Canada – but Icons are the main entrepreneurs. They produce the photos that Pam and Doug Murray organise and that we then sign. The Murrays are freelance agents, but are sort of affiliated to Icons. Everyone over there is great and supports us to the hilt. Thank you one and all. See you soon.

J is for:

January
January is the slow, empty month. Time to be at home and get books finished. Except, and we're back to computers again, I've just had another blocked e-mail. Too late, this time, darn it. It was a last minute invite to a role-playing convention in Cork, Ireland. I was free and I'd have enjoyed it.

K is for:

Kiss
I've racked my brains. I've just the vaguest recollection that, very many years ago, when I was a member of the Perth Repertory Theatre Company (mentioned earlier – and where I met you-know-who), I did kiss the . . . hand of Elizabeth Jill Howard, my leading lady in our production of *Meet Me By Moonlight*, and I certainly buried my head in Valerie Lush's bosom during that same Perth season. The play was Ibsen's *Ghosts*, I was playing Oswald and she was my Mum. But apart

from that I have never kissed anyone, in thespian love, either on stage, TV, or film.

I had an e-mail yesterday from a lady in America, Mary Stadter, who said:

'Looking forward to your joining us in St. Louis for our convention. We've been re-running some of your triumphs. You get killed in nearly all of them.'

So much more satisfying!

Kiss Me Kate

Just wanted to pop this super movie in. It's on Dearly B.'s and my favourite list, we love it. For me anyway, it's Howard Keel and Kathryn Grayson at their very best. And here's a wee extra. *Kiss Me Kate* is dated 1953. The actor who plays Keel's valet – which is a nice, but quite small part – is Claude McAllister who, in 1929, played the co-starring role of Algy, side-kick to Ronald Colman's Bulldog Drummond, in the movie of that name. I'm sure Claude was still loving just being involved in moviemaking in '53, he certainly looks as if he is. I know, I've said before that actors are like soldiers (never dying). Here's hoping we all carry on until we fade away.

L is for:

Love

Oh heavens, it's soppy time again. How many different types of love are there? There's love of my profession, certainly; love of my fellow thespian chums; love of you, the apps, most definitely; but at the end of any day, I'm sure you'll agree, love of a Dearly Beloved and the three wonderful kids she's given me is the very best love of all. Thank you, I'm blushing, so I'll move on!

London

I'll be honest, London is a place I have to visit for work, I like
the theatres and the galleries *et* everything, but I don't like the
place that much. Too busy. We used to live there when we
were first married, in a little basement flat not far from Notting
Hill Gate. And we were burgled. We didn't have much at the
time, I'd only just started to get on to the telly trail.

Amongst other virtually worthless items, such as our small
portable radio, Dearly B. lost a beautiful and treasured
Wedgwood table-lighter (in those days it was fashionable to
smoke, neither of us do now) and I lost one of a pair of
bongo drums which Dearly B. had bought for me on our
honeymoon. I've still got the other, but why nick just one?
Why steal any of it? Daft.

Loony-Tunes

I have a show reel which includes some fifteen minutes of
clips from something in the region of a dozen of my
stupendous portrayals. Well, you remember the cartoon pig
who says, 'Th.. Th.. Th.. That's all folks!'? I've popped him at
the end of the compilation (apologies to the company who
own him – it's not for public display). It comes after a clip
from *The Riddle of the Sands*, to show whoever is watching –
hopefully some very high-powered Hollywood producer – that
this is indeed the end of my tape.

Loonies, I love you. In fact I love all cartoons. I have my
Pooh Bear watch (a birthday gift from the kids), and my Pooh
and Mickey Mouse bow ties (birthday presents from Pam
Clarke and her mates), and this Christmas I received a Sylvester
and Tweety Pie bow tie from my pal, Allan Pal.

Luvvies

A lot of people don't like this word as it suggests that we in my profession are OTT. Bloody daft. Stupid. I don't particularly like the word myself. In fact, only the other day, at a WHSmiths book signing no less, I had a guy say, 'No thank you, I never buy books about luvvies. I don't like the word', and I agreed with him. But what the hell, the word luvvie does explain one aspect of my 'lovely' profession, the one I've been endeavouring to communicate to you throughout these pages. We are a loving profession. We do 'love' each other – in the most 'butch' way and sense of the word of course, especially when it comes to the likes of Uncle Peter and Father Jeremy, Kenny and their ilk!

M is for:

'Manchester Evening News'

They did a nice job when I attended the Fab Café's opening and I thank them for it. There are times, as we all know, when some of the media can stretch things to suit their purpose. (My meeting with a nice gentle hulk of an appreciator on the train to Portsmouth was pulled out of all proportion. It was reported, quite wrongly, that I'd been mugged.) But a lot of the press is fair and their reporters are good eggs and friends. Two papers I would pick out from a vast number, are 'The Manchester Evening News', and that other eveninger, 'The Aberdeen Evening Express'. Thank you, you two, for leading the way.

Moaning

Oh no, please don't. Moaning is destructive. I'm leaving moaning quickly. But please, before I do, don't for goodness sake let us bemoan our lot. I may sound like my daily newspaper's astrologer, but there always has to be something good around the corner. Oh heck, soppy again. Let's move quickly on to . . .

N is for:

Nubrubble

As in 'New' – brubble of course. He just had to get a further mention. I had a call from Danny (Flynn) the other day and he says that the pilot for *Manic Moonsters* is looking even greater.

O is for:

Orchestration

When I was in Wales, Rhyl, I visited a Sci-Fi shop. Well, a Sci-Fi-and-lots-of-other-goodies-as-well shop, like records and posters. I was presented with an excellent compilation of Alice Cooper hits, including 'School's Out', and a poster for that favourite film of mine, Warner's *The Adventures of Robin Hood* – sorry, *Les Aventures de Robin des Bois* – it's in French!

'School's Out' I've spoken of already – at least a couple of times! But it very clearly illustrates how important is the presentation of music. We really zing along to this number at convention discos. Had it been recorded differently I know it wouldn't have that special extra . . . something. In my production of *Shirley Valentine,* I wanted the music from *Zorba the Greek* to introduce the second act, which is set in Greece. Ian, my producer and stage manager, found a recording and brought it along to rehearsal. It was completely wrong, it hadn't the bite of the original, it did nothing for the production and I rejected it. Next week Ian arrived with the track as used in the movie. It is superb.

As I write, I'm remembering one of the epilogues in *Yes, Mr Bronson* where I talk of movie sequels – which were most often made by another producer – and how it's very difficult for a sequel to approach anywhere near the excellence of a first masterpiece, which has prompted the makers to go for a second in the first place. The same can be said of music, it's almost impossible to recapture the passion of a hit, but the record companies keep trying. And cover versions – ugh! Far better to go for something completely different.

Robin des Bois is a remarkable film and I love it, and the joy of Erich Wolfgang Korngold's music is magical and fits this super film like a beautiful satin glove.

OTT

I was going to say 'like wot I've just bin!' But I won't 'cos I mean every word.

It's a strange phenomenon is 'Over the Top'. In the heady days of the early talking picture, everyone thesped away like mad, talking thousands to the dozen and still acting as they'd done in their silent screen days, which of course now comes across as grossly OTT.

Then along came an Englishman named Ronald Colman – mentioned earlier. He'd been using his laid back method of acting during his silent career, but no one had taken a blind bit of notice, then, when talkies arrived, he almost single-handedly, certainly in Dearly B.'s and my opinion, transformed the art of film acting. With his seemingly understated, six inches behind the eyes style, and his beautiful voice, he demonstrated, in his very first talkie, *Bulldog Drummond*, that the secret of film acting was *being*, not acting. (I'm sure, by the way, that *Bulldog D.* was Ronald Colman's first talkie, but if anyone knows differently, do let me know!) The film was made in 1929 by Samuel Goldwyn, and it's the one I already mentioned, in which Algy was played to perfection by Claude McAllister, another Englishman.

It wouldn't be fair if I left OTT without mentioning one group of my thespian buddies who at first glance would seem to be well over the limits of what is natural. The Personalities, with a capital P.

Heavens, let's see: Kenneth Williams, Jack Douglas, Charles Hawtrey, Frankie Howerd, Norman Wisdom, Alistair Sim even, and Lionel Jeffries are just a sprinkling. There are many others – Americans, too! Gene Wilder and Mel Brooks for example. But they still play everything with truth. That's the secret of 'being': truth. They may be playing themselves and their personalities may appear larger than life, but that is how they are. And they are true.

(I confess I'm not quite sure about Robert Newton as Long John Silver, but I think that even he, with his rolling eyes and manic leer, was still truthful – to himself. He most certainly dominated the screen.)

Oscars

For me? Of course not. Not yet anyway! But I have played in three productions which received BAFTA awards as best in their category for the year: *Grange Hill* (best children's); *Caught on a Train* (best single play); *Taking over the Asylum* (best serial): and 'Thieves', the half hour two-hander I did for Scottish Television which won a prestigious accolade in America.

PS from Dearly B: 'I've never seen 'Thieves'. If anyone knows where I can get hold of a copy, I'd be very grateful if you could let me know.'

P is for:

Production

Yes, we still have our production company. A hobby, an extra-curricular little affair, but our own. At this time we have four spankingly good properties in various stages of development and *Maxwell* (see *Yes, Mr B.*) is still the front runner.

Post-synching
This, for me, is the least enjoyable part of my job. How can you hope to create what you did on the set? Mind you, doing a voice from scratch, as in *Manic Moonsters*, or narrating a travelogue, is entirely different. And also mind you, my post synching is still second to none!

Q is for:

Questions
As it was in the last book. I know that the others who tread the convention circuit feel the same as I do about what can be quite a tricky situation. As I said earlier, the 'how can I get into the business' questions are fairly uncommon from appreciators, but they do arise, and when they do, they are more difficult to answer. Because they're more pressing and more searching than those which were asked by the youngsters on *G.H.*. It's possible, too, that I get more 'how do I's than the others, because there's hardly a week goes past without my appearing on the box somewhere.

I promise you, I fully understand those who are eager, even desperate, to perform before the cameras, and my advice has to be the same as that which I gave to the children who reached the top of *Grange Hill* school and were about to leave. If you really, really want to get into show business and it is really, really the only thing you have ever wanted to do, then go for it. If you don't you'll never forgive yourself for not trying. It doesn't matter a hoot if you're two, twenty-two or fifty.

How? Ah, that's the 64,000-dollar question, but if you are really, really, really determined, you'll find a way. Go to The Spotlight, in Leicester Place, London, buy a copy of their booklet, 'Contacts', and write letters – hundreds of them – and knock on doors – thousands of them. Keep smiling, never be discouraged (or if you are don't show it) and Good Luck!

Quarrels

I don't really know why I put this one in. We never quarrel, not on the set, in the bar afterwards, or at home, do we? Ha! Of course we do, everyone does, and if they deny it they're telling porkies. This wonderful, bloody state-of-the-art computer in front of me can bear witness to that. Even Dearly B. and I have had a few tight words as we struggle with its complexities. But they never last, that's the point. Any tiddly problems are usually due to thespian anxieties and nothing else, absolutely nothing. If a fellow actor is having trouble, we listen, or stay clear, as the situation warrants, and then, when the storm has passed, we are 'luvvies' again, no problem. I read in my paper this morning for example, that John Nettles' ex-wife, Joyce, is the all-important casting director on John's series *Midsomer Murders*. It is a lovely profession.

R is for:

Restaurants

Yeah, well, I'm not about to do an Egon Ronay. But I do like to eat well and remember some great feasting houses around the world. I'm not going to single out any specific ones, except perhaps to say that I, personally, have probably encountered more good ones in America. If you're hungry the plates are always piled high. The Americans seem to dine out far more than we do, maybe that's it. And there's always the possibility of a line dance, eh Kenny?!

I was only remarking to Dearly B. this morning that all over the world it seems that the food available is healthier than it used to be. This morning, for example, Sophie (our Sophie – not Aldred!) found a discarded hamburger in the street and I swear even it was a healthier burger than of old. There was masses of salad.

Revenue, as in Tax
Just thought I'd mention that I'm still with Neil (Welch). After my accountant troubles in the past, it's nice to have some stability. He comes over once in the early part of the year, sits on our floor with Sophie (because he likes dogs), and tells us what he's done. Then we sign the forms and he plays with our computer – well, he did this year, he knows about these things you see.

(Although he gave permission for me to include his letter, Neil, by the way, has not yet seen what I've written. I'm keeping him on tenterhooks!)

S is for:

Sci-Fi
Of course it is. It is very fair to say that without Sci-Fi I wouldn't have had anything like the great times I've had.

All of them stand at the front of the line, and I am very grateful to them, and I thank them for opening the convention door. The fact that I've done most of them is, perhaps, the reason why I can cross the bridges to those I have not yet done –being an honoured guest at the *Star Trek* film première for instance. And you wait until I have *First Frontier* and *Manic Moonsters* under my belt. It's just been pointed out by Dearly B. that *Moonsters* is already there! Well, I have done the pilot!

Thank you Sci-Fis all.

Star Wars magazine
Harrison, Luke, Carrie, Peter, Kenny, Jeremy, Dave (and for all I know, old Uncle Ratty) have all featured in the official *Star Wars* magazine, and so have I! And didn't they do me proud? Two full pages, photos, words – very nice ones written by Chris Gardner. The magazine must have done well the week my article appeared, I've lost count of the number of

copies I've autographed at conventions, but it has to be thousands! Marcus Hearn, the editor, sent me a complimentary one. He also gave *Yes, Mr B.* a super review in a later edition. He's done me many kindnesses.

'Sport'
'The Daily Sport' this time as opposed to its sister paper 'The Sunday Sport'.

You'll recall the merry quip that appeared in that publication after my second great evening at the Fab Café in Manchester. Debbie Manley is a nice girl and spends a lot of time in the Fab Café, so she's got good taste too. She rang me yesterday:

'Michael, you know this couple who've been in the news for taking part in a blind wedding?' (A local radio station had held a competition which culminated in an all expenses paid lush wedding and foreign honeymoon for the winners, the twist being that they had never met before the ceremony.)

'Yes,' I replied wondering what on earth was coming, but knowing the sort of paper she works for, having a pretty good idea.

'Well, we're going to hire a top hotel bedroom for the night, add all the trimmings – wonderful dinner, drinks and breakfast – and run a competition for a blind tryst!'

'Yes, Debbie, I get the idea. So how can I help? Sorry, but my Dearly B. wouldn't allow me to be the pot of gold at the end of the rainbow.'

'No, no, of course not. But I'm ringing celebrities to ask them who they'd like to have a blind bedroom date with. (Refined is Debbie.) Who would you like to meet under the sheets?'

'Debbie, I'm sorry luv, I'm terribly square, I guess. I'll meet Dearly Beloved there with very great pleasure.'

And there it was left. Debbie did say she might pop a quote in from Mr Bronson. Something like 'You will take care', but that's up to her. She also added that she would send me some photos for this book. The ones they took in the Fab Café that fabulous night.

Stag

Wow! No, hang on, and let me tell you a story. Before I start, though, I must go on record as saying that what I witnessed on the night in question was real performing, by heck it was. I'm thus very pleased to have this opportunity to propel into the spotlight for a moment a hitherto unsung pocket of my profession. Yes, I know, I talked about naughty movies in *Yes, Mr B.* but I've not mentioned live girlie shows before.

It all started with Aaron, producer Ian Rofe's son, and it went like this:

'Are you there?' Ian always starts with that question when he phones at the crack of night and finds that we've put the answerphone on, 'are you there?'

I reluctantly pick up the phone. 'Yes, I'm here, what is it now? Have you no idea of time? Some of us have been busy you know.'

'Oh yes?'

And so the banter goes on. Finally he gets to the point. 'The Rotary Club are having a dinner and my nipper has some spare seats, do you want to go?'

Now you may well not believe this, but I've never enjoyed putting my nose where its not wanted and stealing another's thunder, honest. I like an evening out, don't we all, but this was a Rotary 'do' and I felt that it would be wrong for me to attend. It was their night, not mine, and most certainly not Bronson's or any of the other parts I've played. So I told Ian my feelings. 'Oh you don't need to worry about that,' he said, 'they won't be bothered with you, they'll be looking elsewhere. This is stag. I'll put you down then. Bye.' And he hung up.

So it was that on a cold evening in October I attended the Pavilion – bowling downstairs, function room above. Large function room, with dance floor in the middle and a well stocked bar behind. We were all dressed in dinner suits. It was a proper pukka 'do'.

The moment Scott Charlton, the compère, strode on to the floor and started his blue patter, I knew it was going to be very stag. (Scott's a damn good comedian and we've since become firm friends, even talked of doing panto together, he as Buttons me as a wicked Mr Bronsonish Baron.)

There were three small, very slim young ladies, who, when they got their kit off – which they did in record time – were completely bald from the neck down. Each did a turn on her own in the first half, which included grabbing a chap from the audience and stripping him and . . . things. In the second half two of the girls did things together, then the third one joined in and they grabbed another seemingly unsuspecting gent and . . . etc – things. There was much laughter, masses of white aerosol foam, and I kept on the move in case they thought it a grand wheeze to grab a celebrity, and the evening finally ended in time for them to catch the last catamaran back to the mainland.

I'm going to the Starfleet Ball in Bournemouth in a couple of weeks. One of the highlights is The Pyjama Party and I'm looking forward to pulling my oversized jamjam top over my suit. But stag isn't my scene. I'm no prude, I'm sure you know that. But – I don't know. Those times when we were re-voicing the porno movies, then we could laugh at the performers and their antics, because it was film. Here we could certainly laugh *with* the girls and *at* their victims. But it would have been wrong to laugh at the girls themselves, because they were there in front of us. All there! And they were working, they were doing their job.

I was returning from filming some six weeks later. I was extremely tired when I got on the catamaran for the short crossing to my Island, so I found a seat, sat down, and closed my eyes. 'Hello Michael.' I reluctantly opened them, looked up, and blow me there was Scott, accompanied by the girls. They were on a return visit because, as one of the three put it when we got chatting:

'That show you came to went really well. Everything worked perfectly just like we'd rehearsed. And don't worry, you were never a target. Scott works out the guys we're going to strip. Didn't you see him standing behind the next one? That's our cue. It's all rehearsed, didn't you know?'

No, I confess I didn't. I didn't think so, but maybe I'm still a wee bit naïve. These lasses and Scott had rehearsed and choreographed their show as tirelessly as we rehearsed *Shirley Valentine*. I may not say 'see you on the green', but I most certainly wish them the very best of Good Luck.

T is for:

The Teviot Students' Union
Conpulsion. Karen and Colin, now Mr and Mrs MacNeil, were at this one, as were Andrew Harman, the writer, together with his missis, and many old friends, so for the life of me I can't put my finger on the reason why it didn't work, either as an event, or as a gaming convention. I just don't know, I don't think the organisers know either.

But I do have a suggestion. When I'm convention bound I always enquire of the organisers how many appreciators they're expecting so that I can gauge the number of books I need to order. On this occasion I was told 350–400. Perhaps that was the reason they did virtually no advertising. They were complacent. Very foolish. Much less than half that number attended.

U is for:

Umbrella
Ever since I was completely drenched on my way to a con in Coventry, right at the start of my trip down the convention lane (my suit was a shambles, thank God for the trouser press in the hotel room) I have carried an umbrella, even when the sun is brightly shining. Only a small one, which fits in my bag, but it's saved the day on many a trip.

Unknown
Soppy time again! We've just installed some new bookcases, and Dearly B. has been busily re-shelving our library. She's found a diary she kept just after we became engaged and we were suddenly separated. Ros went on the Highland Perth Theatre tour and I was on the Lowland. In the few quiet moments she had, she wrote. She described her surroundings of course, but mostly she wrote, very sweetly, about me. About our love and her feelings.

We were completely unknown then. Now, here we are today. She's forging ahead as an artist of increasing renown. She's had her own show, as well as having had her work hung in some of the top exhibitions and art galleries in London, and I, well, I admitted earlier under F that I'm perhaps just a wee bit famous. Oh, yeah, nearly forgot (as if I could), we've also produced along the way, that accountant, that doctor and that history/politics teacher. OK, end of last soppy.

Underground
One of these days soon, a great fiction will be on the bookshop bookshelves. It's been on the Sheard back burner whilst I've been enjoying the writing of *Yes, Mr B.* and this offering. *Day for Death – The Piccadilly Run* however, first in a series of thrillers featuring that ace detective, Superintendent Derek Day, is

written by Dearly Beloved, with the tables turned and just the odd suggested edit from me. It will be with you 'ere very long, so watch out for it.

Why underground? Ah, well, that's where the murdered man plied his blackmailing trade, on the Piccadilly line!

V is for:

Video

I must say a quick word for video, which simply bounds ahead in its capabilities. I've seen feats accomplished on video recently – *Manic Moonsters* for example – which could never have been contemplated even five years ago. The advent of the computer has greatly enhanced the possibilities possible with video.

W is for:

Who

Right, let's get a wee bit less jocular. I've had many letters about this, and even received one this morning, asking about the possibility of my being the next Dr Who. So let me set the record straight as far as I can.

Yes, I did receive a phone call, which was followed by a letter of intent, asking if I'd be interested in playing Dr Who. If, and it is a very huge if, the rights to the Peter Cushing *Dr Who* movies could be obtained. Three were optioned, only two were made.

I would love to play the part and I've said that many times, but all I can add is that the independent producer who first called me is still in deep and seemingly endless negotiations. Tell you what, perhaps you could write to Auntie Beeb and tell her that you want me to be the next Who . . . not a bad idea. In fact a blooming excellent one. Casting by appreciator power. I love it!

Who – again!

Now then, this only came up a couple of days ago. It has been suggested that there should be a third volume from the keyboard of Sheard. You've had *Yes, Mr Bronson*, still one of my publishers' bestsellers, now *Yes, Admiral* is with you, what about . . . 'Yes, Rhos, Dr Summers, Lowe, Scarman, Mergrave and The Headmaster'?

Hmm. If there is to be another one, which does now seem likely, I'd prefer . . . 'Yes, Who?' What do you think?

Let me know. Heavens, if I'm going to be cast by you, you should certainly have a say in the title of my book.

X is for:

The X Files

I couldn't think of an X, so Dearly B. came up with this programme – simply because it's a Sci-Fi that I haven't appeared in. Yet!

Y is for:

You

Because you make it all worthwhile.

Z is for:

Zoroaster

As in *Reporting Christ*, a wee series. No it wasn't, it was a great series. And it came right at the start of my TV career, so it's important. Only important here, though, because I couldn't think of a Z either and Dearly B. again suggested it. Zoroaster was around any time between 600 and 6,000 years BC, nobody knows quite when!

Yes, *Reporting Christ* was a good series, I played a modern day TV reporter who travelled back in time – *Dr Who*-wise – to interview people and talk about events as they happened. Another Sci-Fi!

Zany
You wait till I tell you about those costumes at the Starfleet Ball. The Ball hasn't happened yet, but it will, in a fortnight's time. I'm going to finish with the Starfleet Ball.

And here it is Boom – BOOM!
I've just returned with aching limbs from all that dancing at the Starfleet Ball – there were three dances on successive evenings! On the opening night we had the pyjama party and I'd like to name just five out of hundreds who attended. First, the very likeable and very large Ramsden brothers, Matt and Adam, and their small chum Dave. These three were the first to buy my book, almost before I'd got in the door, and I promised I'd give them a mention. Matt's invited me to his wedding in September. I wonder what he'd like as a present? The new book perhaps!

The other two I want to present are Melanie Hill, who was extremely fetching in a baby-gro, and Andy, who made a delightful Andy Pandy. I mention these two because not only were their costumes excellent and home made, but here are two of those few appreciators who really would like to go further and get into show business. We were able to have a chat on the Monday (going home day) morning. I hope I helped with my: 'Do you want to be an actor?' question, followed, when the answer was a resounding yes, by: 'But do you *need* to be one? Because, if you can't also answer yes to that, don't even try it.' Both answered with very firm affirmatives I'm pleased to say. I think they should have a go.

Here's a wee addition I'm dropping in during my final edit. I couldn't do so before, because, until two days ago, I'd not had the lady's permission to include an incident from the Cardiff charity film première of *Star Trek – Insurrection*. The lady in question being the above mentioned Melanie.

If you remember I was the auctioneer, with a little help from my friends. I was standing on a chair and in full swing, when Melanie, who'd been sitting on the floor to my right, got up and walked in front and, as I was on the chair, beneath me. Thing was, she was wearing the most gorgeous pale pink low cut ball gown – very low. And as I looked down, nothing was left to my imagination, I could see all the way to her feet. How everything stayed in place – or perhaps it should be, inside – I shall never know. Melanie caught my eye – almost literally, for it sure was down with her – giggled like a schoolgirl, clasped the top of the dress to her, and cried, 'Oops! Sorry.'

'Not at all,' I said, 'it was my pleasure.'

Everyone laughed, including Melanie, who then proceeded serenely on her way, without turning a hair. That's show(wo)manship.

The Masked Ball was held on the second evening and was preceded by a most excellent dinner – presented to over two hundred of us by the Moat House, in Bournemouth, where the convention was held. The Ball has to be the pinnacle of an exceptional weekend. The mostly period costumes – I recall particularly some superb seventeenth-century examples – were quite fantastic.

Mind you, the karaoke on the last night was great, too. (Everything was.) This gave everyone a chance to let their hair down. I found an Iain, an Aberdonian like me (hence the Scottish spelling), among the attendees and with his help I reprised 'The Northern Lights', just for Richard Arnold, the

Star Trek expert, who was also a guest at this one. Remember him? Last time, in Aberdeen, at the closing ceremony, I'd got the audience to join me in singing this lovely song. Richard was next in line to say his goodbyes and could only splutter, 'How the hell do I follow that?' But he must be learning; Richard has promised to join in at the next rendition!

Oh heck, there's so much more to tell and so little time. I'm due in Honiton next weekend – as I've said already, doesn't time fly – and I tried so hard at the Starfleet Ball to make myself heard above the music that even I have virtually no voice left. (I know, the answer is to talk 'under' it in a whisper, but that's not always practicable.)

The three dances at Starfleet didn't finish until well after midnight. Then it was off to the bar, which (Dearly B. please note), I was *told* didn't close until five a.m. at the earliest. I was a good boy, I left, oh, by at least three-forty-five.

So even though I got to my bed early-ish, I'm still quite bushed, and I've still the epilogue to do.

Let me close on the Starfleet Ball by saying that there *is* more. It's hoped that *First Frontier* will celebrate its launch there next year, and my love and gratitude for a wonderful three days go to Anne Lindup (the Boss), Paul Rouse (thanks for putting up with my fledgling e-mail efforts, mate), B., James, Annie, and every blessed one of you. One three day visit is not nearly long enough. As Dave Prowse would say, please ask me back.

(And it does go happily on. I checked for e-mails just now, before leaving for my publishers with everything ready, and there was a lovely letter from two super ladies, Chris and Jude, whom I've met at several conventions – MidCon, Continuum, etc. They said they were sorry to have missed the Starfleet Ball, but were looking forward to meeting up with me again at Supernova and other up and coming events, and next year's Ball. It's really great to have so many friends. Now I must run!)

Epilogue 1

Talk about the last minute! We've just got back from Spain, Dearly B. and I. I had a convention in Barcelona and D.B. happily joined me. We've only a very few minutes before I have to leave for Chichester and the publishers, with everything ready, but I thought it would be nice if Dearly B. could quickly give her impressions of our little holiday as we stayed on for a few days after the con.

Here follow, therefore, the only lines not written by me, except of course for Epilogue 2 which was typed ages ago. Over to Dearly B. . . .

IMPRESSIONS OF BARCELONA

Tracking down a spot of lunch for Michael, through the streets of Barcelona, on the setting-up day of the convention at Placa de Sants, and discovering that a baguette was called a 'bikini'. 'Fancy a bikini for lunch?' I asked, raising his hopes!

Exploring the city while Michael worked his socks off. Intrigued by some of the names of metro stations – 'Hospital Clinic'?

Getting delightfully lost exploring the narrow alleyways of the Gothic quarter, some of them so mediaeval that, except for the odd motorbike that suddenly whizzes past, you can imagine *Romeo and Juliet* being played out then and there.

Sitting in the Placa del Pi surrounded by tall six-storey buildings, pink and yellow, all with wrought-iron balconies looking down on the people seated outside the many cafés enjoying, as we did later, lunch of various delicious tapas snacks and local wine.

The wonderful meal we were all invited to at Casa Nostra (I thought it was Cosa Nostra) by the lovely members of the

Star Wars fan club of Spain, and having fun trying to communicate with those who spoke no English.

And the less than lovely meal we had on the Sunday, accompanied by Chris and Fran Baylis. Fran and Chris were sensible and ordered pizza. I was trying to be too clever, with forgotten French and even rustier Latin.

'Oh,' I said to Michael, as I tried to read the menu, '*carne* will be meat. *Pesce* something, must be fish.'

I thought I'd helped him to order a green salad starter (*verde*) followed by a steak. But his starter turned out to be a large plate of sweet mushy peas, and his 'steak' was a slab of bread with small slices of salami that looked like shoe-leather. By the end of the meal we were all dissolved in giggles, helped no doubt by the vino, and the generous measures of spirits dispensed in the hotel bar before this ten p.m. meal.

How we missed Robbie Bulloch – fluent in Spanish – who'd come over with Jeremy to act as interpreter for the guests. This was the one evening we were all doing our own thing.

When the convention had finished, Michael was able to explore the city for himself. We went our separate ways in the mornings and met at lunchtime, as I thought he'd find this more interesting than standing around watching me sketch or going with me to the Picasso museum. And he did! Mind you, he said it was quite by chance that he ended up in the red light district being propositioned by Catalan prostitutes. He beat a very hasty retreat!

The work of artist and architect Antoni Gaudi is in evidence everywhere in Barcelona. Once seen, the Sagrada Familia is never forgotten. His amazing, intricately ornate style is unique.

I must now settle down and plan a painting for Michael as a souvenir. I think he'd like one of La Rambla, the broad thoroughfare that runs through the middle of the old town. The tree-lined central pedestrian walkway is constantly crowded with Spanish and foreign sightseers, jostling with street-theatre performers in all manner and colour of elaborate costume and make-up, including living statues in mediaeval armour.

The brightly coloured Bouqueria market. Beggars parade well-behaved dogs – and even cats – in home-made handcarts. The animals appear to be enjoying themselves – no sign of hardship. Narrow lanes of fast-moving traffic flank the central walkway, and narrow alleyways branch off in every direction into the Gothic quarter. There are tables and chairs everywhere and waiters, with laden trays, dodge the traffic to reach their customers. Noise and colour and life.

It was a lovely trip. I think I'll do Michael's painting on one of the rolls of canvas I couldn't resist buying at that little art shop off the Placa del Pi . . .

Ros Sheard
April 1999

Epilogue 2

Letter from Al Samujh. Dated 3rd April.

> 'Dear Mr Sheard,
> . . . As a child, Sundays and Bank Holidays
> were often spent near Wombourne, on
> Highgate Common. Highgate backs on to
> a small aerodrome, Halfpenny Green . . .'

Right, I promised I'd return to what is fast becoming a detective story of mammoth and fascinating proportions. If you recall I posed the question in *Yes, Mr B.* about whether the aerodrome I guarded during my National Service, name of Halfpenny Green, was the same aerodrome featured in that great movie, *The Way to the Stars*, which was called Halfpenny Field. I've had masses of letters which have endeavoured to unravel the mystery, so many indeed that I'm staggered. Delighted, but decidedly nonplussed.

I imagined that the answer would have been simple. At the end of the day, there are several of the cast and crew still going for heaven's sake. But no, no one can remember for certain. The nearest I've got is when I was working with Johnny Mills and I asked him. He *thought* he was sure that some scenes were shot at Halfpenny Green.

The most sterling detective work has been undertaken by Al Samujh who has become a good chum over the, well, it's almost years already. Golly, doesn't time fly?

Here then are the bulk of two of his letters, which apart from anything give a fascinating glimpse of a country at war, but a country that still managed to produce some cracking movies during those years.

The Way to the Stars was made by Two Cities (Anatole de Grunwald), written by Terence Rattigan and Anatole de Grunwald, and included that wonderful poem by John Pudsey which begins, 'Do not despair for Johnny head in air'. It was directed by Anthony Asquith, and starred John Mills, Rosamund John, Michael Redgrave, Douglass Montgomery, Basil Radford, Stanley Holloway, Joyce Carey, Renee Asherson, Felix Aylmer, Bonar Colleano, Trevor Howard (in I believe his first film role), and Jean Simmons (certainly in hers). It's a corker.

> '. . . We always used to attend the Bank Holiday
> Air Races/Displays at Halfpenny Green.
> You might recall that Prince William
> of Gloucester lost his life in an Air Race
> there in the early seventies. Airfield
> stories abounded – my grandfather had been
> employed in the construction of Lancaster
> bombers – grandma and my mother used to tell
> of the big planes that used Halfpenny Green
> during the war. To us it always seemed too
> small – forgetting that in the '60s the
> third runway had been cut in two by a road;
> an attempt by the Aero Club to avoid paying
> rates. The unused half of the old runway
> is still concrete hardcore and still looks
> very World War II.
> *The Way to the Stars* is one of my favourites,
> too. I like Bonar Colleano, who died far too
> young, as did his widow Susan Shaw.
> I've heard the story many times, from many
> people, that *The Way to the Stars* was filmed
> here at HPG. Finally, after all these years and
> spurred by your memoirs, I went to the town

library's archives. They almost didn't have
anything on Halfpenny Green – it really belongs
to Wombourne Parish. After a little digging,
however, there it was – written evidence that
The Way to the Stars was at least part filmed
at HP Green. And yes, Halfpenny Green was a
large enough airfield. The principal shots
covered here were of the B17s taking off and
landing . . .'

But in Al's letter dated 3rd September . . .

'Dear Michael,
This will set down the details of my search thus
far regarding your question about the film *The
Way to the Stars.*
Several airfields claim a piece of the action in
respect of this film, including our own Halfpenny
Green. As you know, I grew up with the local
legend that the film was in fact shot here and I
was a regular visitor to the airfield on show days
and on Sundays, just to watch the aircraft.
Opinion locally is as divided as ever. One
'expert' claims that none of the film was shot
here, yet the airport's current publicity still
speaks of the link. What is certain is that the
heavy bomber scenes could not have been shot here
– even with its wartime runways open, HPG could
never have been big enough. So, in spite of what
our library archives say, I was right on that
point.
I've tracked the bomber scenes down to a USAAF
airbase at Grafton Underwood, near Kettering in
Northamptonshire. This was the base of several 8th

Army Airforce units during the war and *The Way to the Stars* was made with the co-operation of the 834th heavy bomber group – B17 Flying Fortresses. *The Way to the Stars* is claimed to be the only World War II movie shot using an actual aerial combat unit. Filming is said to have taken place across April and May of 1945. This fact would tie in with the film's release date.

Back to Halfpenny Green. HPG was originally known as Bobbington aerodrome. The name was changed in the war years. The reasons for this are not known but it is assumed that it was to avoid confusion with the southern Bovingdon base.

During the war HPG's principal role was as a beam training school – that is to say, for pilots coming in on a homing beacon assisted landing. The squadron based here was mainly Avro Anson aircraft.

Now . . . ! Several Ansons are seen at the beginning of *The Way to the Stars*, it's the type of aircraft from which John Mills emerges, and these are seen without B17s in the background. So it is perfectly feasible that the scenes featuring the Ansons were filmed at Halfpenny Green, even if the B17 scenes were not. Working on the theory that an active unit, such as the 834th bomber group at Grafton Underwood would have had to be disrupted as little as possible.

One thing that all 'experts' do agree on is the fact that a film *was* made at HPG in the war years, so the library's archives were correct.

Unfortunately no one can remember what it was! So, if you want to believe in the things you were

told as a child (or in a romantic notion
engendered by memories and a cosy old film on the
telly) who's to stop you? After all Halfpenny
Green isn't a million miles away from Kettering.
As you'll undoubtedly appreciate, military
personnel moved about an awful lot at that time –
Terence Rattigan (*The Way to the Stars* writer) flew
for the RAF, and David Tomlinson (he played Prune)
was an RAF instructor for a time. So it's highly
likely they could have come across Halfpenny Green
at some point and Rattigan could well have set his
story there. Halfpenny Field, the airfield,
featured in *The Way to the Stars*, is such a
distinctive name that no matter where the movie
was shot, I think it to be far more than mere
coincidence.
In closing on the subject for the moment – I
haven't finished digging yet by a long chalk – I
will quote from my correspondence with Graham
Beale, the airport's current director: "I was very
interested in reading of yet another person of
character who has had contact and involvement with
HPG in the past. We would be delighted if Mr
Sheard wished to visit the airport."
So there you are, if you ever feel like a revisit. Incidentally, RAF Bridgenorth, where
5050481 A/C 2nd class Sheard did his National
Service basic training, took over HPG on September
14th, 1953. So now you can place your 'ownership'
of it in historical perspective . . .'

I'm deeply indebted to Al for giving me the OK to include
his letters. Thanks mate.

And thank you, all of you. I'm going to be soppy again, but what the hell. I'm grateful to everyone. I can't possibly list you all here, but thanks particularly to Dearly Beloved, always first and foremost, Uncle Pete, Kenny, Father Jeremy and Nick again, for their super forewords, and THANK YOU SUMMERSDALE for having the nonce once again to take a chance – on a certainty!

It's funny you know, or there again perhaps it's very understandable, but I'm getting withdrawal symptoms already!

Yours Aye – see you all in 'Yes, Who?'

Epilogue 3

No, wait. There's an EPILOGUE THREE! And it's unique to this edition, 'cos it's only just happened.

Can you imagine me, gobsmacked? Impossible, I hear you chorus, nothing could flummox you. Well I have to admit, I've been gobsmacked twice this year. Twice in ten short days! The second Smack will appear in my next volume, and in fact I'll not dwell too long on the first, because I think the lady herself should have the honour of telling you about it.

I would say, though, before she starts, that it was one of the most wonderful surprises I've ever had, and that includes getting the part of Ozzel in *The Empire Strikes Back*!

Here then are the words of Mrs Karen (Quincy) Gillett, my Number One Appreciator, as they appear in 'ShearDelight' – read about that in the next tome, too!

'On stage, Ms Gillett, please!'

'I am probably unique in the "Sheard Chums' Society" because Michael and I had never met or even spoken to one another.

'At the beginning, a very long time ago, there was a lot of Michael's work being shown on TV and I was fascinated by the contrasts. So I decided to write to Michael to tell him how much I was enjoying his work and to grovel for a signed photo. Very soon after, a reply arrived complete with photo. I wrote a letter back to thank him and the rest, as they say, is history.

'After a few years of being kept up-to-date with Michael's work and exchanging birthday and Christmas cards, I decided to send him a calendar of Liverpool for Christmas. It turned out to be the perfect gift. Unbeknown to me, Michael's aunt had died earlier in the year and she had always sent him a calendar for Christmas. He seemed quite chuffed with it, so I've carried on the tradition and sent a calendar every year since.

'BUT I STILL HADN'T MET HIM!

'And so we come to Tuesday 14th December this year. That was a day to remember on Merseyside. No, not the Paul McCartney concert at the 'not-the-original' Cavern. No, not even a number 61 bus actually turning up at the bus stop on Knowsley Road, Bootle. Believe it or not, the day is memorable for just one thing. It's the day Michael Sheard was left *speechless!* Honest, and I should know because I did it!

'The whole thing started on December 2nd, my 21st birthday. Oh sorry, it's a true story not a fairy tale isn't it . . . Well, in amongst the birthday cards was a letter from Newcastle. I was baffled, as I didn't know any Geordies. When I opened it, it was from a lady called Pam (Clarke) asking me to do a little piece for a certain Christmas surprise for Michael. *(That's the second Smack, see the next book! – me)*

'Several e-mails and phone calls later it transpired that Michael was to be at a small convention in Southport soon. And so the great conspiracy began. I e-mailed Michael to say that I wasn't well, in case he'd thought of inviting me. The Southport organiser, Andy, was happy to help with the surprise. All was arranged and with three days to go it was set up – as Michael was!

'Tuesday came and I felt OK-ish. Andy picked me up and off we drove to the coastal town. On arrival at the hotel my bottle was on the verge of going. "I hope I'm not going to regret this," I thought.

'"I'll tell him you're on the mobile," said Andy.

'I stood in the hallway and in he went to the lounge.

'Andy deserved an Oscar. He asked Michael who his number one fan was. My name was given in reply and Andy handed over the phone. "She's on the phone. Here."

'Michael took the phone, which was, not surprisingly, dead.

'"Oh, is she not there?" Andy asked. "Well, that's probably because she's outside. Come in Karen." Deep breath – and in I wandered.

'Michael looked a bit stunned, then that big grin spread over his face and he walked over, arms outstretched.

'We greeted each other with a big hug, like old (well, not that) friends. Everyone in the room knew all about this, but him. The plot had worked to a tee. The whole day was amazing.'

Dear Number One. Thank you. Thank you all. I still wake up in the wee small hours and am amazed at the many wonderful friends I have.

Bless you, every flippin' one of you.

We'll see much more of each other in the next wonderful Sheard production!